Excel

Revise in a Month

Year 4
NAPLAN*-style
Tests

T0359318

PASCAL
PRESS

* This is not an officially endorsed publication of the NAPLAN program and is produced by Pascal Press independently of Australian governments.

Lyn Baker & Alan Horsfield

© 2014 Lyn Baker, Alan Horsfield and Pascal Press
Reprinted 2015
Conventions of Language questions updated 2016
Reprinted 2019

Revised in 2020 for the NAPLAN Online tests

Reprinted 2020, 2021, 2022

ISBN 978 1 74125 424 2

Pascal Press
PO Box 250
Glebe NSW 2037
(02) 8585 4050
www.pascalpress.com.au

Publisher: Vivienne Joannou
Project editor: Rosemary Peers
Edited by Rosemary Peers
Answers checked by Peter Little and Dale Little
Cover and page design by DiZign Pty Ltd
Typeset by Dizign and Grizzly Graphics (Leanne Richters)
Printed by Vivar Printing/Green Giant Press

Disclaimer
While information in this book is correct at the time of going to press, students should check the official NAPLAN website and ask their teachers about the exact requirements or content of the tests for which they are sitting, as this may change from year to year.

All efforts have been made to obtain permission for the copyright material reproduced in this book. In the event of any oversight, the publisher welcomes any information that will enable rectification of any reference or credit in subsequent editions.

The publisher thanks the Royal Australian Mint for granting permission to use Australian currency coin designs in this book.

Notice of liability
The information contained in this book is distributed without warranty. While precautions have been taken in the preparation of this material, neither the authors nor Pascal Press shall have any liability to any person or entity with respect to any liability, loss or damage caused or alleged to be caused directly or indirectly by the instructions and content contained in the book.

Table of Contents

NAPLAN and NAPLAN Online

WHAT IS NAPLAN?

- NAPLAN stands for National Assessment Program—Literacy and Numeracy.
- It is conducted every year in March and the tests are taken by students in Years 3, 5, 7 and 9.
- The tests cover Literacy—Reading, Writing, Conventions of Language (Spelling, Grammar and Punctuation)—and Numeracy.

WHAT IS NAPLAN ONLINE?

Introduction

- In the past all NAPLAN tests were paper tests.
- From 2022 all students will take the NAPLAN tests online.
- This means students will complete the NAPLAN tests on a computer or on a tablet.

Tailored test design

- With NAPLAN paper tests, all students in each year level took exactly the same tests.
- In the NAPLAN Online tests this won't be the case; instead, every student will take a tailor-made test based on their ability.
- Please visit the official ACARA site for a detailed explanation of the tailored test process used in NAPLAN Online and also for general information about the tests: https://nap.edu.au/online-assessment.
- These tailor-made tests will mean broadly, therefore, that a student who is at a standard level of achievement will take a test that is mostly comprised of questions of a standard level; a student who is at an intermediate level of achievement will take a test that is mostly comprised of questions of an intermediate level; and a student who is at an advanced level of achievement will take a test that is mostly comprised of questions of an advanced level.

Different question types

- Because of the digital format, NAPLAN Online contains more question types than in the paper tests. In the paper tests there are only multiple-choice and short-answer question types. In NAPLAN Online, however, there are also other question types. For example, students might be asked to drag text across a screen, measure a figure with an online ruler or listen to an audio recording of a sentence and then spell a word they hear.
- Please refer to the next page to see some examples of these additional question types that are found in NAPLAN Online and how they compare to questions in this book. As you will see, the content tested is exactly the same but the questions are presented differently.

NAPLAN Online question types

Additional NAPLAN question types	Equivalent questions in this book
Comparing	

Comparing

Four girls compare ribbons. Meg's ribbon is the longest. Nora's ribbon is longer than Mia's but shorter than Kim's.

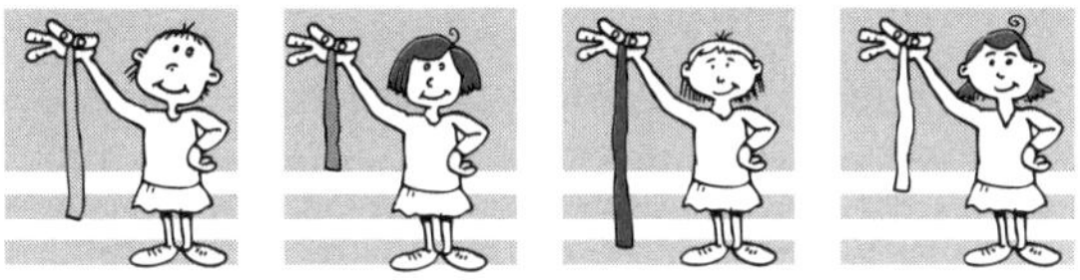

Move each picture beneath the correct name.

Meg

Nora

Mia

Kim

Four girls compare ribbons. Meg's ribbon is the longest. Nora's ribbon is longer than Mia's but shorter than Kim's. Write the name of each girl under her picture.

Drag and drop

The *Indian Pacific* makes four stops on the trip from Sydney to Perth.

Drag these places to show the order in which they happened in the text. Use the tab to read the text.

1
2
3
4

Broken Hill   Kalgoorlie   Cook   Adelaide

The *Indian Pacific* makes four stops on the trip from Sydney to Perth.

Write the numbers 1 to 4 in the boxes to show the order of the stops.

Broken Hill   Kalgoorlie   Cook   Adelaide

Measuring

How long is this nail in the picture below? Use the online ruler to measure the length of the picture in millimetres.

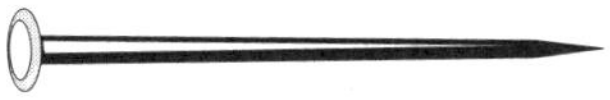

○ 57   ○ 52   ○ 67   ○ 62

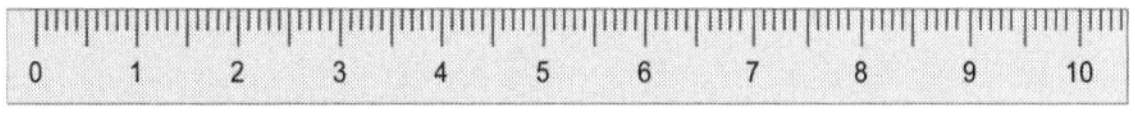

How long is this nail in millimetres?

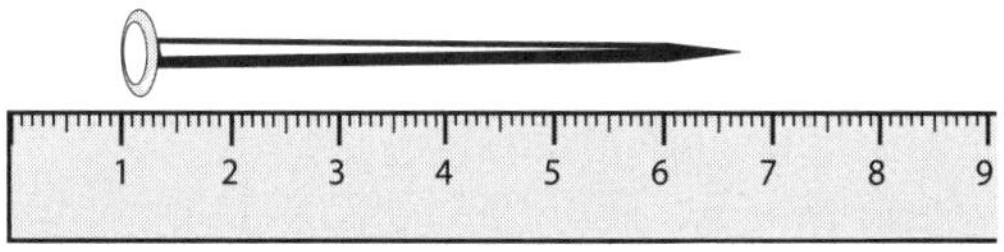

A 57   B 52   C 67   D 62

Text entry

"It is now time for your _____ piano lesson," said Ms Taylor.

Click on the play button to listen to the missing word.

0.08 / 0.09

Type the correct spelling of the word in the box.

Please ask your parent or teacher to read to you the spelling words on page 210. Write the correct spelling of each word in the box.

Word	Example
1. daily	"It is now time for your daily piano lesson," said Ms Taylor.

Maximise your results in NAPLAN Online

STEP 1: USE THIS BOOK

How *Excel* has updated this book to help you revise

Tailored test design

- We can't replicate the digital experience in book form and offer you tailored tests, but with this series we do provide Intermediate and Advanced NAPLAN Online–style Literacy and Numeracy tests
- This means that a student using these tests will be able to prepare with confidence for tests at different ability levels.
- This makes it excellent preparation for the tailored NAPLAN Online Literacy and Numeracy tests.

Remember the advantages of revising in book form

There are many benefits to a child revising using books for the online test:

- One of the most important benefits is that writing on paper will help your child retain information. It can be a very effective way to memorise. High-quality educational research shows that using a keyboard is not as good as note-taking for learning.
- Students will be able to prepare thoroughly for topic revision using books and then practise computer skills easily. They will only succeed with sound knowledge of topics; this requires study and focus. Students will not succeed in tests simply because they know how to answer questions digitally.
- Also, some students find it easier to concentrate when reading a page in a book than when reading on a screen.
- Furthermore it can be more convenient to use a book, especially when a child doesn't have ready access to a digital device.
- You can be confident that *Excel* books will help students acquire the topic knowledge they need, as we have over 30 years experience in helping students prepare for tests. All our writers are experienced educators.

STEP 2: PRACTISE ON *Excel Test Zone*

How *Excel Test Zone* can help you practise online

We recommend you go to www.exceltestzone. com.au and register for practice in NAPLAN Online–style tests once you have completed this book. The reasons include:

- for optimal performance in the NAPLAN Online tests we recommend students gain practice at completing online tests as well as completing revision in book form
- students should practise answering questions on a digital device to become confident with this process
- students will be able to practise tailored tests like those in NAPLAN Online, as well as other types of tests
- students will also be able to gain valuable practice in onscreen skills such as dragging and dropping answers, using an online ruler to measure figures and using an online protractor to measure angles.

Remember that *Excel Test Zone* has been helping students prepare for NAPLAN since 2009; in fact we had NAPLAN online questions even before NAPLAN tests went online!

We also have updated our website along with our book range to ensure your preparation for NAPLAN Online is 100% up to date.

About the NAPLAN tests and this book

ABOUT THE TESTS

Test results

- The test results are used by teachers as a diagnostic tool. The results provide students, parents and teachers with information that can be used to improve student learning.

- The Student Report provides information about what students know and can do in the areas of Reading, Writing, Conventions of Language (Spelling, Punctuation and Grammar) and the various strands of Numeracy. It also provides information on how each student has performed in relation to other students in their year group and against the national average and the national minimum standard.

- NAPLAN tests are not aptitude or intelligence tests. They focus on what has been achieved, especially on the knowledge and skills taught in the syllabus. These are often called KLAs (key learning areas).

- Official tests are trialled on selected groups to test the reliability of the questions. The questions in this book are representative of questions that you can expect to find in an official test. They have been prepared by professionals who have an understanding of teaching and of testing procedures.

- The NAPLAN results present an objective view of student performance and form the basis from which schools can make informed educational decisions about further school learning programs.

- Because NAPLAN tests are national tests they provide authorities with sufficient information to track student educational development from primary to high school, or when transferring from one Australian school to another.

TYPES OF TESTS

- There are four different types of tests in Year 5 NAPLAN Online.
  1 The Numeracy Test (50 minutes)
  2 The Conventions of Language Test (45 minutes)
  3 The Reading Test (50 minutes)
  4 The Writing Test (42 minutes)
  Tests 2–4 form the Literacy component of the test.

- The Writing Test is held first, followed by the Reading Test, the Conventions of Language Test and finally the Numeracy Test.

USING THIS BOOK

- This book is designed to be used over four weeks, with weekly exercises in various aspects of literacy and numeracy.

- Each session gives students an opportunity to Test their Skills, revise Key Points and practise a Real Test on a specific aspect of the curriculum.

- In a month the student will have covered much of the material that could be included in a NAPLAN Online test.

- Finally there are two Sample Test Papers based on the content used in past Year 5 NAPLAN test papers.

- Because NAPLAN tests are timed tests, times have been suggested for completing the various units in this book.

> Please note there are no Year 4 NAPLAN tests. This book will help you prepare for the Year 5 NAPLAN tests a year early.

Let's start to revise!

Week 1

This is what we cover this week:

Day 1   **Number and Algebra:**   ◎ Numbers

Day 2   **Number and Algebra:**   ◎ Patterns and number sentences

Day 3   **Spelling:**   ◎ Making singular verbs and plural nouns

            Grammar and Punctuation: ◎ Types of sentences and articles

Day 4   **Reading:**   ◎ Understanding narratives
                     ◎ Understanding poetry
                     ◎ Understanding information reports

Day 5   **Writing:**   ◎ Narratives

NUMBER AND ALGEBRA
Numbers

30 MIN

Write down the number represented by each set of blocks.

1 ☐

2 ☐

3 ☐

4 ☐

Fill in the blanks.

5 732 = ☐ hundreds, ☐ tens and ☐ ones

6 509 = ☐ hundreds, ☐ tens and ☐ ones

7 9234 = ☐ thousands, ☐ hundreds, ☐ tens and ☐ ones

8 2506 = ☐ thousands, ☐ hundreds, ☐ tens and ☐ ones

9 7019 = ☐ thousands, ☐ hundreds, ☐ tens and ☐ ones

10 6120 = ☐ thousands, ☐ hundreds, ☐ tens and ☐ ones

Write in words.

11 256 ☐

12 6423 ☐

13 1006 ☐

14 2017 ☐

15 3200 ☐

Write using numbers.

16 one hundred and fifty-two ☐

17 four hundred and eighty ☐

NUMBER AND ALGEBRA
Numbers

(continued)

18 three thousand, seven hundred and eighty-six

19 one thousand, two hundred and one

20 eight thousand and sixty-four

Write down each number.

21 300 + 20 + 7 =

22 4000 + 600 + 30 + 2 =

23 1000 + 400 + 70 =

24 900 + 5 =

25 7000 + 60 + 3 =

After each number below, write the next (whole) number.

26 89

27 600

28 309

29 999

30 6499

Look at these numbers: **135, 47, 684, 82**.

31 Which number is the smallest?

32 Which number is the largest?

33 Which numbers are odd?

34 Which numbers are even?

Look at these numbers: **4283, 5671, 3908**.

35 Which number is the largest?

36 Which number is the smallest?

37 Which number is even?

What number is the arrow pointing to on each number line?

38
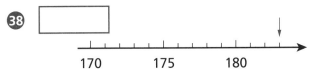

39
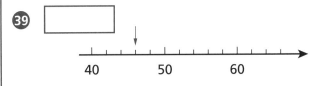

40
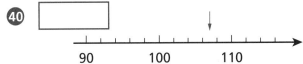

NUMBER AND ALGEBRA
Numbers

1 **Sets of blocks can be used to represent numbers.**

= 100 | = 10 | ☐ = 1

Example:

This is 4 tens and 7 ones or 47.

Example:

This is 2 hundreds, 1 ten and 3 ones or 213.

Example:

This is 1 hundred, 7 tens and 5 ones or 175.

Example:

This is 1 hundred and 2 ones. There are no tens.
So the number is 102.

2 **The digits from 0 to 9 are used to make numbers.**

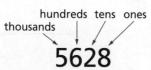

hundreds tens ones
thousands
5628

When numbers are written, the position of the digits tells us what the number is. The last column on the right is ones, the next to the left is tens, then hundreds, thousands, ten thousands, and so on.

3 **Place value is the value of a digit in a number.**

In 732 the value of the 7 is hundreds (700). The value of the 3 is tens (30).
So 732 = 7 hundreds, 3 tens and 2 ones.
If there are 0 tens, for example, then they don't get named in the number.
509 is five hundred and nine.

Examples:
- 509 = 5 hundreds, 0 tens and 9 ones
- 9234 = 9 thousands, 2 hundreds, 3 tens and 4 ones
- 2506 = 2 thousands, 5 hundreds, 0 tens and 6 ones
- 7019 = 7 thousands, 0 hundreds, 1 ten and 9 ones
- 6120 = 6 thousands, 1 hundred, 2 tens and 0 ones

4 **Learn how to correctly write numbers in words.**
First learn the names of the digits: 1 one, 2 two, 3 three, 4 four, 5 five, 6 six, 7 seven, 8 eight, 9 nine.
Then learn the special names for 10 ten, 11 eleven and 12 twelve and for the 'teens', 13 thirteen, 14 fourteen, 15 fifteen, 16 sixteen, 17 seventeen, 18 eighteen and 19 nineteen.
The tens have special names too: 20 twenty, 30 thirty, 40 forty, 50 fifty, 60 sixty, 70 seventy, 80 eighty and 90 ninety.
Once you know all the names and the place values then the numbers can be easily written in words.

Examples:
- 256 is two hundred and fifty-six.
- 6423 is six thousand, four hundred and twenty-three.
- 1006 is one thousand and six.
- 2017 is two thousand and seventeen.
- 3200 is three thousand two hundred.

5 **Also learn how to change numbers written in words to numbers.**
Examples:
- One hundred and fifty-two is 152.
  [1 hundred, 5 tens and 2 ones]
- Four hundred and eighty is 480.
  [4 hundreds, 8 tens and 0 ones]
- Three thousand, seven hundred and eighty-six is 3786. [3 thousands, 7 hundreds, 8 tens and 6 ones]
- One thousand, two hundred and one has 1 thousand, 2 hundreds, 0 tens and 1 one. So one thousand, two hundred and one is 1201.
- Eight thousand and sixty-four has 8 thousands, 0 hundreds, 6 tens and 4 ones. It is 8064.

Key Points

6 If we know how many thousands, hundreds, tens and ones in a number then it is easy to write a **single number**.

Examples:
- 300 + 20 + 7 = 327
- 4000 + 600 + 30 + 2 = 4632
- 1000 + 400 + 70 = 1470 [There are no ones.]
- 900 + 5 = 905 [There are no tens.]
- 7000 + 60 + 3 = 7063 [There are no hundreds.

7 **Learn to count up to at least 10 000.** (That doesn't mean you should practise counting all the way from 0 to 10000. You must be able to continue from any starting point.)

Examples:
- The next number after 89 is 90.
- The next number after 600 is 601.
- The next number after 309 is 310.
- The next number after 999 is 1000.
- The next number after 6499 is 6500.

8 **When you can count and understand place value, it is easy to place numbers in order from largest to smallest** and to find the largest or smallest of a group of numbers.

Example:
- So the numbers 135, 47, 684, 82 can be placed in order from lowest to highest. 47, 82, 135, 684
- The smallest of those numbers is 47 because it has no hundreds and, of the numbers without hundreds, it has the smallest number of tens.
- The largest of those numbers is 684.

Example:
- When the numbers 4283, 5671, 3908 are placed in order from lowest to highest we get 3908, 4283 and 5671.
- The largest of those numbers is 5671.
- The smallest of those numbers is 3908.

9 **An even number is one that can be divided by two with no remainder.** If we have an even number of objects they can be arranged in pairs or groups of two.

Example:

12 is an even number.

Even numbers end in 0, 2, 4, 6 or 8.
An odd number is a number that cannot be divided by two evenly. There will always be a remainder (of one) when an odd number is divided by two. An odd number of objects will always have one object left over when arranged in pairs.

Example:

11 is an odd number.
Odd numbers end in 1, 3, 5, 7 or 9.

Examples:
- So in the group of numbers 135, 47, 684 and 82, two numbers are even and two are odd. The odd numbers are 135 and 47 and the even numbers are 684 and 82.
- In the numbers 4283, 5671 and 3908 only one number is even. The even number is 3908.

10 **A number line shows numbers written in order.** Every number has a position on a number line.

Fractions and decimals can also be placed on a number line.
Sometimes positions are marked but the numbers are missing. We can work out what the numbers are by filling in, or imagining, the missing numbers.

Example:
Here the arrow points to 183.

170   172   174 175   177   179 180   182
   171   173   176   178   181   183

Sometimes a number line can show numbers increasing by twos, fives, tens or some other number. We use the given numbers to work out what the missing numbers must be.

Example: ↓

40 42 44 46 48 50 52 54 56 58 60 62 64 66

This arrow points to 46.

Example:

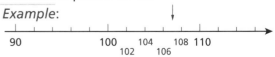

90   100   104   108 110
                     102   106

This arrow is pointing halfway between 106 and 108. So it is pointing to 107.

Real Test

NUMBER AND ALGEBRA
Numbers

20 MIN

For some questions you will need to write the answer in the box. For other questions you need to circle the correct answer.

1 Which one of these equals 687?

A 6 + 8 + 7   **B** 600 + 70 + 8
C 600 + 80 + 7   **D** 700 + 80 + 6

2 Write nine hundred and twenty-four as a number.

3 Mary has twelve crayons and James has eighteen crayons. Isabel has more crayons than Mary but not as many as James. How many crayons could Isabel have?

A 9   **B** 11   **C** 15   **D** 19

4 Which group of blocks shows the number thirty-two?

A   **B**   **C**   **D**

5 Which number is closest to 90?

A 88   **B** 99   **C** 86   **D** 93

6 Which number is seven thousand and forty-five?

A 7450   **B** 745   **C** 7405   **D** 7045

7 Julie has these 4 cards.

| 8 | 2 | 1 | 9 |

How could Julie place the cards to make the largest possible **even** number?

8 Write down the next number after 1099.

9 How many odd numbers are between 40 and 64?

A 11   **B** 12   **C** 13   **D** 23

10 6208 =

A 6 hundreds + 2 tens + 8 ones
B 6 thousands + 2 tens + 8 ones
C 6 thousands + 2 hundreds + 8 tens
D 6 thousands + 2 hundreds + 8 ones

11 Which number is at the position of the arrow?

12 Daisy has these four cards.

| 9 | 5 | 0 | 4 |

What is the closest number to 5000 that Daisy can make with her cards?

13 Write six thousand and eighteen as a number.

14

450   630

What number is exactly halfway between 450 and 630?

15 Peter has these three cards.

| 1 | 2 | 3 |

How many different **odd** numbers can Peter make using all three of his cards?

16 Lisa has this list of numbers: **17, 35, 42, 83, 112, 150, 207, 333**.

How many of Lisa's numbers are odd?

A 3   **B** 5   **C** 6   **D** 8

17 Which is 9027?

A nine thousand and twenty-seven
B nine hundred and twenty-seven
C nine thousand, two hundred and seven
D nine thousand, two hundred and seventy

18 7 + 60 + 500 =

A 765   **B** 756   **C** 567   **D** 576

☞ **Answers and explanations on page 160**

NUMBER AND ALGEBRA
Patterns and number sentences

30 min

Here is a pattern of shapes:

△○□◆ △○□◆ △○□◆ △○□◆ △○...

1 How many different shapes are in the pattern before it repeats?

2 Which shape will come next?

Here is a pattern of beads:

●○○●○●○○●◎●○○●○●○○●◎●○○●○●○○●◎●○○●

3 How many beads are in the pattern before it repeats?

4 Which bead will come next in the pattern?

5 How many ● are needed for each ◉ ?

This is a pattern of numbers:

5, 8, 11, 14, 17, …

6 By how much are the numbers going up each time?

7 What is the next number in the pattern?

Here is a pattern of numbers:

19, 25, 31, 37, 43, …

8 By how much are the numbers going up each time?

9 What is the next number in the pattern?

This is a number pattern: **26, 22, 18, 14, …**

10 By how much are the numbers going down each time?

11 What is the next number in the pattern?

Look at the numbers in this pattern:

4, 11, 18, ? , 32, 39, …

One of them is missing.

12 By how much are the numbers going up each time?

13 What is the missing number?

14 What will the next number in the pattern be?

The first number in a pattern is 7.

The numbers go up by 5 each time.

15 What is the second number in the pattern?

16 What is the third number?

17 What is the fourth number?

18 What is the tenth number?

NUMBER AND ALGEBRA
Patterns and number sentences

(continued)

Hamish makes this pattern with sticks.

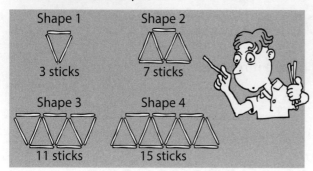

Shape 1 — 3 sticks
Shape 2 — 7 sticks
Shape 3 — 11 sticks
Shape 4 — 15 sticks

19 How many more sticks are used in Shape 2 than in Shape 1?

20 How many more sticks are used in Shape 3 than in Shape 2?

21 How many more sticks are used in Shape 4 than in Shape 3?

22 How many extra sticks are used each time?

23 How many sticks will be needed for Shape 5?

24 How many sticks will be needed for Shape 6?

Lily is making tree diagrams with sticks.

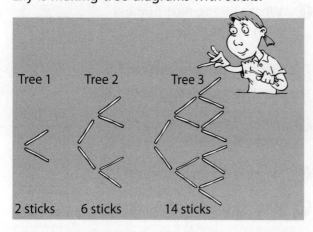

Tree 1 — 2 sticks
Tree 2 — 6 sticks
Tree 3 — 14 sticks

25 How many more sticks are needed for Tree 2 than for Tree 1?

26 How many more sticks are needed for Tree 3 than for Tree 2?

27 How many more sticks will be needed for Tree 4 than for Tree 3?

28 How many sticks will be needed for Tree 4?

29 How many sticks will be needed for Tree 5?

Fill in the blanks.

30 $7 + \boxed{} = 11$

31 $9 + \boxed{} = 12$

32 $\boxed{} + 6 = 14$

33 $24 - \boxed{} = 15$

34 $7 \times \boxed{} = 35$

35 $48 \div \boxed{} = 8$

36 $\boxed{} - 7 = 6$

37 $\boxed{} \times 4 = 28$

38 $\boxed{} \div 6 = 2$

Key Points

NUMBER AND ALGEBRA
Patterns and number sentences

① **Patterns can be found in shapes and numbers.** If a pattern is made with shapes, we look to see how many shapes are in the pattern before it repeats.

Example:

△○□◆△○□◆△○□◆△○□◆△○…

This pattern has 4 shapes that are being repeated. We can break the pattern into the group of 4 so that they can be more clearly seen:

△○□◆　△○□◆　△○□◆　△○□◆　△○

The final group of shapes has only two of the four that repeat. The next shape is the third shape in the group. The shape that comes next is □.

Example:

●○●○●○●◎○●○●○●○◎○●○●○●○◎●○●…

In this pattern of beads there are 8 beads in each of the repeating groups.

●○●○●○●◎　●○●○●○◎　●○●○●○◎　●○●…

[There are only 4 different beads, but some of those are used more than once in the pattern before it begins to repeat.] The final group has just 3 beads. The next bead will be the fourth bead in the pattern. The next bead will be ○.
There is only one ○ in the group of 8 repeating beads, but there are four ●. So there are 4 ● for each ○.

② **In the most common number patterns, the same number is being added each time**.

Example:

5, 8, 11, 14, 17, …

In this pattern the numbers are going up by 3 each time.

$5 + 3 = 8$, $8 + 3 = 11$, $11 + 3 = 14$, and so on.

Once we have found the pattern it is then easy to find the next number or any missing numbers.

So in this pattern the next number will be $17 + 3 = 20$.

Example:

19, 25, 31, 37, 43, …

In this pattern the numbers are going up by 6 each time.

The next number will be $43 + 6$. So the next number is 49.

Example:

26, 22, 18, 14, …

In this pattern, we can immediately see that the numbers are going down not up. This means that a number is being taken away each time. To find the number that is being taken away we can subtract or count backwards.

The numbers in this pattern are going down by 4 each time. The next number in the pattern is $14 − 4$ so it is 10.

Example:

4, 11, 18, ? , 32, 39, …

This pattern has a number that is missing. (It is replaced by a question mark.) We use the other numbers to find the pattern. The pattern is to add 7 each time.

Now $18 + 7 = 25$.

So the missing number is 25. We can check that this is correct.

$25 + 7 = 32$, which fits the pattern. So the missing number is 25. The next number in the pattern is $39 + 7$ or 46.

③ **A number pattern can be described by its starting number and a rule.**

Example:

If the first number in a pattern is 7 and the numbers go up by 5 each time, then the second number will be $7 + 5$ or 12.
The third number will be $12 + 5$ or 17.
The fourth number will be $17 + 5$ or 22.
So we now know the pattern:
7, 12, 17, 22, 27, 32, 37, 42, 47, 52, 57, …
The tenth number in the pattern is 52.

④ **Often a pattern will involve shapes made from objects** such as sticks, pins or beads. **There might then be two patterns in one,** a pattern of shapes and a pattern of the number of objects that make up each shape.

Example:

Shape 1	Shape 2	Shape 3	Shape 4
3 sticks	7 sticks	11 sticks	15 sticks

In this pattern there is a pattern of triangles and a pattern of sticks for each shape.

NUMBER AND ALGEBRA
Patterns and number sentences

(continued)

- There are 3 sticks used in Shape 1 and 7 sticks used in Shape 2, so there are 4 more sticks used in Shape 2 than in Shape 1.
- There are 11 sticks used in Shape 3, so because $11 - 7 = 4$, there are 4 more sticks used in Shape 3 than in Shape 2.
- There are 15 sticks used in Shape 4, so because $15 - 11 = 4$, there are 4 more sticks used in Shape 4 than in Shape 3.
- So there are 4 extra sticks used each time. [This can also be seen from the pattern because 2 extra sticks are placed at each side of the previous shape.]

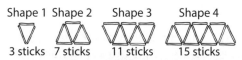

Shape 1 Shape 2 Shape 3 Shape 4
3 sticks 7 sticks 11 sticks 15 sticks

- The number of sticks needed for Shape 5 will be $15 + 4$ or 19.
- The number of sticks needed for Shape 6 will be $19 + 4$ or 23.

5 Not all number patterns involve adding (or subtracting) the same number each time. **Patterns involving objects can also change by different amounts each time.**

Example:

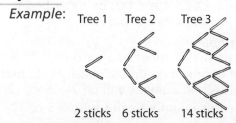

Tree 1 Tree 2 Tree 3
2 sticks 6 sticks 14 sticks

- In this pattern 2 sticks are used for Tree 1 and 6 sticks are used for Tree 2. So 4 more sticks are needed for Tree 2 than for Tree 1.
- 14 sticks are used for Tree 3. So 8 more sticks are needed for Tree 3 than for Tree 2.
- To be sure of the pattern we need to look at the diagrams to see where the extra sticks are being placed each time.

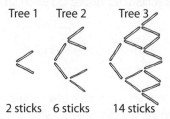

Tree 1 Tree 2 Tree 3
2 sticks 6 sticks 14 sticks

- The extra sticks are being placed at the end of the branches on the right side of each tree. There are 2 sticks at the end of each branch.
- Tree 1 has 2 branches, so Tree 2 needed 2 lots of 2 sticks or 4 extra sticks. Tree 2 then has 4 branches on the right, so Tree 3 needed 4 lots of 2 sticks or 8 extra sticks.
- Tree 4 will need 8 lots of 2 or 16 extra sticks. Now $14 + 16 = 30$. So Tree 4 will need 30 sticks altogether.
- Tree 5 will need 16 lots of 2 or 32 extra sticks. So Tree 5 will need 62 sticks altogether.

6 **It might be necessary to find a missing number in a number sentence.** Sometimes we can **see** the answer straight away. For example, to find the missing number in the question $7 + \square = 11$, you might know that $7 + 4 = 11$ so immediately you know that the missing number must be 4.

With questions involving addition another way to find the answer is by counting on. For example, to find the missing number in the question $9 + \square = 12$, we count on from 9 until we get to 12. (10, 11, 12) so the answer is 3.

Sometimes we can use the opposite operation to answer a question. The opposite of adding is subtracting. So in the question $\square + 6 = 14$, we can take away 6 from 14. $14 - 6 = 8$ so the missing number is 8. [You can check that the answer is correct: $8 + 6 = 14$. ✓]

Another way to find the missing number in a number sentence is to think of it as 'What number?' So for example, to find the missing number in $24 - \square = 15$, think 'What number can be taken away from 24 and leave 15?' The answer is 9.

Example: To find the missing number in $7 \times \square = 35$ ask yourself '7 multiplied by what number is 35?' The answer is 5.
$48 \div 6 = 8$
$13 - 7 = 6$
$7 \times 4 = 28$
The opposite of multiplying is dividing. So to find $\square \div 6 = 2$ we can multiply 2 by 6.
$12 \div 6 = 2$

Real Test

NUMBER AND ALGEBRA
Patterns and number sentences

1 What is the next number in this pattern? **3, 7, 11, 15,** ⬚

2 ✻ ⌘ ✾ ✧ ⌘ ✻ ✧ ✾ ⌘ ✻ ✻ ⌘ ✾ ✧ ⌘ ✻ ✧ ✾ ⌘ ✻ ✻ ⌘ ✾ ✧ ⌘ ✻

What comes next in this pattern?

A ✻ ⌘ ✻ ✾   **B** ✻ ✾ ⌘ ✻   **C** ✧ ✻ ⌘ ✾   **D** ✧ ✾ ⌘ ✻

3 Alice made a pattern. She added 6 each time. Which could be Alice's pattern?
Select **all** possible patterns.

A 6, 9, 12, 15, …   **B** 6, 12, 24, 48, …   **C** 2, 8, 14, 20, …   **D** 5, 11, 17, 23, …

4 What number must be added to 9 to give 15? ⬚

5 **4, 8, ?, 16, 20, 24**

What is the missing number in this pattern? ⬚

6 Tess is making a pattern with pins.

Shape 1   Shape 2   Shape 3

4 pins   7 pins   10 pins

How many pins will Tess need for Shape **5**? ⬚

7 **1, 2, 3, 6, 11, 20, ?**

Each new number in this pattern is found by adding together the three numbers before it in the pattern. What is the next number in the pattern?

A 29   **B** 37   **C** 39   **D** 57

8 ⅂ ⊓ ⊥ ⅃ ⅂ ⊓ ⊥ ⅃ ⅂ ⊓

Which shape comes next in this pattern?

A ⅂   **B** F   **C** ⊥   **D** ⅂

9 What number can be taken away from 17 to leave 12? ⬚

☞**Answers and explanations on pages 160-161**

Real Test

NUMBER AND ALGEBRA
Patterns and number sentences

(continued)

10 43, 36, 29, 22, 15, ...

How could you describe this pattern?

A counting backwards by 7   **B** counting backwards by 8
C counting forward by 7   **D** counting forward by 8

11 Look at this pattern: ✸ ⊞ ✸ ★ ✸ ◯ ✸ ⊞ ✸ ★ ✸ ◯ ✸ ⊞ ✸ ★ ✸ ◯

How many ✸ are needed for each ★ ?

A 1   **B** 2   **C** 3   **D** 4

12 William starts with a number. He doubles it and adds 7.

William's answer is 15. What number did he start with?

A 4   **B** 6   **C** 11   **D** 16

13 Daniel put his spanners in order of length. The lengths made a pattern.

How long is Spanner 4?

A 16.75 cm
B 17.25 cm
C 17.5 cm
D 17.75 cm

Spanner 1   10 cm
Spanner 2   12.5 cm
Spanner 3   15 cm
Spanner 4   ? cm
Spanner 5   20 cm

14 Levi is 7 years old. In three years time Levi's dad will be 4 times Levi's age.

How old is Levi's dad now? ☐

15 1, 2, 4, 7, 11, 16, 22, ?

What number comes next in this pattern?

A 30   **B** 29   **C** 28   **D** 27

16 Brooke is making a pattern using sticks.

Shape 1
3 sticks

Shape 2
9 sticks

Shape 3
18 sticks

How many sticks will Brooke need for Shape **5**? ☐

☞ **Answers and explanations on pages 160-161**

Key Points and Test Your Skills

SPELLING
Making singular verbs and plural nouns

15 MIN

Most spelling rules have exceptions. English words have many different origins (e.g. *café* comes from France and *kindergarten* comes from Germany).

Key Points — Plural nouns

1 With most nouns to make the plural form you simply add an *s*.
Examples: dollars, displays, paintings

2 To make the plural form of nouns that end with a consonant + *y* change the *y* to *i* and add 'es'.
Examples: jelly ➜ jellies, canary ➜ canaries

3 To make the plural form of nouns that end with *s*, 'ss', *x*, 'zz', 'ch' and 'sh' add 'es'.
Examples: gas ➜ gases, glass ➜ glasses, box ➜ boxes, church ➜ churches

4 To make the plural form of some nouns that end with *o*, add 'es'.
Examples: potato ➜ potatoes, echo ➜ echoes
(Note there are many exceptions to this 'rule', e.g. radio ➜ radios, solo ➜ solos.)

5 There are some nouns whose singular and plural forms are the same.
Examples: deer, fish, sheep, tuna, you (pronoun)

6 To make the plural form of some nouns that end with *f* or 'fe', change the *f* to *v* and add 'es'.
Examples: life ➜ lives, wharf ➜ wharves

7 There are quite a few nouns that have unusual plural forms. You just have to know these.
Examples: child ➜ children, tooth ➜ teeth, man ➜ men, goose ➜ geese, mouse ➜ mice

8 There are some nouns that simply refer to the substance's mass. The plural form is only used in special circumstances.
Examples: water, rice, flour, air

Key Points — Singular verbs

1 With most verbs to make the singular form you simply add an *s*.
Examples: weeps, runs

2 To make the singular form of verbs that end with a consonant + *y* change the *y* to *i* and add 'es'.
Examples: try ➜ tries, copy ➜ copies

3 To make the singular form of verbs that end with *s*, 'ss', *x*, 'zz', 'ch' and 'sh' add 'es'.
Examples: fix ➜ fixes, buzz ➜ buzzes, push ➜ pushes

4 To make the singular form of some verbs that end with *o* add 'es'.
Examples: go ➜ goes, do ➜ does

5 There are some verbs whose singular and plural forms are the same.
Examples: ate, saw, said

Test Your Skills

Learn the words below. A common method of self-testing is the **LOOK, SAY, COVER, WRITE, CHECK** method. Any mistakes should be rewritten three times correctly and immediately. By rewriting each word correctly you become familiar with the correct spelling. If a word is particularly troublesome, rewrite it several more times or keep a list of words that you can check regularly.

memory _____	volcano _____	communities _____
sketches _____	memories _____	volcanoes _____
shelves _____	journey _____	illness _____
prefix _____	speeches _____	journeys _____
illnesses _____	prefixes _____	studios _____

Write any troublesome words three times: _____

Real Test

SPELLING
Common misspellings

15 min

Please ask your parent or teacher to read to you the spelling words on page 209.
Write the correct spelling of each word in the box.

1 The music teacher has two _____ in her house.

2 Driving in the city _____ out my big sister.

3 The butcher _____ the meat he has for sale in a glass case.

4 Emma _____ she will get one hundred per cent for spelling.

5 The bank has two _____ in Parramatta.

6 Jay _____ that people who litter should be put in jail!

Each line has one word that is incorrect. Write the correct spelling
of the underlined word in the box.

7 A <u>mechanick</u> looked at the engine while we waited in the park.

8 The nail was removed from the wood using a pair of <u>plires</u>.

9 A <u>spaner</u> is used to tighten nuts and bolts.

10 We have two <u>assembleys</u> at school each week before lessons start.

11 I had <u>gastrick</u> pains all night after eating a green apple.

12 Morgan has a blister on the big toe of her <u>wright</u> foot.

Each sentence has a spelling mistake.
Write the correct spelling of that word in the box.
There is only one mistake in each line.

13 "David, you must <u>conplete</u> that work tonight!" stated the teacher.

14 Sam slipped in the gravell and grazed his knees.

15 The family watched the zeberas at the Western Plains Zoo.

16 I don't think it was reel but Angela had a photo of a dinosaur.

17 The pirates drew two crossers on the old treasure map.

18 Bannana muffins and orange pastries are my favourites.

☞ **Answers and explanations on pages 161-162**

Key Points and Test Your Skills

GRAMMAR AND PUNCTUATION
Types of sentences and articles

15 MIN

Key Points

① **There are four main types of sentences.**
All sentences begin with a capital letter.

a **Statements** end with a full stop. A simple statement contains one verb and makes sense on its own.

Example: The dog <u>ran</u> across the road.

More complex sentences can contain two or more verbs and two or more ideas.

Example: The dog <u>ran</u> across the car when it <u>saw</u> the dogcatcher arrive.

Note: Full stops are also used for shortened words, often titles, where the last letter is not the last letter of the word (e.g. Capt. (Captain) but Rd (Road)).

b **Questions** end with a question mark. Questions usually need answers.

Example: Where <u>are</u> you going? (Answer: I am going home.)

c **Exclamations** end with an exclamation mark. Exclamation sentences are often quite short.

Example: <u>Look</u> at the strange bird!

d **Commands** end with a full stop (unless they are particularly sharp, in which case they use an exclamation mark).

Example: <u>Bring</u> your work over here.

② **The words *the*, *a* and *an* are called articles.**

a The word *the* is used before specific objects or people. It is called a **definite article** because it refers to a definite object or person.

Examples: Dad put his coat on <u>the sofa</u> in the study. (This means that Dad put his coat on one special sofa, not any old sofa.)

<u>The 8:30 bus</u> is always on time. (In this sentence the writer is referring to one special bus at one special time, not just any bus.)

b The word *a* is an **indefinite article**. It is used before words beginning with a consonant sound when referring to no particular object or person or to things in general.

Examples: <u>A bus</u> should come along soon. (In this sentence the writer is not referring to any particular bus—he or she doesn't know which one.)

Dad put his coat on <u>a chair</u> in the kitchen. (You are not told if it was a particular chair.)

c The word *an* is an **indefinite article**. It is used before nouns and adjectives that start with a vowel sound (e.g. an umbrella, an ice cream, an old lady). Take care with silent *h* (e.g. an hour).

Example: Dianne took <u>an apple</u> from the bowl. (The writer means that Dianne took no particular apple from the bowl; she just took an apple in general.)

Test Your Skills

① Put the correct punctuation in the brackets at the end of these sentences.

a Will Jemma catch the early bus (_____)
I don't think so (_____)

b Ms Corby collected the money for the excursion (_____)

c Mother wondered if all the old fruit would be tossed out (_____)

d Put the plates on the sink then you can sit down (_____)

e Quick, help (_____)

② Write *a*, *an* or *the* in the spaces.
Mr Bosley has _____ old car. It is _____ bright green MG. Every day he drives his MG down _____ main street before turning onto _____ highway. _____ highway is very busy but Mr Bosley usually gets to work on time. His place of work is _____ office block. Of all _____ offices in _____ building, Mr Bosley has _____ view that fills _____ other workers with envy. He has _____ oversized desk!

Real Test

GRAMMAR AND PUNCTUATION
Types of sentences and articles

15 min

1 Which of the following correctly completes this sentence?
I keep my dog in our backyard. Last night the dog made a hole under ▮▮▮▮▮▮ back fence!
A an   B a   C one   D the

2 Which of the following correctly completes this sentence?
Leslie is a great swimmer. She is ▮▮▮▮▮▮ than everyone else in the class.
A gooder   B best   C better   D more better

3 Which of the following correctly completes this sentence?
The boys ▮▮▮▮▮▮ all the leftover cherries for themselves!
A kept   B keeped   C keep   D keept

4 Which of the following correctly completes this sentence?
A sermon was given by ▮▮▮▮▮▮ O'Keefe before he retired from church duties.
A fr.   B Fr   C Fr.   D father

5 Read this sentence.

Jerry, my big brother, left for high school early this morning!

Write any verbs from the sentence in the boxes. Use as many boxes as you need.

6 Which of the following correctly completes this sentence?
Your dog chased our cat over the lawn and ▮▮▮▮▮▮ the dusty shed!
A into   B in   C through   D inside

The writing below has some gaps. Choose the best option to fill each gap.

Inexpensive ways to celebrate

Explore ways your family can enjoy time together without spending a fortune.

It's ▮▮▮▮▮▮ good idea to check community

7
a	the	are	an
A	B	C	D

noticeboards, local newspapers ▮▮▮▮▮▮

8
but	yet	or	nor
A	B	C	D

online for free community events ▮▮▮▮▮▮

9
full stop	comma	question mark	exclamation mark
.	,	?	!
A	B	C	D

church programs or local markets. ▮▮▮▮▮▮

10
Christmas	christmas	Christ mas	Christ Mass
A	B	C	D

is a great time to see lights and even ▮▮▮▮▮▮

11
fireworks,	fireworks!	fireworks?	fireworks.
A	B	C	D

These ▮▮▮▮▮▮ provide happy memories for the whole family.

12
have	is	has	will
A	B	C	D

☞ **Answers and explanations on pages 162-163**

GRAMMAR AND PUNCTUATION
Types of sentences and articles

(continued)

13 Which sentence should end with a question mark (**?**)?

A How John worked that out I'll never know

B How to get to Albany from here is quite easy

C How many minutes are in two hours

D How I wish I were rich

14 Which sentence has the correct punctuation?

A Prof Sinclair has lessons only on Friday afternoon.

B Prof. Sinclair has lessons only on Friday afternoon.

C prof. Sinclair has lessons only on Friday afternoon.

D Prof Sinclair has Lessons only on Friday Afternoon.

15 Which of the following correctly completes the sentence?

Steve needed ______ eight-hour break between his exams to drive between colleges.

A a

B the

C an

D and

16 Write the correct verb in the space to complete this sentence.

Last night frogs [   ] croaking and a cricket was chirping near my bedroom window.

17 Which sentence is correctly punctuated?

A "Where will we stay for the night?" asked Mum as we arrived in Mildura.

B Where will we stay for the night asked Mum as we arrived in Mildura.

C "Where will we stay for the night," asked Mum as we arrived in Mildura.

D Where will we stay for the night asked Mum, "As we arrived in Mildura?"

18 Choose the letter to show where the missing comma (**,**) should go.

Joella had to find her school (A) books, her pencils (B) a spare lunch box (C) and a money (D) purse.

Answers and explanations on pages 162-163

Test Your Skills

READING
Understanding narratives

10 MIN

A narrative is a form of prose writing that tells a story. Its main purpose is to entertain. Writers of narratives create experiences that are shared with the reader. To do this the writer uses literary techniques. Such techniques include figurative language (similes and metaphors), variety in sentence length and type, variety in paragraph length, and direct speech. In many narratives the author is the person who wrote the story. The narrator is the person (*I*) in the story who tells the story.

Read the narrative *The tent* and answer the questions.

1 **The tent**

2 We all looked at the
3 lopsided sign on the
4 side of an old tent,
5 which was covered
6 in stains and sun-
7 bleached blotches.
8 The fading sign was
9 composed of stars,
10 comets and cards,
11 around a big glowing,
12 fortune-telling glass
13 sphere. Behind the
14 sphere was the shadowy shape of a fortune-teller
15 covered in swirls of mist. In the bottom corner was
16 a $3 price sign that had been roughly drawn over
17 in white paint by a larger $5 price.

18 "Let's give it a go?" said Angela.

19 "If you go first," I dared. Megan didn't say
20 anything.

21 "Come on Tracey, it was your idea!" Angela
22 argued. She was right!

23 We hesitated for a minute outside the flap of
24 the tent which had another cracked-paint sign.
25 This one carried a promise of 'Future happiness
26 revealed, the secrets of wealth and success
27 unlocked NOW'.

28 "Isn't this a bit <u>old hat</u>," offered Megan timidly.
29 "It's in the Stars every day in the paper. Mum
30 reads hers but I don't always read mine. I'm
31 a Capricorn."

32 "That's all made up. Like on the computer
33 when you type in your birthday! It's not for you
34 personally!" stated Angela.

35 I smiled sweetly and said, "This way could be a
36 lark! Okay! I'm game. Let's go."

37 As I pulled back the flap of the tent and entered
38 the eerie gloom a sinister voice said, "Welcome to
39 your future Tracey." She knows my name!

1 Who is the narrator of the passage? Write your answer in the box.

2 When Megan described the fortune-telling as *old hat* she meant it was
A not worth paying for.
B an embarrassment.
C a trick of some sort.
D old-fashioned.

3 Which term best describes Megan's behaviour?
A cautious
B annoyed
C confident
D daring

4 What surprised the narrator most?
A the change of price
B the fortune-teller saying her name
C the condition of the tent
D Angela's behaviour

5 The girls decided to enter the tent because they
A had tickets.
B wanted to know their future.
C thought it might be fun.
D knew the fortune-teller.

6 The girls most likely thought the fortune-teller would be
A genuine.
B frightening.
C reasonable.
D phoney.
E enlightening.

Answers: 1 Tracey 2 D 3 A 4 B
5 C 6 D

☞ **Explanations on page 163**

Read this passage from *Alice's Adventures in Wonderland* (1865) by Lewis Carroll (1832–98) and then answer the questions.

1 **Alice's Adventures in Wonderland**

2 *Alice was sitting with her sister on the bank of a stream when*
3 *suddenly a White Rabbit with pink eyes ran close by her. Now*
4 *read on.*

5 There was nothing so very remarkable in that; nor did Alice think
6 it so very much out of the way to hear the Rabbit say to itself,
7 "Oh dear! Oh dear! I shall be too late!" (when she thought it over
8 afterwards it occurred to her that she ought to have wondered at
9 this, but at the time it all seemed quite natural). When the Rabbit
10 actually took a watch out of its waistcoat-pocket, and looked at it,
11 and then hurried on, Alice <u>started</u> to her feet, for it flashed across
12 her mind that she had never before seen a rabbit with either a
13 waistcoat-pocket, or a watch to take out of it. <u>Burning with curiosity</u>,
14 she ran across the field after it, and was just in time to see it pop
15 down a large rabbit-hole under the hedge.

16 In another moment down went Alice after it, never once
17 considering how in the world she was to get out again.

18 The rabbit-hole went straight on like a tunnel for some way, and then dipped suddenly down, so
19 suddenly that Alice had not a moment to think about stopping herself before she found herself
20 falling down what seemed to be a very deep well.

1 What was the White Rabbit doing when Alice first saw it?
  A It was taking a watch from its waistcoat-pocket.
  B It was complaining to itself.
  C It was coming out of a hole under the hedge.
  D It was popping down a large rabbit-hole.

2 The author says that Alice was [B]*urning with curiosity*. This means she was
  A getting hot.
  B running out of energy.
  C unable to think clearly.
  D desperately wanting to find out.

3 What did Alice find most unusual about the White Rabbit? Write your answer on the lines.

_____

_____

4 A good title for this particular passage would be
  A Hole under the hedge.
  B Waistcoat-pocket watch.
  C Into the unknown.
  D Trapped in a well.

5 Alice's decision to follow the White Rabbit could best be described as
  A courageous.   **B** practical.
  C rude.   **D** reckless.

6 When Alice began falling down the hole she was
  A not worried.   **B** terrified.
  C joyful.   **D** excited.

7 The word *started* suggests that Alice
  A made a sudden, surprise move.
  B caught her breath as she stood up.
  C thought about standing up.
  D moved her feet before standing up.

☞**Answers and explanations on pages 163-164**

Real Test

10 MIN

Read the narrative *Clean-up* and answer the questions.

1 **Clean-up**

2 The after-lunch bell had rung. 4G straggled to lines. Ms Green stood
3 on the small classroom landing, her hands on her hips, her whistle in
4 her mouth. She tapped her foot.

5 Pete Morgan (called Morgue behind his back) was first in the
6 boys' line, his eyes level with Ms Green's feet. Cheekily he tapped
7 his foot too.

8 Ms Green blew her whistle. "We are still waiting," she said primly,
9 "for *some* boys. Hurry into place!"

10 "We always have to wait for Smudger," gently complained Anna.

11 Ms Green looked down at her. "He *has* a proper name Anna."

12 "Smudger's okay," growled Smudger.

13 "Really?" said Ms Green with raised eyebrows. "Now we are settled
14 I want you to look at the playground. Turn and have a good look!
15 That's right. What do you see?"

16 "Smudger and Greg left litter on the grass, Ms Green," said Bob,
17 raising his hand.

18 "Not true," brayed Smudger. "My scraps are in the bin!"

19 "I don't really care," said Ms Green sweetly as she <u>descended</u> the steps. "We must KEEP THE
20 SCENE CLEAN. It's like a pigsty. Off you go everyone. Ten papers or scraps. Not you Bob. You get a
21 carton from the classroom and bring it here. That's a good boy!"

22 The children scampered as Ms Green walked around the lunch area supervising.

1 What did Ms Green want cleaned up?
  A the classroom   B a pigsty
  C the playground   D a classroom landing

2 Which of the options could replace *descended* without affecting the meaning?
  A stamped on   B came down
  C strode along   D described

3 Which student did Ms Green regard as reliable?
  A Smudger   B Pete   C Bob   D Anna

4 Pete Morgan was called Morgue behind his back. This is most likely because
  A Pete didn't like being called by the name.
  B no one could pronounce his name correctly.

C Ms Green told her class to do it.
D Pete wouldn't know who was saying it.

5 What was Anna's complaint about Smudger?
  A He left litter on the grass.
  B He didn't put scraps in the bin.
  C He called out too much.
  D He was often late for lines.

6 Which word would best describe Smudger?
  A helpful   B bold
  C shy   D snobby

7 Why did Ms Green stand on the landing with her hands on her hips?
  A She was becoming impatient.
  B She was looking at the pigsty.
  C She couldn't decide what to do.
  D She didn't know the correct time.

☞ **Answers and explanations on pages 164-165**

Poetry can take many forms. It can tell a story (narrative verse), paint a word picture, or be the format for a play. Poets create experiences that are shared with the reader. To do this poets uses literary techniques. Such techniques include figurative language (similes and metaphors), rhyme and rhythm. Poetry does not have to rhyme.

Poetry is often described as the most personal form of expression. Poets choose their words carefully and economically to create images and feelings with words.

Read the poem *Possum* by Elaine Horsfield and then answer the questions.

1 **Possum**

2 A possum's living in our roof—
3 I'm sure you will agree,
4 It's not the kind of place you'd think
5 A possum ought to be.

6 He spends the day just sleeping.
7 He's quiet as a mouse,
8 But when it's time for us to sleep
9 He wakes up the whole house.

10 He <u>clomps</u> around the rafters
11 Then jumps onto the shed
12 And leaps into the tree outside
13 The window by my bed.

14 One night he asked his mates along
15 They partied half the night.
16 You should have heard the noise they made—
17 It ended in a fight.

18 Dad said we'll get a possum house
19 And put it near the shed.
20 And then when he has parties,
21 I'll sleep quietly in my bed.

1 This poem
A tells a story.
B creates a feeling.
C describes a scene.
D describes a problem.

2 You are going to compare the texts *Clean-up* (page 20) and *Possum* (page 21). What is a feature of each text? Tick **two** options for each text.

	Clean-up	Possum
is a narrative	☐	☐
is in the first person	☐	☐
is written to entertain	☐	☐

3 Which word has a similar meaning to *clomps* as used in the poem?
A stomps   B crashes
C stumbles   D jumps

4 How did the narrator's father react to the possum problem?
A He gave the possums a party.
B He took no notice and slept all night.
C He trapped the possum.
D He said he'd put a possum house by the shed.

5 Where is the tree the possum jumps into?
A close to the bedroom window
B above the roof of the house
C behind the shed
D near the mousehole

6 The possum makes the most noise when he
A jumps onto the shed.
B plays in the trees.
C fights with his mates.
D clomps around the rafters.

☞**Answers and explanations on page 165**

Real Test

READING
Understanding information reports

10 MIN

An information report is a factual text that uses detail to provide a better understanding about a living or non-living subject.

Read the information report *Border towns* and answer the questions.

1 **Border towns**
2 Border towns, those that sit on the border of
3 two states, can be interesting. The twin towns
4 of Albury–Wodonga sit on opposite sides of the
5 Murray River that forms the border between
6 New South Wales (postcode 2640) and Victoria
7 (postcode 3689). Albury has more people.

8 Tweed Heads, NSW (2485), is next to the
9 Queensland border, <u>adjacent</u> to the 'Twin Town' of
10 Coolangatta (4225) on the Gold Coast. As a bit of
11 fun it is known as a town where you can change
12 time zones simply by crossing the street (during
13 daylight-saving months in NSW).

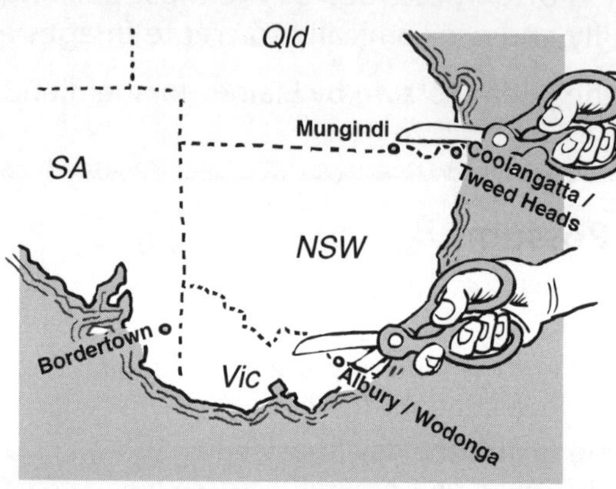

14 Mungindi (Mung-in-di) is a town of 700 people on the New South Wales/Queensland border
15 near Moree. Mungindi (NSW postcode 2406) is the only border town in the southern hemisphere
16 with the same name on both sides of the border. Most of Mungindi is in New South Wales but a
17 quarter of the population live in Queensland. The border itself is the Barwon River. Locals take
18 the centre of the bridge as being the border, although no border marker exists. Some residents
19 have a NSW address and phone number but live in Queensland.

20 <u>Bordertown (5268)</u> in South Australia is 20 km west of the border. There is no twin town over
21 the border.

Map labels: Qld, SA, NSW, Vic, Mungindi, Coolangatta / Tweed Heads, Bordertown, Albury / Wodonga

1 Which of the border towns does the writer find most interesting?
   A Coolangatta B Mungindi
   C Wodonga D Moree

2 The odd point made about some Mungindi residents in Queensland is that they
   A live on the opposite riverside to NSW residents.
   B have closer neighbours than the NSW residents.
   C have to cross a bridge to get into NSW.
   D have a NSW address and postcode.

3 Which of these listed towns is not separated from a 'twin' by a river?
   A Mungindi
   B Albury
   C Tweed Heads
   D Wodonga

4 In which state is Bordertown? Write your answer in the box.

5 The word *adjacent* means
   A near. B linked.
   C adjusted. D similar.

6 Bordertown is unusual in that it
   A has daylight saving.
   B is not on a river.
   C has its own postcode.
   D is not at a border.

7 In the text the number *(5268)* follows the name *Bordertown*. This number is the
   A border river's length.
   B town's postcode.
   C town's population.
   D distance east to a border.

☞ **Answers and explanations on pages 165-166**

GENERAL WRITING TIPS

Each weekly writing plan provides four exercises. It is strongly suggested that you **attempt only three of the four exercises** in each practice period. This allows for three 42-minute writing sessions. The exercise not attempted in each unit can be used as additional practice at another time.

Writing Tests are designed to test your ability to express ideas, feelings and points of view.

You will be assessed on:

● the thought and content of your writing

● the structure and organisation of your ideas

● the expression, style and appropriate use of language of your writing

● the amount you write in the given time.

To get the best results, follow these steps.

Step 1—Before you start writing

● **Read the question.** Be sure you understand the type of writing requested by the assessors. If you are expected to write an explanation, there is little point in writing a story. Read the instructions carefully. Ask yourself if you should be describing, explaining, entertaining, telling a story, expressing a point of view, expressing an emotion or persuading the reader.

● **Check the stimulus material carefully.** Make sure the stimulus material forms the basis of your writing. You will likely be given a topic, picture, words/phrases, short poem or prose extract as stimulus material.

● **What writing style?** If you are given a choice of writing styles (text types), pick the style you are most comfortable with.

● **Warning:** Don't try to make a pre-planned response fit the stimulus material given.

Step 2—Jot down points

Give yourself a few minutes before you start to get your thoughts in order and jot down points. You won't have time to write a draft. Depending on the style required, jot down points on:

● who (characters), why (reasons for action), where (setting), when (time)

● sequences of events/arguments/points

● any good ideas you suddenly have

● how to include the senses and your feelings.

Remember: You can discard ideas that don't fit into your final approach.

Step 3—Make a brief outline

List the points or events in order. This will become your framework. It can be modified as you write.

GENERAL WRITING TIPS

Step 4—Start writing

- Make your **paragraphing** work for you. New incidents in stories may require a new paragraph. Changes in time or place require new paragraphs. Descriptions that move from one sense to another (e.g. from sight to sound) require new paragraphs.

- The quality and extent of your **vocabulary** is being tested. Don't use unusual words or big words just to impress the assessor. A mistake here will expose your ignorance.

- It is important that you **complete your piece of writing**. Unfinished work will lose you marks, as will extremely short responses.

- Get as much of the **punctuation, spelling and grammar** right as you can, but allow yourself a couple of minutes after you finish to proofread your work. You won't have time for detailed editing.

- If you are writing a story, know the **ending** before you start. Your ending should not be trite or clichéd (e.g. *I woke up and found it was just a dream!*).

- If you are asked to give a **point of view**, think through the evidence you can use to support your 'argument' so that you can build to a strong conclusion.

- If you are including **descriptions** in your writing, think about the importance and relevance of all the senses—sights, smells, tastes, sounds and physical feelings. You may also include an **emotional response**.

- Have a **concluding sentence** that 'rounds off' your work.

- Keep your **handwriting** reasonably neat (i.e. readable).

Step 5—When you finish

When you finish, **re-read** your work and do a quick check for spelling, punctuation, capital letters and grammar.

> **Check the Writing section** (www.nap.edu.au/naplan/writing) **of the official NAPLAN website for up-to-date and important information on the Writing Test**. Sample Writing Tests and marking guidelines that outline the criteria markers use when assessing your writing are also provided. Please note that, to date in NAPLAN, the types of texts that students have been tested on have been narrative and persuasive writing.
>
> The Australian Curriculum for English requires students to be taught three main types of texts:
> - imaginative writing (including narratives and descriptions)
> - informative writing (including procedures and reports)
> - persuasive writing (expositions).
>
> Informative writing has not yet been tested by NAPLAN. The best preparation for writing is for students to read a range of texts and to get lots of practice in writing different types of texts. We have included information on all types of texts in this book.

TIPS FOR WRITING NARRATIVES

A **narrative** is a form of prose writing that tells a story. Its main purpose is to entertain. Writers of narratives create experiences that are shared with the reader. To do this the writer uses literary techniques. Such techniques include figurative language (similes, metaphors, alliteration, onomatopoeia, rhetorical questions and repetition), variety in sentence length and type, variety in paragraph length, and direct speech.

In any narrative, the author is the person who wrote the story. The narrator is the person (*I*) who is both in the story and who tells the story.

When writing narratives it is best to keep the following points in mind. They will help you get the best possible mark.

Before you start writing

- Read the question and check the stimulus material carefully. *Stimulus material* means the topic, title, picture, words, phrases or extract of writing you are given to base your writing on.
- Write about something you know. Don't try to write about something way outside your experience.
- Decide if you are going to be writing in the first person (you become a character in your story) or in the third person (about other characters). When writing in the first person be careful not to overuse the pronoun *I* (e.g. I did this, I did that).
- Take a few moments to jot your ideas down on a piece of paper. Write down the order in which things happen. These could be the points in your story where you start new paragraphs.
- Remember: Stories have a beginning, middle and end. It sounds simple but many stories fail because one of these three parts is not well written.

The introduction

- Don't start with *Once upon a time*—this is too clichéd and predictable.
- Don't tell the reader too much in the beginning. Make the reader want to read on to find out more. The beginning should introduce a problem to be solved.

The body

- In the middle of your story include events that make solving the problem more difficult or doubtful. This makes the story interesting.
- Use a setting that you are familiar with, e.g. home, school, sport, holiday place or shopping centre. You will then be able to describe the setting realistically.
- Choose characters that are like people you know because they are easier to imagine. You don't have to use their real names—it's probably best not to!
- Use your imagination to make the story more interesting, but don't try to fill it with weird or disgusting events.
- Enhance your story with the use of literary techniques, e.g. similes, metaphors, onomatopoeia and alliteration.
- Make your paragraphing work for you. New paragraphs are usually needed for new incidents in your story, changes in time or place, descriptions that move from one sense to another, or changes in the character who is speaking.

The conclusion

- The ending is the hardest part to write because it has to have something to do with the beginning.
- Never end your stories with: *and it was just a dream; I was saved by a superhero (or by magic); I was dead; and they lived happily ever after!* Endings like these just tell the marker that you don't have a creative way to end your story.

When you have finished writing give yourself a few minutes to read through your story. Now is the time to check spelling and punctuation, and to insert words that have been accidentally left out.

Year 4 Sample Writing
(a sample answer to the question on page 28)

The Fortune-teller

Bylawang has a show every year. Everyone in town goes to the show. This particular year I was allowed to go with Sylvia and Tegan. After a day of rides and looking at the farm displays we ended up behind an old tent, feeling bored.

"What can we do now?" Sylvia moaned quietly. She was getting tired of wandering around.

"I don't know! How much money have you got left Mia?" growled Tegan, looking at me.

I licked my lips and said slowly, "Only two dollars. I'm just about skint."

"Mia, you must have more than two dollars," Tegan said loudly. I shook my head sadly.

With drooping shoulders we wandered around towards the front of the tent. A brass band was playing jazz nearby.

There was a lopsided sign on the tent. We all looked at the sign silently as if we were Year 1 kids just learning to read. The fading sign was composed of stars and comets and cards, around a big, glowing glass ball. Behind the sphere was the shadowy shape of a fortune-teller covered in swirls of mist.

"Let's give it a go?" said Tegan. Sylvia made a funny little moan.

"If you go first," I dared, wondering if we had enough money. Sylvia didn't say anything.

"Come on Mia, it's better than doing nothing! She *might* be real," Tegan argued. She was right!

We hesitated for a minute outside the flap of a tent that had another cracked-paint sign. This one carried a promise of 'Future happiness revealed, the secrets of wealth and success unlocked NOW'. We pushed back the flap and tiptoed in. There, behind a small table, was an older lady in strange clothes and with, what looked like, a fake tan and a fake smile!

"Come in Mia," she wheezed. "It is $5 to have your palm read—but for you, I do it for two!"

She knew my name and how much money I had left! I was amazed and shocked. Then it dawned on me. We had been talking quite loudly behind her tent—less than a metre from where she sat! At least *that* was a bit of excitement before going home.

Structure

Audience
- Children who go to local shows will relate to the situation.

Character and setting
- The reader is quickly told about *what*, *who*, *when* and *where*.

Text structure
- The problem (orientation) is introduced early in the writing.
- Some information is held back by the writer.
- A series of events are related in the order in which they happen. The girls are trying to find something to do.

Paragraphing
- New paragraphs are used for when someone speaks and to show different time periods.

Cohesion
- One problem is solved.
- The ending ties in with the beginning (being bored then finding a bit of excitement).
- The girls have different personalities. The last sentence rounds off the story.

Language and ideas

- The story is written in the first person. The story is told by *I* (the first person). The writer has used a familiar subject and setting.

Vocabulary
- Adjectives and adverbs are used to enhance the story.
- A variety of 'said' words are used. Verbs are used imaginatively.

Sentence structure
- The writer includes a simile to improve meaning. A variety of sentence beginnings add interest. Interesting detail is included (e.g. swirls of mist).

Ideas
- The writer makes good use of 'sounds' in the setting and repetition.

Punctuation
- Exclamation sentences are used for effect.
- Correct grammar is used throughout.

Spelling
- There are no errors in punctuation and spelling.

This text is beyond what would be expected of a typical Year 4 student. It is provided here as a model. The assessment comments are based on the marking criteria used to assess the NAPLAN Writing Test.

© Pascal Press ISBN 978 1 74125 424 2

Real Test

WRITING
Narrative 1

Before you start, read the **General Writing Tips** on pages 23–24 and the **Tips for Writing Narratives** on page 25.

Today you are going to write a narrative or story. It will be about the unexpected discovery of an animal.

Choose one of the following phrases and use it as the basis for a story:

- a puppy on the doorstep
- a butterfly at the school assembly
- a mouse in the classroom
- a cockroach under the table.

- a goanna in the garden
- a budgie on the windowsill

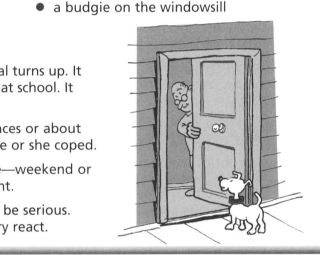

Think about where the unexpected animal turns up. It could be around the home or it could be at school. It might be at someone else's home.

Your story might be about your experiences or about those of another person and how well he or she coped.

Think about when your story takes place—weekend or schoolday, summer or winter, day or night.

Your story might be amusing or it might be serious. Think about how the people in your story react.

Before you start to write, think about:
- where your story takes place
- the characters and what they do in your story
- the events that take place in your story and the problems that have to be resolved
- how the story begins, what happens in your story and how your story ends.

Remember to:
- plan your story before you start writing
- write in correctly formed sentences and take care with paragraphing
- pay attention to the words you use, your spelling and punctuation
- write neatly but don't waste time
- quickly check your story once you have finished.

Start writing here or type in your answer on a tablet or computer.

_____

_____

_____

_____

☞ **Marking guide on page 166**

Real Test

42 MIN

Before you start, read the **General Writing Tips** on pages 23–24 and the **Tips for Writing Narratives** on page 25.

Today you are going to write a narrative or story.

Look at the picture on the right.

The idea for your story is about a surprise. You (or someone else) could be caught in automatic sprinklers, standing on an ants' nest or walking into a spider's web. It might be someone you meet unexpectedly or who knows something you wouldn't have predicted.

Think about where your story takes place. It could be at a beach, by a lake or river. It could be in a park or camping grounds.

Think about when your story takes place—daytime or dusk, summer or winter, holidays or schooldays, mealtime.

Your story might be amusing or it might be serious. Think about how other people in your story might react.

Before you start to write, think about:
- where your story takes place
- the characters and what they do in your story
- the events that take place in your story and the problems that have to be resolved
- how the story begins, what happens in your story and how your story ends.

Remember to:
- plan your story before you start writing
- write in correctly formed sentences and take care with paragraphing
- pay attention to the words you use, your spelling and punctuation
- write neatly but don't waste time
- quickly check your story once you have finished.

Start writing here or type in your answer on a tablet or computer.

_____

_____

_____

_____

_____

☞ Go to page 26 to see a sample answer to this question.

☞ Marking guide on page 166

Real Test

WRITING
Narrative 3

42 MIN

Before you start, read the **General Writing Tips** on pages 23–24 and the **Tips for Writing Narratives** on page 25.

Today you are going to write a narrative or story. Sometimes you may be given a picture to stimulate your storywriting imagination.

Look at the picture on the right and use it to write a story. It may be about yourself or a person in the picture.

Before you start to write, think about:
- where your story takes place
- the characters and why they are where they are and what they do in your story
- the events that take place in your story and the problems that have to be resolved
- how the story begins, what happens in your story and how your story ends.

Remember to:
- plan your story before you start writing
- write in correctly formed sentences and take care with paragraphing
- pay attention to the words you use, your spelling and punctuation
- write neatly but don't waste time
- quickly check your story once you have finished.

Start writing here or type in your answer on a tablet or computer.

_____

_____

_____

_____

_____

☞ **Marking guide on page 167**

Real Test

42 min

Before you start, read the **General Writing Tips** on pages 23–24 and the **Tips for Writing Narratives** on page 25.

Today you are going to write a narrative or story. Sometimes you may be given a topic to stimulate your storywriting imagination.

Today's topic is **The Visitor.**

Your visitor may be someone you know, a stranger with some amazing news, a person needing help, an alien or some being from a fantasy world.

Use your imagination to select the visitor you want to write your story about. You may be a character in your story or your story could be about someone else.

Before you start to write, think about:
- where your story takes place
- who the visitor is and why that visitor came visiting
- the events that take place in your story and the problems that have to be resolved
- how the story begins, what happens in your story and how your story ends.

Remember to:
- plan your story before you start writing
- write in correctly formed sentences and take care with paragraphing
- pay attention to the words you use, your spelling and punctuation
- write neatly but don't waste time
- quickly check your story once you have finished.

Start writing here or type in your answer on a tablet or computer.

_____

_____

_____

_____

_____

☞ **Marking guide on pages 167-168**

What's next ?

Week 2

This is what we cover this week:

Day 1 **Number and Algebra:** ◎ Adding, subtracting, multiplying and dividing

Day 2 **Number and Algebra:** ◎ Fractions, decimals and money

Day 3 **Spelling:** ◎ Adding 'ing' or 'ed' to verbs and 'er' and 'est' to adjectives

 Grammar and Punctuation: ◎ Types of nouns and adjectives and use of commas and brackets

Day 4 **Reading:** ◎ Understanding persuasive texts
 ◎ Understanding posters
 ◎ Understanding cartoons
 ◎ Understanding explanations

Day 5 **Writing:** ◎ Persuasive texts

Test Your Skills

NUMBER AND ALGEBRA
Adding, subtracting, multiplying and dividing

30 MIN

Add.

1 $2 + 3 + 6 =$ ☐

2 $4 + 3 + 5 =$ ☐

3 $6 + 7 + 8 + 2 =$ ☐

4 $1 + 4 + 6 + 9 =$ ☐

Subtract.

5 $9 - 2 =$ ☐

6 $12 - 5 =$ ☐

7 $17 - 4 - 3 =$ ☐

8 $13 - 6 - 7 =$ ☐

Complete the following.

9 $57 + 25 = 57 + 20 +$ ☐

$=$ ☐ $+$ ☐ $=$ ☐

10 $32 + 47 = 30 + 40 +$ ☐ $+ 7$

$= 70 +$ ☐ $=$ ☐

11 $62 - 26 = 62 - 20 -$ ☐

$=$ ☐ $-$ ☐ $=$ ☐

12 $3200 + 760 = 3200 + 700 +$ ☐

$=$ ☐ $+$ ☐ $=$ ☐

13 $37 + 45 = 37 + 3 +$ ☐

$=$ ☐ $+$ ☐ $=$ ☐

14 $58 + 39 = 58 + 40 -$ ☐

$=$ ☐ $-$ ☐ $=$ ☐

Add.

15 $\begin{array}{r} 624 \\ + 371 \\ \hline \end{array}$ ☐

16 $\begin{array}{r} 3265 \\ + 428 \\ \hline \end{array}$ ☐

17 $\begin{array}{r} 28\,327 \\ + 5\,176 \\ \hline \end{array}$ ☐

Subtract.

18 $\begin{array}{r} 975 \\ - 432 \\ \hline \end{array}$ ☐

19 $\begin{array}{r} 2563 \\ - 387 \\ \hline \end{array}$ ☐

20 $\begin{array}{r} 43\,508 \\ - 6\,243 \\ \hline \end{array}$ ☐

Multiply.

21 $2 \times 7 =$ ☐

22 $4 \times 8 =$ ☐

23 $5 \times 9 =$ ☐

24 $6 \times 7 =$ ☐

25 $8 \times 3 =$ ☐

26 $9 \times 0 =$ ☐

Divide.

27 $10 \div 2 =$ ☐

28 $40 \div 5 =$ ☐

29 $28 \div 4 =$ ☐

30 $27 \div 9 =$ ☐

31 $56 \div 7 =$ ☐

32 $36 \div 6 =$ ☐

Complete the following.

33 $34 \times 9 = 30 \times 9 +$ ☐ $\times$ ☐

$=$ ☐ $+$ ☐ $=$ ☐

34 $264 \div 8 =$ ☐ $\div 4$

$=$ ☐ $\div 2 =$ ☐

Use the fact that $137 \times 6 = 822$ to answer the following questions.

35 $138 \times 6 =$ ☐

36 $822 \div 137 =$ ☐

Find the answers.

37 What is the sum of 7 and 8? ☐

38 What is 11 take away 7? ☐

39 How much more than 4 is 13? ☐

40 What is the difference between 9 and 4? ☐

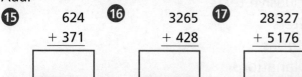

NUMBER AND ALGEBRA
Adding, subtracting, multiplying and dividing

(continued)

1 It is important to be able to quickly and easily **add two or more single-digit numbers**.

Examples:

$2 + 3 + 6 = 11$ and $4 + 3 + 5 = 12$

When adding numbers, remember that it can be done in any order.

Examples: $6 + 7 + 8 + 2 = 13 + 10 = 23$

- $1 + 4 + 6 + 9 = 20$ because $1 + 9 = 10$ and $4 + 6 = 10$. It is easiest to add those pairs of numbers first.

2 **When subtracting, we take away one number from another.**

Examples: $9 - 2 = 7$. We might say 9 take away 2 or take 2 away from 9.

- $12 - 5 = 7$. We might say 12 minus 5 is 7.
- Now $17 - 4 - 3 = 13 - 3 = 10$. We get the same answer if we subtract 3 from 17 first and then subtract 4, but we cannot subtract the 3 from the 4. [If we do that we get the wrong answer. $4 - 3 = 1$ and $17 - 1 = 16$.]
- $13 - 6 - 7 = 7 - 7 = 0$

3 **There are many ways to make adding and subtracting easier.** For example, one or more of the numbers can be broken into **hundreds, tens and ones**.

Examples:

- $57 + 25 = 57 + 20 + 5 = 77 + 5 = 82$
- $32 + 47 = 30 + 40 + 2 + 7 = 70 + 9 = 79$
- $62 - 26 = 62 - 20 - 6 = 42 - 6 = 36$
- $3200 + 760 = 3200 + 700 + 60$
  $= 3900 + 60$
  $= 3960$

The numbers could also be split some other way. For example, we might **take an amount from the second number to make the first number a multiple of ten**.

Example:

$37 + 45 = 37 + 3 + 42 = 40 + 42 = 82$

Or we might **add a number larger than the one we want, and then subtract the extra amount**.

Example:

$58 + 39 = 58 + 40 - 1 = 98 - 1 = 97$

4 Also learn **to add numbers written out in a formal addition**.

$$\begin{array}{r} 624 \\ + \ 371 \\ \hline 995 \end{array}$$

Remember to carry over excess tens and hundreds.

Examples: In this next sum we begin by adding 5 and 8 to get 13. The '3' belongs in the ones position so we write that down but the '1' is actually 'one ten' so we add one to the tens position.

$$\begin{array}{r} {}^{1} \\ 3265 \\ + \ 428 \\ \hline 3693 \end{array}$$

We must continue this process for hundreds and thousands as well as tens.

$$\begin{array}{r} {}^{1}\ {}^{11} \\ 28\,327 \\ + \ 5\,176 \\ \hline 33\,503 \end{array}$$

5 **We must also be able to perform formal subtractions.** The process is simple if every digit in the bottom is smaller than the corresponding digit above.

$$\begin{array}{r} 975 \\ - \ 432 \\ \hline 543 \end{array}$$

But it might be necessary to trade some of the numbers in order to be able to subtract.

Example: Look at the subtraction below. We cannot take 7 items away from only 3. So we take one of the tens from the next column so that instead of 6 tens and 3 ones we have 5 tens and 13. We can now take 7 away from 13 to leave 6 ones. In the tens column we now want to take 8 (tens) away from 5 (tens), but again that cannot be done. We take one of the hundreds from the hundreds column so that we can do the subtraction.

$$\begin{array}{r} {}^{4}\ {}^{15}{}^{13} \\ 2\,\cancel{5}\,\cancel{6}\,3 \\ - \ 3\,8\,7 \\ \hline 2\,1\,7\,6 \end{array}$$

Key Points

NUMBER AND ALGEBRA
Adding, subtracting, multiplying and dividing

(continued)

We must **take special care when there is a 0 in the numbers**, although the same method is used in the subtraction.

$$\begin{array}{r} ^{3}\cancel{4}\,^{13}\cancel{3}\,^{4}\cancel{5}\,^{10}\cancel{0}\,8 \\ -\;\;6\;2\;4\;3 \\ \hline 3\;7\;2\;6\;5 \end{array}$$

We can always **check a subtraction by adding the answer to the amount that was taken away**.

6 It is very important to be able to **multiply** numbers together. Learn to immediately know the answer to any multiplication up to 10 × 10.

Examples: 2 × 7 = 14 because 2 lots of 7 is 7 + 7 or 14.

4 × 8 = 32 because 8 + 8 + 8 + 8 is 32.

It is important to understand the process of multiplication, but it is not necessary to go through this process every time you want to multiply.

Learning your **tables** is perhaps the best thing you can do to help you with numeracy and your studies of mathematics when you are older.

So 5 × 9 = 45, 6 × 7 = 42 and 8 × 3 = 24.

Take care when multiplying by 0. The answer is always 0 (e.g. 9 × 0 = 0).

7 **Division is simply a process of splitting amounts into groups of certain sizes.**

Examples: 10 ÷ 2 = 5 because if 10 objects are divided into 2 groups there will be 5 objects in each group.

So 40 ÷ 5 = 8 and 28 ÷ 4 = 7.

Division is related to multiplying. It is the opposite process. So if you can multiply, you can divide.

Examples: If you know that 3 × 9 = 27 then you also know that 27 ÷ 9 = 3 and 27 ÷ 3 = 9.

56 ÷ 7 = 8 because 8 × 7 = 56.

36 ÷ 6 = 6

8 **There are many ways we can make multiplying and dividing simpler too.** For example, you can break a two-digit number into the tens part and ones part and multiply each part separately.

Example:

34 × 9 = 30 × 9 + 4 × 9 = 270 + 36 = 306

You can change the order in which you multiply and you can find the factors of a number to make a question easier.

Example: 14 × 15 = 2 × 7 × 5 × 3

$$\begin{aligned} &= 2 \times 5 \times 7 \times 3 \\ &= 10 \times 21 \\ &= 210 \end{aligned}$$

To divide by two you just need to halve the number. To divide by 4 you halve the number and then halve it again.

Examples: 264 ÷ 8 = 132 ÷ 4 = 66 ÷ 2 = 33

You can use known facts to help you work out unknown facts.

Example: So if 137 × 6 = 822, then 138 × 6 is just one more lot of 6. Now 822 + 6 = 828 so 138 × 6 = 828.

Because division is related to multiplication, then if 137 × 6 = 822 it must follow that 822 ÷ 137 = 6.

9 It is important to understand the language of mathematics. For example, **to find the sum means to add**. So the sum of 7 and 8 is 7 + 8 or 15.

To find the product means to multiply, so the product of 6 and 3 is 6 × 3 or 18.

We must read questions carefully. For example, 11 **take away** 7 means the same as take 7 away from 11. It is important to do it the right way. You subtract 7 from 11. 11 − 7 = 4.

13 is 9 **more** than 4 because 13 − 4 = 9.

To find the difference between two numbers subtract the smaller number from the larger. So the difference between 9 and 4 is 9 − 4 or 5.

Real Test

NUMBER AND ALGEBRA
Adding, subtracting, multiplying and dividing

20 MIN

1 Joel had 25 cards. He gave 7 to Francis and 8 to Harry. How many cards did Joel have left?

2 Susan puts strawberries into 20 equal groups. Each group has 5 strawberries.

How many strawberries are there altogether?

A 100 **B** 25 **C** 15 **D** 4

3 These ear tags are sold in packets of 100.

Beth needs an ear tag for each of her 232 cows. What is the least number of packets Beth needs?

A 1 **B** 2 **C** 3 **D** 4

4 Kylie has 76 books. Ella has 85 books. How many books do they have altogether?

5 Sally puts cans of drinks in packs. She puts 6 cans in a pack like this:

Sally has 30 cans altogether. Which of these shows how Sally could work out how many packs she will have?

A 30 + 6 **B** 30 − 6 **C** 30 × 6 **D** 30 ÷ 6

6 There are 24 children in kindergarten. There are 4 more boys than girls. How many girls are in kindergarten?

7 Thomas and Oliver both have the same total number of cars and trucks. Thomas has 37 cars and 28 trucks. Oliver has 52 cars. How many trucks does Oliver have?

8 17 + 35 has the same value as 20 + ☐ .

9 Ryan has 9 marbles. Billy has 5 times as many marbles as Ryan. What is the difference between the number of marbles Billy has and the number of marbles Ryan has?

10 Here are 4 number cards.

| 1 | 2 | 3 | 4 |

Use each card once to make this true.

☐ ☐ ☐ × ☐ = **1248**

11 Jenna, Daisy and Lucy together have 32 stickers.

Daisy has 4 more stickers than Jenna. Lucy has 3 more stickers than Daisy. How many stickers does Daisy have?

12 6 × 5 = ☐ × 3

13

Complete this number sentence to show the total number of eggs in the picture.

☐ × 12 = ☐

14 A group of children were given 4 balloons each. Altogether there were 116 balloons. How many children were in the group?

15 3 × 7 = 12 + ☐

16 There are 145 photos in Ken's albums. There are between 25 and 30 photos in each album. How many albums does Ken have?

A 4 **B** 5 **C** 6 **D** 7

☞ **Answers and explanations on pages 168-169**

Test Your Skills

NUMBER AND ALGEBRA
Fractions, decimals and money

30 MIN

What fraction of each rectangle is shaded?

 **1**

 **2**

 **3**

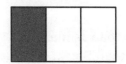 **4**

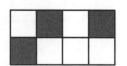 **5**

 **6**

These oranges could be cut into how many:

7 halves?

8 quarters?

This shape could be divided into how many:

9 thirds?

10 tenths?

11 hundredths?

12 Write two different fractions to describe the shaded part of this shape.

and

$\frac{1}{4}$ of each shape is shaded. True or false?

13

14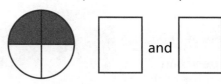

Write the next three numbers in each pattern.

15 $\frac{1}{2}$, 1, $1\frac{1}{2}$, 2, $2\frac{1}{2}$, ____ , ____ , ____

16 $\frac{1}{3}$, $\frac{2}{3}$, 1, $1\frac{1}{3}$, $1\frac{2}{3}$, ____ , ____ , ____

17 $\frac{1}{4}$, $\frac{1}{2}$, $\frac{3}{4}$, 1, $1\frac{1}{4}$, ____ , ____ , ____

NUMBER AND ALGEBRA
Fractions, decimals and money

(continued)

Which arrow is pointing to:

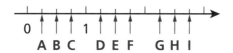

0   A B C   1   D E F   G H I

18 $\frac{1}{4}$? ☐

19 $\frac{3}{4}$? ☐

20 $1\frac{1}{2}$? ☐

21 $2\frac{3}{4}$? ☐

What fraction is each arrow pointing to?

22
0   1   ☐

23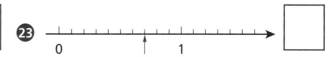
0   1   ☐

Write a number in each box.

24 $0.3 = \dfrac{\Box}{10}$

25 $0.7 = \dfrac{\Box}{\Box}$

26 $0.01 = \dfrac{\Box}{100}$

27 $0.09 = \dfrac{\Box}{\Box}$

Add.

28 $6 + 0.9 =$ ☐

29 $0.7 + 0.05 =$ ☐

30 $4 + 0.3 + 0.08 =$ ☐

31 How much money is this? ☐

Add these amounts together.

32 $5.20 + $2.50 ☐

33 $14.65 + 30 cents ☐

34 $9.45 + $6.70 ☐

What is the change from $10.00 if you spend:

35 $7.00? ☐

36 $9.75?

37 $4.38? ☐

Key Points

NUMBER AND ALGEBRA
Fractions, decimals and money

(continued)

1 **When something is divided into equal parts each of those parts is a particular fraction of the whole thing.**

Example: If something is divided into 2 equal parts then each part is one-half of the whole.

So $\frac{1}{2}$ of the rectangle is shaded.

If the shape is divided into 4 equal parts then each part is one-quarter or one-fourth or $\frac{1}{4}$ of the whole.

Examples: So $\frac{1}{4}$ of the rectangle is shaded.

- This rectangle has three of its four equal parts shaded.

  The fraction that is shaded is $\frac{3}{4}$.

- This rectangle has one of three parts shaded. The shaded fraction is one-third $\left(\frac{1}{3}\right)$.

- This rectangle has three out of eight parts shaded.

  The fraction shaded is $\frac{3}{8}$.

- This rectangle has two out of four parts shaded.

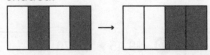

  But if the two parts that were shaded were put together, then we could see that one out of two parts or $\frac{1}{2}$ is shaded.

2 Any object can be broken up into fractions. As one-half is one part out of two, **there are two halves in every whole.**
So every orange could be divided into two halves. Three oranges could be divided into 6 halves.

As one-quarter is one part out of four, **there are four quarters in every whole.**
So every orange could be broken into 4 quarters. Three oranges could be divided into 12 quarters.

Any shape can be divided into 3 thirds, 10 tenths or 100 hundredths.

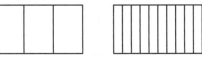

3 This circle has $\frac{2}{4}$ or $\frac{1}{2}$ shaded.

$\frac{2}{4}$ and $\frac{1}{2}$ are **equivalent fractions** because they **are the same amount.**

Any fraction that is equivalent to $\frac{1}{2}$ could also be used. For example, $\frac{4}{8}$ or $\frac{6}{12}$.

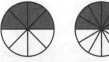

4 But remember, **the shape must be divided into equal parts.**

So the shape on the right has $\frac{1}{4}$ shaded, but the shape below does not because the parts are not all the same size.

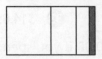

5 It is important to **learn to count with fractions.**

Example: $\frac{1}{2}$, 1, $1\frac{1}{2}$, 2, $2\frac{1}{2}$, 3, $3\frac{1}{2}$, 4

When counting you should be able to use **mixed numerals**, which **are a mixture of whole numbers and fractions.**

Examples: $\frac{1}{3}$, $\frac{2}{3}$, 1, $1\frac{1}{3}$, $1\frac{2}{3}$, 2, $2\frac{1}{3}$, $2\frac{2}{3}$

or $\frac{1}{4}$, $\frac{1}{2}$, $\frac{3}{4}$, 1, $1\frac{1}{4}$, $1\frac{1}{2}$, $1\frac{3}{4}$, 2

Key Points

NUMBER AND ALGEBRA
Fractions, decimals and money

(continued)

⑥ Also learn to find the position of fractions on the **number line**.

Examples:

On the number line above, 1 whole is divided into 4 equal parts so each part is $\frac{1}{4}$.

So A points to $\frac{1}{4}$ and C points to $\frac{3}{4}$.

E points to $1\frac{1}{2}$ and I points to $2\frac{3}{4}$.

- On the number line below, 1 whole is broken into 3 equal parts, so each part is $\frac{1}{3}$. The arrow is pointing to $\frac{2}{3}$.

- On this number line, 1 whole is broken into 10 equal parts. Each part is $\frac{1}{10}$ and the arrow is pointing to $\frac{7}{10}$.

⑦ **The place value system can be extended to numbers after a decimal point**. The first digit after the decimal point represents tenths and the second digit after the decimal point represents hundredths.

thousands   tens   tenths

1234.56

hundreds   units   hundredths

So 0.3 is three-tenths or $\frac{3}{10}$ and 0.7 is $\frac{7}{10}$.

0.01 is one-hundredth or $\frac{1}{100}$ and 0.09 is $\frac{9}{100}$.

$6 + 0.9 = 6.9$ because it is 6 units plus nine-tenths.

$0.7 + 0.05 = 0.75$ (seven-tenths plus five-hundredths)

$4 + 0.3 + 0.08 = 4.38$ (four units plus three-tenths plus eight-hundredths)

⑧ It is very important to learn **to recognise all the different coins and notes that make up our money**. You should **also** be able to **count amounts of money**.

Example: Here there are two 50c coins, three 20c coins, one 10c coin and three 5c coins.

Altogether there is $1.85.

⑨ **When adding amounts of money, we can add the cents together and add the dollars together.**

Examples: $5.20 + $2.50 = $7.70 because $5 + $2 = $7 and 20c + 50c = 70c.

- To add $14.65 + 30c we add the cents together. $65 + 30 = 95$
So $14.65 + 30c = $14.95.

- To add $9.45 + $6.70 we could write it out as a sum and add.

$$\begin{array}{r} {}^{1}\ \ \\ \$9.45 \\ + \ \$6.70 \\ \hline \$16.15 \end{array}$$

Or we could take 30c from the first amount and add it to the second.
$9.45 + $6.70 = $9.15 + $7.00 = $16.15

⑩ **To find the change we can subtract the cost from the amount of money.**

So the change from $10.00 if you spend $7.00 is $3.00 because $10 - 7 = 3$.

You can also count forward from the amount. $9.75 + 25c = $10.00 so the change from $10.00 when you spend $9.75 is 25c.

Remember that change must be calculated to the nearest 5c. Now $4.38 is close to $4.40. You need another 60c to make $5 and then another $5 to make $10. The change from $10.00 when you spend $4.38 is $5.60.

Real Test

NUMBER AND ALGEBRA
Fractions, decimals and money

1 Ben has these pencils.

He gives half of the pencils to Casey.
How many pencils does Ben have left?

2 Angus has these coins.

He buys a drink for $2.85. How much money does Angus have left?

A $1.25   B $1.15   C $0.95   D $1.05

3 How many quarters are there in three and a half apples?

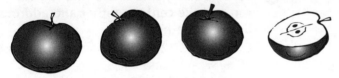

A 10   B 11   C 13   D 14

4 Which arrow is closest to 0.75 on this number line?

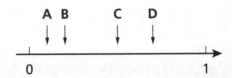

5 Jay has $8.45. He doesn't have enough money to buy this toy truck.

He needs another 25 cents. How much is the truck? $

6 Grace feeds her calves. Together they eat half a bale of hay every day. How many bales of hay will Grace need to feed her calves for two weeks?

A 5   B 7   C 10   D 14

7 April is making sandwiches. She cuts these into halves.
How many halves does she have altogether?

A 2
B 4
C 6
D 8

☞ **Answers and explanations on page 169**

Real Test

NUMBER AND ALGEBRA
Fractions, decimals and money
(continued)

8 Put the numbers 0.3, 0.03, 0.13 and 0.103 in order from smallest to largest.

smallest   largest

9 This shape is made with 8 triangles.
What fraction of the shape is shaded?

A $\frac{2}{6}$ B $\frac{1}{2}$

C $\frac{1}{4}$ D $\frac{1}{6}$

10 Lily bought a book and a pen.

What is the correct change

from $5.00? $ [ ]

$2.25 $1.65

11 Twelve people share these pizzas equally.
What fraction of a pizza will each person get?

A $\frac{1}{2}$ B $\frac{1}{3}$

C $\frac{1}{4}$ D $\frac{1}{12}$

12 What is 6 tens, 8 ones and 3 hundredths equal to?
A 368   B 68.3   C 68.03   D 683

13 Which arrow points to $\frac{1}{5}$ on this number line?

0   A B   C   D   1

14 A shopkeeper charged Jack $4.35 for a magazine. Jack got $1.65 in change. What amount of money did Jack give the shopkeeper?
A $5   B $6   C $7   D $10

15 Some shapes are made by joining squares. All the squares are the same size. Which shape has one-third of its squares shaded?

A    B    C 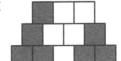   D

☞ **Answers and explanations on page 169**

SPELLING
Adding 'ing' or 'ed' to verbs and 'er' and 'est' to adjectives

15 min

 Most spelling rules have exceptions. English words have many different origins (e.g. *bunyip* comes from Aboriginal Australia and *sarong* comes from Malaysia).

Key Points

1 With most words you simply add the 'ing' or 'ed'.

Examples: camp, camping, camped; paint, painting, painted; peep, peeping, peeped

2 **a** Simply add 'ing' to words that end with a consonant + **y**.

Examples: try ➜ trying; bury ➜ burying; carry ➜ carrying

b Before adding 'ed' to words that end in a consonant + **y**, change the **y** to **i**.

Examples: tally ➜ tallied; cry ➜ cried

3 For words ending with a consonant + **e**, you drop the **e**, then add 'ing' or 'ed'.

Examples: hope ➜ hoping, hoped; wave ➜ waving, waved; snore ➜ snoring, snored

4 For short words ending in a single vowel + a consonant, simply double the last letter.

Examples: hop ➜ hopping, hopped; stab ➜ stabbing, stabbed; beg ➜ begging, begged
The main exceptions are words ending in **w**, **x** and **y**.

Examples: know ➜ knowing, knew; box ➜ boxing, boxed; play ➜ playing, played

5 The same rules apply when adding 'er' and 'est' to make comparative adjectives.

Examples: fast ➜ faster, fastest; happy ➜ happier, happiest; hot ➜ hotter, hottest

Test Your Skills

Learn the words below. A common method of self-testing is the **LOOK, SAY, COVER, WRITE, CHECK** method. Any mistakes should be rewritten three times correctly and immediately. By rewriting the word correctly you become familiar with the correct spelling. If the word is particularly troublesome, rewrite it several more times or keep a list of words that you can check regularly.

copy _____	copying _____	copied _____
answer _____	answering _____	answered _____
address _____	addressing _____	addressed _____
reply _____	replying _____	replied _____
type _____	typing _____	typed _____
study _____	studying _____	studied _____
quick _____	quicker _____	quickest _____

Write any troublesome words three times: _____

Real Test

SPELLING
Common misspellings

15 MIN

Please ask your parent or teacher to read to you the spelling words on page 209. Write the correct spelling of each word in the box.

1 It was late in the _____ when Uncle James arrived.

2 The school has a boy _____ this year.

3 The butcher has _____ for sale on white trays.

4 Dad buys packets of mixed nuts that include _____.

5 We use _____ water to make our coffee.

6 Tulips are _____ that flower well in cool regions.

Each line has one word that is incorrect. Write the correct spelling of the underlined word in the box.

7 If there is <u>climarte</u> change then some people will suffer.

8 The oranges were <u>juicey</u> but the flavour was weak.

9 "<u>Whear</u> did you put the DVD we borrowed?" asked Mum.

10 We need to make a <u>decisson</u> before we start driving.

11 Sometimes I <u>wander</u> what I am going to do with you!

12 Are lemons and oranges <u>citerus</u> fruits?

Each sentence has a spelling mistake. Write the correct spelling of that word in the box. There is only one mistake in each line.

13 After a <u>lieftime</u> of adventure Jill thought it was time to relax.

14 Matthew was stung by a <u>whasp</u> while climbing the tree.

15 The pilot guided the ship into the narrow harbor.

Read the text *Hospital visit.* Each line has a word that is incorrect. Write the correct spelling of the word in the box.

Hospital visit

16 We went to see Grandpa in hospital. The only flowers we could buy were daisys.

17 "He looks a lot better today," said the nerse as we entered the ward. "I checked

18 his head wund. It's okay. Soon we will only see a small scar." This was good news for everybody.

☞**Answers and explanations on page 170**

Key Points and Test Your Skills

GRAMMAR AND PUNCTUATION
Types of nouns and adjectives and use of commas and brackets

15 MIN

Key Points

1 There are four types of nouns.

a **Common nouns** are the names of everyday things around us.

Examples: coat, clouds, toe, elephant, desert

b **Proper nouns** begin with a capital letter and are the names of a particular person, place or thing.

Examples: Napoleon, Melbourne, Ford, Opera House, Christmas Day, Russians

c An **abstract noun** is a type of noun that refers to something a person cannot physically interact with.

Examples: beauty, hate, amazement, sadness, peace, exhaustion, health

d **Collective nouns** are used to name groups of individuals, places or things.

Examples: crowd, batch, bunch, herd, flock

2 **a** **Adjectives** are words that tell us more about nouns or describe them.

Examples: <u>weak</u> cordial, <u>ugly</u> boxer, <u>ten</u> houses, <u>brown</u> paint, the sky is <u>blue</u>

b **Proper adjectives** are formed from proper nouns.

Examples: Italy → Italian, France → French, Japan → Japanese

c Adjectives have three degrees of comparison.

Examples: tall, taller, tallest

Joan is <u>tall</u>. (One person is tall.); Bill is <u>taller</u> than Joan. (Two people are compared.); Helen is the <u>tallest</u> person in our class. (Three or more people are compared.)

3 **Commas** are used in a series of items or adjectives or to indicate a pause. There is no comma between the last two items in a series that are separated by *and*.

Examples: Commas in series: For school, Jim has books, pens, pencils and paste. Commas for pauses: My teacher, Ms Dhondy, has written a book.

4 **Brackets** are used to include additional information that may be useful.

Example: Emma Peggle (1960–2006) wrote ten novels in her short life.

Test Your Skills

1 Name the type of noun (common, proper, abstract or collective) for each word.

hair _____, idea _____,

Broome _____, gang _____

2 Draw a line through the adjectives in this sentence.
He was an old Tasmanian farmer living in the small coastal town of Cygnet.

3 Write the correct word in the space.

a That was the _____ film I have ever seen! (funny, funnier, funniest)

b It's been _____ this year than any year since 1998. (wet, wetter, wettest)

4 Add commas to these sentences and write the number of commas you used in the box.

a Justine has four long purple ribbons. ☐

b Leon an old friend is not feeling well. ☐

c Anna Meg Belle Yvonne and Susie all won ribbons at the carnival. ☐

5 Add the brackets required in this sentence.
The pindan wattle *acacia tumida* grows in Australia's north-west corner.

Real Test

GRAMMAR AND PUNCTUATION
Types of nouns and adjectives and use of commas and brackets

15 min

1 Choose the letter to show where the missing comma (**,**) should go.

Kathy Freeman, an Australian sprinter won a gold medal in the 2000 Olympics.

Ⓐ   Ⓑ   Ⓒ   Ⓓ

2 Which of the following correctly completes this sentence?
Chad is a great runner. He is ▨▨▨▨ than all of his brothers.

A fast   B more fast   C faster   D fastest   E more faster

3 Which of the following correctly completes this sentence?
John was ▨▨▨▨ by a huge black ant when he sat on a stump.

A bit   B bited   C bitted   D bitten

4 Which of the following correctly completes this sentence?
There were several doctors on duty but we managed to see ▨▨▨▨ Khan.

A dr   B Dr.   C Dr   D doctor

5 Which word is the collective noun in this sentence?

The coach and a team of cricketers had a meeting with our school teachers.

Write your answer in the box.

6 Brackets are required in this sentence.
Which part should be enclosed in brackets?

Charles 'Woody' Herman 1913–1987, the big band leader, also played clarinet.

Ⓐ   Ⓑ   Ⓒ   Ⓓ

7 Which of the following correctly completes this sentence?
I wondered who was at the ▨▨▨▨ The voice was familiar.

A door.   B door   C door,   D door?

8 Choose the word that is **not** required in this sentence.
We all meet together in the dining room to discuss the food supply.

A all   B together
C dining   D supply

9 Which of the following correctly completes this sentence?
Bonny didn't want curry ▨▨▨▨ was spicy, ▨▨▨▨ she had pasta with meatballs.

A which—so   B what—so
C what—because   D which—as

10 Choose the letter to show where the missing apostrophe (**'**) should go.

Ⓐ   Ⓑ   Ⓒ   Ⓓ

His book of tests was left with the atlas in his dads office.

☞ **Answers and explanations on pages 170-171**

GRAMMAR AND PUNCTUATION
Types of nouns and adjectives and use of commas and brackets

(continued)

11 Choose the word that *who* refers to in this sentence.

Brad and Don wanted to go swimming without Lee. Bret had the bus fares. He was the one <u>who</u> decided what to do!

Write your answer in the box. [   ]

12 Which of the following correctly completes this sentence?
You'll still go fishing ▆▆▆▆ of the weather!

  A because
  B regardless
  C despite
  D even though

13 Which sentence should have a question mark (**?**)?

  A What you get is what you deserve
  B What caused the accident is a police matter
  C What a great concert that was
  D What harm can it do if it's not dangerous

14 Eni thought Greg was going to join her in the grandstand.
Which sentence shows this?

  A "This is an unexpected meeting!"
  B "When did you decide to come?"
  C "I didn't know you'd be so late."
  D "Did you know I would be here?"

15 Which of the following correctly completes the sentence?
Kevin needed ▆▆▆▆ hour to clean the car inside and out after the picnic.

  A an   **B** the
  C a   **D** ah

16 Which of the following correctly completes the sentence?
The band, with two drummers, ▆▆▆▆ belting out rock songs all night.

  A is   **B** are
  C was   **D** were

17 Which sentence is correctly punctuated?

  A "Today," warned the bus driver, "you will wear a seatbelt."
  B Today warned the bus driver, "You will wear a seatbelt."
  C "Today, warned the bus driver, you will wear a seatbelt."
  D Today, "warned the bus driver," you will wear a seatbelt.

18 Shade a bubble to show where the missing comma (**,**) should go.

Two four and six are all even numbers less than ten.

   Ⓐ   Ⓑ   Ⓒ Ⓓ   Ⓔ

☞ **Answers and explanations on pages 170-171**

Persuasive texts are used to 'argue' the case for or against a particular action or plan or to provide a point of view—to persuade others to see it your way. They may also be to persuade others to do something.

Read the persuasive text *Dogs in towns* and answer the questions.

1 **Dogs in towns**

2 Only a few towns and places have bans on dogs. I believe most
3 dogs in towns and cities should be banned. I don't include farm
4 dogs. They help farmers. Nor do I include dogs such as guide dogs,
5 sniffer dogs or police dogs, but I do include all those dogs that
6 spend most of their time imprisoned in small yards or <u>poky</u>
7 little flats, many floors from the ground.

8 Our family has a walk every evening at dusk. It is amazing how
9 many dogs run along fences barking at people for simply using
10 public footpaths. Many don't stop until well after you have
11 passed by. It's a form of harassment. The big ones with bared
12 teeth look as if they could climb over any <u>flimsy fence</u> and attack
13 at the first chance. Their behaviour is threatening—and scary.

14 Not all people walk in daylight hours. If something stirs it up
15 at night, a <u>yap, yap, yapping</u> mutt will carry on for ages! Have you tried doing homework or
16 sleeping when next door's pet won't be quiet?

17 Then there's the problem when an inconsiderate owner leaves dog droppings on the footpath or
18 the verge. Have you ever trod on one? They are disgusting.

19 Think of all the money that could be used for people if money wasn't spent on obese dogs and
20 unnecessary dog operations.

21 Many town dog owners have lost all commonsense and respect for others.

1 The writer is most upset about dogs that
 A are kept locked up in yards.
 B have to work on farms.
 C bark unnecessarily.
 D leave droppings in the street.

2 Which word best describes how the writer feels about town dogs?
 A insulted　　　　B understanding
 C disappointed　　D indignant

3 Which of these dogs does the writer feel most concern for?
 A dogs in flats　　B police dogs
 C obese dogs　　　D farm dogs

4 A *flimsy fence* is one that is
 A made of wood.　　B full of holes.
 C starting to fall over.　D not very strong.

5 The word *poky*, as used in the text, means
 A smelly.　　B cramped.　　C airless.
 D dark.　　　E lonely.　　　F quiet.

6 The writer repeats the word *yap* to show how
 A much some dogs bark.
 B loudly some dogs bark.
 C dogs react to being locked up.
 D inconsiderate dog owners are.

7 For what reason does the writer exclude guide dogs, sniffer dogs and police dogs from her criticism?
 A She doesn't want to offend owners.
 B They are kept on farms.
 C She prefers large dogs to small dogs.
 D They assist people.

Answers: 1 C 2 D 3 A 4 D 5 B 6 A 7 D

☞ **Explanations on page 171**

Read the persuasive text *Pet cemeteries* and answer the questions.

1 Pet cemeteries

2 For pets there are few private cemeteries and even fewer public cemeteries. I think there should
3 be more. To me they are just as important as people cemeteries.

4 Pet owners have feelings. For many people a pet is a friend and companion. Older people are
5 more at ease if they own a pet. They can become very attached to their cat, dog or budgie. Lonely
6 or single people find pets give them an easy way to <u>interact</u> with neighbours. They provide an
7 opportunity for a conversation. Pets are more than something to own like a car or a TV.

8 City people will say, "There is nowhere to put a pet
9 cemetery!" There is! Australia is a big place. A cemetery
10 doesn't have to be in the city. Country councils could make
11 money out of providing space for pet cemeteries. Most
12 people would not want to visit a cemetery every day but
13 the occasional trip to the country could be a pleasant drive.

14 Pets are an important part of many people's lives. People
15 depend upon them and respect them. It is important to
16 have proper cemeteries for pets. They give people an
17 opportunity to remember their loved companions.

18 Pets are more than farm animals. Everyone should
19 contact their local council and ask them to provide public
20 pet cemeteries.

1 To get more cemeteries for pets, the writer suggests people should write to

A pet owners.
B country councils.
C their local council.
D pet cemetery caretakers.

2 What is the main reason for having pet cemeteries in the country?

A Cemeteries in the country are easy to visit.
B Country councils could make money from pet cemeteries.
C People don't want any more cemeteries in the cities and towns.
D There is plenty of space for cemeteries in country areas.

3 Which word best describes how the writer feels about the shortage of pet cemeteries?

A nervous   B concerned
C excited   D puzzled

4 The writer wouldn't expect a pet cemetery to be used for a

A calf.   B bird.   C cat.   D dog.

5 As used in the text, the word *interact* means

A behave.   B visit.
C communicate.   D avoid.

6 The writer is trying to persuade people to

A get a pet for company.
B visit a private pet cemetery.
C go for a country drive.
D have more public pet cemeteries.

7 Which statement is correct according to the writer?

A Single people don't need pets.
B It is better to have a pet than own a TV.
C Farm animals are more important than pets.
D Pet cemeteries are not needed by city people.

☞ **Answers and explanations on page 172**

Real Test

READING
Understanding posters

10 MIN

Many organisations put up posters to advertise coming events. Posters and fliers are meant to capture the reader's attention and provide information with a minimum of words. Gaylene saw this poster in a store window in Wambalong.

Look at the poster and answer the questions.

1 The purpose of the poster is to persuade people to
A spend money.
B find out about Australia Day.
C learn how to play games.
D celebrate an event.

2 At what time will visitors be able to get lunch?
Write your answer in the box.

3 More information about the Wambalong Fun Day could be obtained from
A Dwyers General Store.
B Wambalong Clubhouse.
C Wambalong School.
D Pioneer Park.

4 The sporting events on the Fun Day are intended to
A be entertaining.
B improve players' skills.
C find a champion.
D fill in time before the Talent Quest.

5 A sponsor is a person or organisation that
A has something to sell.
B provides funds for an event.
C wants to be important.
D is in charge of the event.

6 What event is being held in Rocky River?
A water skiing
B swimming
C novelty races
D fishing

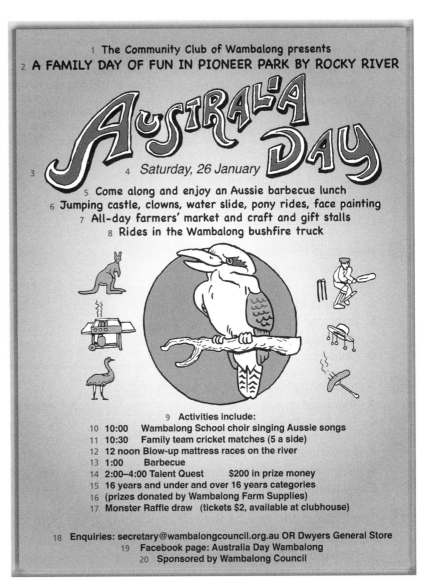

1 The Community Club of Wambalong presents
2 A FAMILY DAY OF FUN IN PIONEER PARK BY ROCKY RIVER

AUSTRALIA DAY

3 4 *Saturday, 26 January*
5 Come along and enjoy an Aussie barbecue lunch
6 Jumping castle, clowns, water slide, pony rides, face painting
7 All-day farmers' market and craft and gift stalls
8 Rides in the Wambalong bushfire truck

9 Activities include:
10 10:00 Wambalong School choir singing Aussie songs
11 10:30 Family team cricket matches (5 a side)
12 12 noon Blow-up mattress races on the river
13 1:00 Barbecue
14 2:00–4:00 Talent Quest $200 in prize money
15 16 years and under and over 16 years categories
16 (prizes donated by Wambalong Farm Supplies)
17 Monster Raffle draw (tickets $2, available at clubhouse)

18 Enquiries: secretary@wambalongcouncil.org.au OR Dwyers General Store
19 Facebook page: Australia Day Wambalong
20 Sponsored by Wambalong Council

☞ **Answers and explanations on pages 172-173**

Pictures, as well as text, can be used to convey meaning.

Look at the cartoon and answer the questions.

1 This cartoon is intended to
   A warn readers about being marooned.
   B make readers smile.
   C give hope to people who are lost.
   D advise readers to be careful.

2 The men are stranded on the island.
   What is a likely estimate of how long they have been stranded?
   Write your answer on the line.

   _____

3 How does the man with the note feel after reading the note?
   A impressed
   B annoyed
   C disbelieving
   D relieved

4 A suitable caption for the cartoon would be
   A Two men and a note.
   C The best holiday.
   B Friends.
   D A spell on a desert island.

5 It is most likely that the Year 4 teacher
   A was a thoughtful teacher.
   C wanted to help her ex-student.
   B had a long memory.
   D was very understanding.

6 The look on the face of the man not holding the note suggests that he is
   A slightly amused by the teacher's reply.
   B worried by the note's comments.
   C not very interested in his companion's feelings.
   D shocked and about to panic.

7 What will be the marooned men's main task after reading the note?
   A correcting the spelling mistakes
   C mending their clothes
   B building a boat
   D finding food to stay alive

☞ **Answers and explanations on page 173**

Real Test

10 MIN

The purpose of an explanation is to tell how or why something happens. Explanations can be about natural or scientific phenomena, how things work or events.

Read the explanation *What are mantis shrimps?* and answer the questions.

---

1   **What are mantis shrimps?**

2   Mantis shrimps are crustaceans, like crabs, lobsters
3   and other shrimps. They have the most complex eyes
4   in the animal kingdom. They can see colours other
5   animals cannot see. They can see <u>ultraviolet</u>, visible and
6   infra-red light and different levels of polarised light.
7   Their eye shape allows them to see things with three
8   different parts of the eye at once.

9   Mantis shrimps are <u>lightning-fast</u> predators. They
10   are either 'spearers', who use their forelimbs with
11   numerous barbs to capture soft-bodied prey like fish
12   and other types of shrimps, or 'smashers' that possess
13   club-like limbs to crush hard-shelled animals such as
14   crabs, clams and snails. They can deliver a blow that is
15   equivalent to the speed and force of a rifle bullet. The
16   strike from a mantis shrimp's forelimb is considered to
17   be one of the fastest movements known in the animal
18   kingdom. Larger mantis shrimps can reach speeds of
19   10 metres per second.

Sources: http://www.marineparks.wa.gov.au/fun-facts/69-mantis-shrimp.html
        http://www.bbc.co.uk/nature/blueplanet/factfiles/crustaceans/mantis_shrimp_bg.shtml

---

1 The writer says mantis shrimps are *lightning-fast*. This means they are very
   A bright.   **B** dangerous.   **C** abrupt.   **D** quick.   **E** flashing.

2 When catching their prey, mantis shrimps are either spearers or
   A killers.   **B** clubbers.   **C** shooters.   **D** stalkers.

3 What is the first paragraph about?
   A crabs and lobsters   **B** different colours of light
   C mantis shrimps' eyes   **D** mantis shrimps as predators

4 The barbs on the mantis shrimp's forelimbs are most likely used to
   A hold their prey.   **B** spear soft-bodied fish.
   C provide protection.   **D** frighten off predators.

5 *Ultraviolet* is the name given to a
   A plant.   **B** colour.   **C** fish.   **D** speed.

6 Which of the two paragraphs describes the shrimps'
   hunting behaviour? Write your answer in the box. Paragraph [   ]

7 This text was most likely written by someone interested in
   A the animal kingdom.   **B** sources of food.
   C marine adaptation.   **D** complex eye features.

☞**Answers and explanations on pages 173-174**

TIPS FOR WRITING PERSUASIVE TEXTS

Persuasive texts (expositions or opinions) are used to 'argue' the case for or against a particular action, plan or point of view—to *persuade* others to see it your way. Persuasive texts need to be well organised and clear so that readers will understand and be convinced of your arguments.

When writing persuasive texts it is best to keep the following points in mind. They will help you get the best possible mark.

Before you start writing

■ Read the question carefully. You will probably be asked to write your reaction to a particular question or statement, such as *Dogs should be kept out of parks*. Most of the topics that you will be asked to comment on are very general. This means you will probably be writing about something you know and can draw upon your experience. When writing your personal opinion you may include such phrases as *I think, I believe* and *It is important*. Remember to sound confident. Some common ways for the question to be worded are: *Give your opinion on ...; Do you agree or disagree?; What do you think is/are ... ?; What changes would you like to see ... ?; Is ... a good idea or a bad idea?*

■ You will be expected to give your reasons. Sometimes the question may actually state *Give your reasons*. Remember: the stance taken in a persuasive text is not wrong, as long as the writer has evidence to support his or her opinion. How the opinion is supported is as important as the opinion itself.

■ Give yourself a few minutes before you start writing to get your thoughts in order and jot down points.

The introduction

■ Right from the beginning it is important to let the reader know what position you have taken or what you believe. You can do this via the title or in the first line or paragraph, which may include a brief preview of the main arguments and some background information.

The body

■ Follow the structure of persuasive texts. As persuasive texts aim to convince readers, your reasons must be logical and easily understood. You must provide both arguments (points) and evidence to support the arguments.

■ Correctly paragraph your writing. Use paragraphs with topic sentences to organise your information. Without paragraphs your arguments become confused and difficult to follow. Use one paragraph for each idea or argument. Arguments can be ordered according to your choice. They can be 'numbered', e.g. *firstly, secondly, finally*.

■ Make sure your arguments (or points) are relevant. They must add to your case. 'Waffle' and unnecessary detail don't improve a persuasive text. It is better to stick to the facts without getting sidetracked. Once you have made a point there is no need to repeat it.

■ Use interesting, precise words. Include strong persuasive words such as *must, believe, important* or *certainly*. Avoid common words that carry little or no meaning, such as *good*. You can state your arguments using sentences beginning with words such as *firstly, furthermore* or *finally*.

■ Vary the types and lengths of sentences and the words that begin each sentence. If your writing includes a personal opinion, try to avoid too many sentences starting with *I*.

■ Use impersonal writing, although personal opinions can be part of the text.

The conclusion

■ The final paragraph must restate your position more forcefully and wrap up your case. It can include a recommendation.

When you have finished writing give yourself a few moments to read through your persuasive text. Quickly check spelling and punctuation and insert any words that have been accidentally left out. Direct speech is not a feature of persuasive texts. Indirect speech (reported speech) does not have speech marks (" ").

Vocabulary

- A wide variety of precise **verbs** are used to establish strong, informed points.
- **Nouns** are used to make specific statements.
- **Adverbs** and adjectives are well selected to qualify statements. The pronoun *I* is used sparingly.

Sentence structure

- Sentence beginnings (e.g. *because, firstly*), sentence types and lengths are varied. A topic sentence is used to introduce the main idea in some paragraphs.
- Questions and exclamations are used to effect. A rhetorical <u>question</u> is used to full effect.

Ideas

- Points are well made to create a sense of rational, logical assessment.
- A personal opinion is expressed with careful choice of words.
- Ideas are presented forcefully and positively.

Punctuation

- Punctuation, including apostrophes, exclamation marks and stops, is correctly applied.

Spelling

- There are no spelling mistakes of common or unusual words.

Year 4 Sample Writing
(a sample answer to the question on page 57)

The Best Place to Live

Because my parents are teachers I have lived in many places. The place where we live right now is the best. It's Smiths Lake on the north coast of NSW.

Firstly, the climate is so good. It never gets too cold in winter. I've never seen a frost. In summer the temperature rarely rises above 30°. On most hot summer evenings a cool breeze wafts in from the ocean.

The town is small. That's good! No massive malls with all their hassle. There are only six shops in Smiths Lake but you can purchase most things you need. There is heaps of free parking anytime.

The scenery at Smiths Lake is fantastic. From the top of the small hill where most houses are you can see the lake, a beach, the ocean and a national park. The scenery changes with the weather and the boats that are using the water. On the lake, on weekends, there are water skiers, sailboarders, sailing boats and people fishing happily from dinghies.

On the ocean we often see yachts and fishing boats. Container ships and cruise ships slide along the horizon.

There are no hotels in Smiths Lake. The closest school is a short bus trip away. The village is very quiet and safe. The streets are litter free.

Finally, best of all are the beaches, not only at Smiths Lake but at nearby villages, all within a short drive from home. If one beach is too rough it is easy to find another that is safer. And they are not like Bondi! They are not crowded.

Would I want to live anywhere else? For me, Smiths Lake is the best place to live. I hope Mum and Dad don't decide to move too soon.

This text is beyond what would be expected of a typical Year 4 student. It is provided here as a model. The assessment comments are based on the marking criteria used to assess the NAPLAN Writing Test.

Audience

- The audience is readily identified (people interested in living locations).
- Brief statements outline the issue to be discussed.
- Background information is provided to give context to the points raised

Persuasive techniques

- Arguments supporting the writer's opinion are in separate paragraphs.
- Points raised are obviously important to the writer in a personal way.
- Evidence and examples are used to support the argument.
- Objectivity is maintained throughout the writing.

Text structure

- The text contains a well-organised introduction, body and conclusion.
- The writer refers regularly to words used in the topic.

Paragraphing

- New paragraphs, with topic sentences, are used for new points and a summary.

Cohesion

- The final paragraph refers to the topic and re-establishes how the writer feels.
- There is a strong, personal concluding sentence.

© Pascal Press ISBN 978 1 74125 424 2

Real Test

WRITING
Persuasive text 1

42 min

Before you start, read the **General Writing Tips** on pages 23–24 and the **Tips for Writing Persuasive Texts** on page 52.

Today you are going to write a short speech. You want your class to make you class captain. You have to persuade the other students to vote for you. It will be in first person, that is, you will use the word 'I' quite often. You may include some humour. Try to make your writing convincing.

Before you start to write, think about:
- an appropriate greeting and introduction
- two or three clear points as to why you would make a good class captain
- a concluding paragraph briefly reminding the class of your worthy qualities
- a concluding appeal to the class to vote for you and an appropriate thanks for listening.

Remember to:
- plan your speech before you start writing
- write in correctly formed sentences and take care with paragraphing
- choose your words carefully and pay attention to your spelling and punctuation
- write neatly but don't waste time
- quickly check your speech once you have finished.

Start writing here or type in your answer on a tablet or computer.

_____

_____

_____

_____

_____

_____

☞ **Marking guide on page 174**

Real Test

WRITING
Persuasive text 2

42 min

Before you start, read the **General Writing Tips** on pages 23–24 and the **Tips for Writing Persuasive Texts** on page 52.

Today you are going to write a letter to the school council. The school council is concerned that many students remove articles of clothing, such as hats and footwear, once they leave the school grounds. They are planning to introduce rules and punishments for students to ensure this does not happen. You do, or do not, agree with this plan. Write to the school council outlining your reasons.

Remember, persuasive texts can be used to 'argue' the case **for** or **against** a particular plan—to persuade others to see something your way.

The address for your letter is given below.

Before you start to write, think about:
- the students (including you) that this plan could affect
- the effect the decision may have on the school's reputation
- how other people, including parents, may feel about the plan
- two or three clear points supporting your feelings about the plan
- how to complete your letter.

Remember to:
- plan your 'arguments' before you start writing—make a list of points you wish to make
- write in correctly formed sentences and take care with paragraphing
- choose your words carefully and pay attention to your spelling and punctuation
- write neatly but don't waste time
- quickly check your letter once you have finished.

Start writing here or type in your answer on a tablet or computer.

The President
Eastdale School Council
Eastdale Public School

_____

_____

_____

_____

☞ **Marking guide on pages 174-175**

Real Test

WRITING
Persuasive text 3

[42 min]

Before you start, read the **General Writing Tips** on pages 23–24 and the **Tips for Writing Persuasive Texts** on page 52.

Today you are going to write a persuasive text. Some of the students at your school want an area of the school playground set aside for a skateboard launch ramp and grind box. Your teacher wants you and the other students in her class to express their opinions in writing.

She has provided the first sentence.

Before you start to write, think about:
- how you feel about the idea—are you for or against it?
- two or three clear 'arguments' supporting your opinion
- any examples of events that have happened that support why you feel a particular way
- a concluding paragraph briefly reminding of how strongly you feel about the idea
- trying to make your writing convincing.

Remember to:
- plan your writing before you begin
- write in correctly formed sentences and take care with paragraphing
- choose your words carefully and pay attention to your spelling and punctuation
- write neatly but don't waste time
- quickly check your work once you have finished.

Start writing here or type in your answer on a tablet or computer.

Some students at our school who have skateboards want a launch ramp and grind box put in the school grounds. To me this (is / is not) a good idea.
(delete one)

_____

_____

_____

_____

_____

☞ **Marking guide on page 175**

Real Test

WRITING
Persuasive text 4

42 min

Before you start, read the **General Writing Tips** on pages 23–24 and the **Tips for Writing Persuasive Texts** on page 52.

You have come across this competition and decided to submit an entry.

NEW WRITING COMPETITION

Topic: The best place for a holiday!

Prizes to be won for each age group.

Open to all primary school pupils.

NO ENTRY FEE

You may prefer to write **the best place to live** as your competition topic.

Before you start to write, think about:
- where the holiday place is—it can be a place you have been to or a place where you would like to have a holiday
- two or three clear 'arguments' supporting your opinion
- a short concluding paragraph briefly restating your choice
- trying to make your writing convincing.

Remember to:
- plan your writing before you begin
- write in correctly formed sentences and take care with paragraphing
- choose your words carefully and pay attention to your spelling and punctuation
- write neatly but don't waste time
- quickly check your work once you have finished.

Start writing here or type in your answer on a tablet or computer.

_____

_____

_____

_____

_____

☞ Go to page 53 to see a sample answer to this question.

☞ Marking guide on page 175

We're halfway there!

Week 3

This is what we cover this week:

Day 1   **Measurement and Geometry:** ◎ Units of measurement

Day 2   **Measurement and Geometry:** ◎ Shape and angles

Day 3   **Spelling:** ◎ Making adverbs, adding the
                              suffix 'ful', and 'ie' and 'ei' words

        Grammar and Punctuation: ◎ Verbs, tense and use of commas

Day 4   **Reading:** ◎ Understanding descriptions

        Reading: ◎ Understanding recounts

        Reading: ◎ Understanding poetry

        Reading: ◎ Understanding timetables

Day 5   **Writing:** ◎ Recounts

        Writing: ◎ Descriptions

MEASUREMENT AND GEOMETRY
Units of measurement

What is each instrument used to measure?

(Choose from length, mass, time, temperature.)

1 [ ]   **2** [ ]   **3** [ ]   **4** [ ]

Look at these lines.

A ▬▬▬▬▬▬▬
B ▬▬▬▬▬▬▬▬▬▬
C ▬▬▬▬▬▬▬▬▬
D ▬▬▬▬▬▬▬▬
E ▬▬▬▬▬▬

5 Which line is the longest? [ ]

6 Which line is the shortest? [ ]

7 Which line is longer than line A but shorter than line C? [ ]

Use this ruler to answer these questions.

cm 1 2 3 4 5 6 7 8 9 10

8 How many centimetres long is the pencil? [ ]

9 How many centimetres long is the key? [ ]

10 How many millimetres long is the toy car? [ ]

Which has the greater mass (A or B)?

11 [ ]   **12** [ ]

MEASUREMENT AND GEOMETRY
Units of measurement

(continued)

13 What is the mass of this block in kilograms? [ ]

How many litres of juice are in each jug?

14 [ ]   **15** [ ]   **16** [ ]

What time is shown on each clock? Write your answer in two different ways.

17 [ ] [ ]

18 [ ] [ ]

19 [ ] [ ]

20 [ ] [ ]

Match the letter (A, B or C) that is beside the same time as each of these.

21 5:30 [ ]   **22** 2:45 [ ]   **23** 3:15 [ ]

A quarter past three
B quarter to three
C half past five

How many:

24 millilitres in 1 litre? [ ]   **25** millimetres in 1 metre? [ ]

26 grams in 1 kilogram? [ ]   **27** centimetres in 1 metre? [ ]

28 millimetres in 1 centimetre? [ ]   **29** metres in 1 kilometre? [ ]

30 seconds in 1 minute? [ ]   **31** minutes in 1 hour? [ ]

Key Points

MEASUREMENT AND GEOMETRY
Units of measurement

1 **Instruments are used to measure things.**
For example, to measure length we might use a ruler or a tape measure.

To measure mass we use scales. These might be balance scales, bathroom scales or kitchen scales.

To measure capacity we might use a measuring jug.

We use a thermometer to measure temperature.

We might use a clock, watch, timer or stopwatch to measure time.

2 **The length of a shape is a measure of how long it is.**
We can compare shapes using their length without needing to actually measure them.

Example: If we look at the 5 lines at the top of the next column, we can easily see that Line B is the longest. It is the one with the greatest length.

The line with the least length is Line E. So we say that the shortest line is E.

Lines B, C and D are all longer than Line A.
Lines A, D and E are all shorter than Line C.
So the line that is longer than Line A but shorter than Line C is Line D.

We could put the lines in order from shortest to longest.

3 **Length is measured in metres, or parts of metres.**

We can use a ruler or tape measure to measure the length of a shape.

Most rulers have marks allowing us to measure in centimetres or millimetres.

Example: On the ruler below, the numbers show the centimetres. We can see that the pencil is 3 cm long.

- When using a ruler we should measure from the start when possible. But we can still measure objects that aren't measured from the start of the ruler. For example, the key above is 4 cm long. We can work this out by counting the centimetres, or using subtraction:
  $10 - 6 = 4$.

- The smaller units on the ruler are millimetres. Each centimetre is divided into 10 mm.
  Counting the millimetres we can see that the toy car is 17 mm long.

Key Points

MEASUREMENT AND GEOMETRY
Units of measurement

(continued)

④ Mass is a measure of how heavy an object is. We sometimes call this the weight of the object, although the correct name is mass. Using a set of balance scales we can easily tell which object has the greater mass.

These are called balance scales because when the two sides are the same or balanced, the masses are the same.

But if one side is lower than the other, then the mass on that side is greater.

So B has a greater mass than A on these scales.

But A has a greater mass than B on these scales.

On other types of scales we just read the mass. For example, the mass of this block is 4 kg because the needle on the dial is pointing to 4.

⑤ Capacity is a measure of amounts of liquid. Capacity is measured in litres, or parts of litres.

Example: The first jug contains 2 litres of juice and the second jug contains 4 litres of juice.

The third jug holds an amount halfway between 2 litres and 4 litres. So the third jug contains 3 litres of juice.

⑥ There are two different ways of reading time.

Examples: This clock shows 7 o'clock or 7:00. If it is morning it would be 7 am, but if it was night it would be 7 pm.

- This clock has the bigger hand or minute hand pointing to 9 and the smaller (hour) hand is just before 6. The time is a quarter to six. Now this time is 45 minutes after 5 o'clock so it is also called 5:45.

- This clock has the minute hand pointing to 6. (It has moved halfway around the clockface, or through 30 minutes.) The hour hand is halfway between 1 and 2. The time is half past one or 1:30.

- On this clock the minute hand has moved a quarter of the way around the clockface. So the time is quarter past five. We can also see that it has moved 15 minutes so the time is also 5:15.

- We need to be able to tell the time on both types of clocks and be able to change one time to another. For example, 5:30 is half past five; 2:45 is quarter to three; and 3:15 is quarter past three.

⑦ When measurements use parts of metres, litres or kilograms, the parts are usually tens, hundreds or thousands.

Because *milli* means thousandth there are 1000 millilitres in 1 litre, 1000 millimetres in 1 metre and 1000 milligrams in 1 gram.
Because *centi* means hundredth there are 100 centimetres in 1 metre.
There are 10 millimetres in 1 centimetre.
Because *kilo* means thousand there are 1000 grams in 1 kilogram, 1000 metres in 1 kilometre and 1000 litres in 1 kilolitre.
Time is measured differently to length, mass and capacity.
There are 60 seconds in 1 minute.
There are 60 minutes in 1 hour.

Real Test

MEASUREMENT AND GEOMETRY
Units of measurement

20 min

1 Liz got on the train at 3:35 pm. She got off the train at 4:04 pm. For how many minutes was Liz on the train?

A 29   B 31   C 41   D 69

2 What is the temperature shown on this thermometer? ☐ degrees

3 Which of these measurements is the same as 600 cm?

A 6 km   B 6 m

C 0.6 km   D 0.6 m

4 The top has been torn off this calendar. It shows the month of October.

Fred's birthday is on Thursday 3 October. Cate's birthday is on 26 October. What day of the week is Cate's birthday this year?

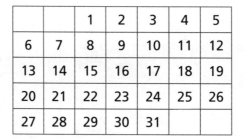

		1	2	3	4	5
6	7	8	9	10	11	12
13	14	15	16	17	18	19
20	21	22	23	24	25	26
27	28	29	30	31		

A Thursday

B Friday

C Saturday

D Sunday

5 Cassie wants to measure the mass of a box. Which of these units should be used?

A metres   B litres   C kilograms   D seconds

6 What time does this clock show?

A 4:45

B 4:09

C 9:04

D 9:24

7 What is the length of this pencil in millimetres?

A 88

B 87

C 82

D 78

8 A movie started at 6:30 pm. It ran for one and a quarter hours. What time did the movie finish?

A 7:15 pm   B 7:30 pm   C 7:45 pm   D 8:15 pm

☞ **Answers and explanations on page 176**

Real Test

MEASUREMENT AND GEOMETRY
Units of measurement

(continued)

9 Four girls compare ribbons. Meg's ribbon is the longest. Nora's ribbon is longer than Mia's but shorter than Kim's. Write the name of each girl under her picture.

10 Which is the same length of time as half a minute?

A 15 seconds   **B** 30 seconds   **C** 45 seconds   **D** 50 seconds

11 Which has the greatest mass?

A   **B**   **C**   **D**

12 Jess is having a cup of tea. Which is closest to the amount that a cup will hold?

A 20 mL

B 200 mL

C 2 L

D 20 L

13 John builds a fence right around this yard.

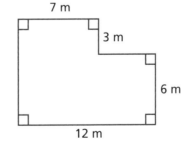

How long is the fence?

A 28 m   **B** 33 m   **C** 37 m   **D** 42 m

14 A recipe uses 750 mL of milk. Bella opens a 2-litre bottle and measures the correct amount of milk.

How much milk will remain in the bottle? ☐ mL

☞ **Answers and explanations on page 176**

MEASUREMENT AND GEOMETRY
Shape and angles

30 MIN

Look at these shapes.

A B C D E F
G H I J K L

1 How many are triangles? ☐

2 How many are quadrilaterals? ☐

3 What shape is A? ☐

4 What shape is B? ☐

5 What shape is L? ☐

6 What shape is C? ☐

7 What letter is in the pentagon? ☐

8 Write a letter that is in a trapezium? ☐

9 Write a letter that is in a rhombus? ☐

10 What letter is in the hexagon? ☐

Look at this shape.

11 The shape is a ☐ .

12 It has been divided into one ☐ and two ☐ .

13 Draw one more line on the diagram to divide the shape into 4 triangles.

Count the shaded squares to find the area of each of these shapes in square units.

14 ☐

15 ☐

16 ☐

Some tiles have been placed on this grid.

17 How many tiles can be placed on the grid altogether? ☐

18 How many more tiles are needed? ☐

MEASUREMENT AND GEOMETRY
Shape and angles

(continued)

Look at these angles.

1 2 3

19 Which angle is a right angle?

20 Which angle is larger than a right angle?

21 Which is smaller than a right angle?

Look at these objects.

A B C D E F
G H I J K L

22 How many are prisms?

23 How many are pyramids?

24 What is E?

25 What is F?

26 What letter is in the cube?

27 What letter is in the sphere?

Look at this object.

Are these views from the front, side or top?

28

29

30

How many cubes are used to make these rectangular prisms?

31

32

Key Points

MEASUREMENT AND GEOMETRY
Shape and angles

1 **We need to know the names of different two-dimensional shapes.** [Some shapes have more than one name.]

Triangles have exactly three sides.

In this group of shapes, shapes I and K are triangles, so there are two triangles in the group.

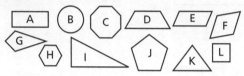

Quadrilaterals have exactly four sides. So shapes A, D, E, F, G and L are all quadrilaterals. There are six quadrilaterals in the group.

Shape A is a special quadrilateral. All of its angles are right angles. It is a **rectangle**.

Shape B is a **circle**.

Shape L is another special quadrilateral. It is a rectangle because all of its angles are right angles. It is a special rectangle because all of its sides are equal. It is a **square**.

Shape C has eight sides. It is an **octagon**.

A **pentagon** has five sides so shape J is a pentagon.

Shape D is the shape that we usually think of when we talk about a **trapezium**. (But shapes A, D, E, F and L are all trapeziums. Shapes A, E, F and L are special trapeziums because they also have other names.)

A **rhombus** has all of its sides equal in length. Shape F is a rhombus. (Shape L is also a rhombus as well as a square.)

A **hexagon** has six sides so shape H is a hexagon.

Shape G is a **kite** and E is a **parallelogram**.

2 **Many figures are combinations of triangles and quadrilaterals.** Other two-dimensional shapes can be divided into common shapes. You need to be able to **compare** and **describe** such figures.

A parallelogram is a quadrilateral with both pairs of opposite sides parallel.

Example: This shape is a parallelogram. It has been divided into one rectangle and two triangles.

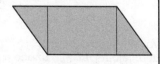

To divide the parallelogram into four triangles altogether we will need to divide the rectangle into two triangles. We can do this by drawing one of the diagonals of the rectangle. Diagonals are lines that go across a shape from one corner (vertex) to another.

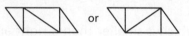 or

3 **Area is a measure of how much space a shape takes up.** One way to compare areas is to find how many squares a shape takes up on a grid.

Examples: By counting, we can see that this shape has 19 squares.

- This shape has 4 rows of squares and 6 squares in each row. Now 4 × 6 = 24. So there are 24 squares altogether.

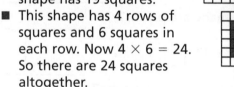

- In some shapes not all squares are completely covered. When counting we match the parts of squares together. In this shape there are 12 full squares. Matching the 'half' squares, there are about another 3 squares. So altogether the area is about 15 squares.

4 **Finding the number of tiles on a grid or stamps on a rectangle is the same as finding the area of the shape.**

Example: This grid will hold 21 tiles altogether. We can find this number by counting, or by multiplying the number of rows by the number in each row: 3 × 7 = 21.

To find the number of tiles still needed we could just count the remaining spaces. But we can see that there are 6 tiles already on the grid. Now 21 − 6 = 15. So 15 more tiles are needed.

5 A right angle is exactly one-quarter of a turn.

Example: So angle 2 is a right angle. In the first angle, one arm has turned through more than one-quarter of a turn from the other arm, so angle 1 is larger than a right angle.

The third angle is less than one-quarter of a turn so angle 3 is smaller than a right angle.

6 We need to know the names of different three-dimensional objects. **Prisms are 3D objects that have two faces that are exactly the same and other faces between those two that are rectangles.**

In the group of objects below, A, B, C, G, H, I and K are all prisms. So there are seven prisms in this group.

[Prisms are named for their identical faces. For example, object A has two identical rectangular faces, so it is a rectangular prism. (In fact it has three pairs of identical rectangles.) Object B has two identical hexagonal faces, so it is a hexagonal prism. Object C has two identical triangular faces, so it is a triangular prism, and so on.]

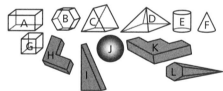

Pyramids have one particular face (after which they are named) and all the other faces are triangles that meet at a point.

In the group of objects above, D and L are pyramids. So there are two pyramids in the group.

[Object D is a rectangular pyramid and object L is a hexagonal pyramid.]

7 Other 3D objects have special names. For example, object E is a **cylinder** and object F is a **cone**. Object G is a special rectangular prism because all of its faces are squares. G is the letter in the **cube**. A round object like a ball is called a **sphere**, so J is the letter in the sphere.

8 **We can look at objects from different positions and see different views.**

Example: Consider this object made from blocks.

If we look at the object from the top we will see this view:

We won't be able to see how high the blocks are stacked, or that they are stacked at different heights.

■ If we look at the object from the front, we will only be able to see the front face. The view from the front is:

■ If we look at the object from the side, we see the height of the blocks. Because this object only has blocks one row deep, the view will be the same from either the right or left side. The view from the side will be:

9 **Volume is a measure of the amount of space taken up by a 3D object.** If an object is built from smaller cubes, then by counting those cubes we can compare volumes.

Example: The prism below only has cubes one row deep.

By counting, there are 12 cubes. We could also find this number by multiplying the number of rows of cubes high, (3), by the number of cubes in each of those rows, (4), by the number of rows deep, (1).

Now $3 \times 4 \times 1 = 12$. So there are 12 cubes altogether.

This prism has $2 \times 5 \times 2$ cubes or 20 cubes.

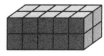

MEASUREMENT AND GEOMETRY
Shape and angles

1 Which of these shows a cone?

   A

   B

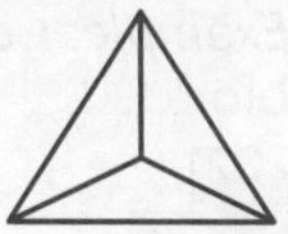

   C

   D

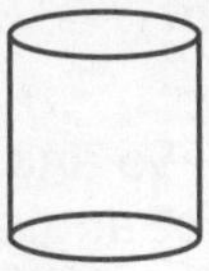

2 Ed made this design using four tiles placed around a square.
The tiles are exactly the same shape and size.
What shape could Ed's tiles have been?

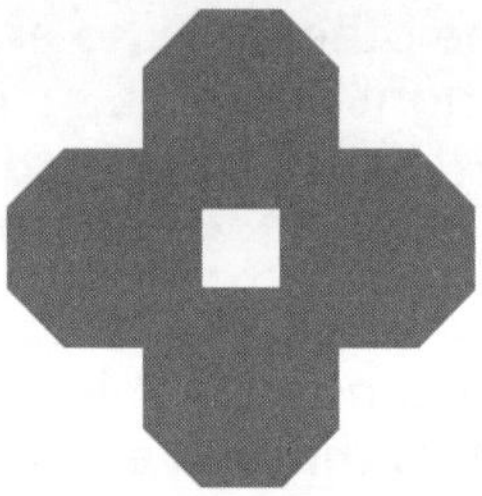

A pentagon

B trapezium

C octagon

D hexagon

3 Jenny is making a pattern by placing stickers on a piece of paper. She has placed 10 stickers.

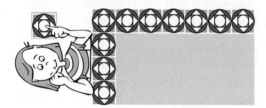

How many more stickers will fit on the paper? _____

4 Nikki cut this piece of cheese. Which of these is the piece of cheese most like?

A triangular prism

B triangular pyramid

C rectangular prism

D rectangular pyramid

5 8 of these blocks fit across the box. They fit 3 high and 5 wide.

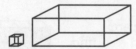

How many blocks will fit in the box? _____

6 Which angle is closest in size to a right angle?

   A

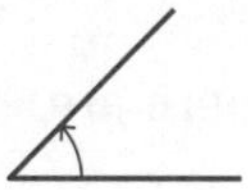

   B

   C

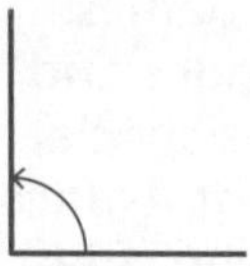

   D

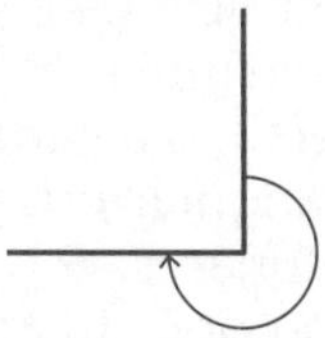

☞ **Answers and explanations on pages 176-177**

Real Test

MEASUREMENT AND GEOMETRY
Shape and angles

(continued)

7 This water tank is in the shape of a cylinder. What is the top view?

A B C D

8 Felix shaded some squares to spell out his name.

Write the letters in order from greatest area to smallest area.

greatest area   **smallest area**

9 Mary stacked cubes to make this object.

top view

How many cubes did Mary use?

10 This prism was made by gluing 16 small cubes together.

Jed picks up the object and counts the faces of the small cubes that he can see. How many of those faces can be seen?

11 A square pyramid has 5 faces. Which shows the 5 faces?

A   B   C   D

12 A cube has a different symbol (⊙, ☼, ❖, ✽, ★, ●) on each of its faces. Here are two pictures of the cube.

Which symbol is on the face opposite ⊙?

A ☼   B ❖   C ✽   D ★   E ●

☞ **Answers and explanations on pages 176-177**

 Most spelling rules have exceptions. English words have many different origins (e.g. *balaclava* comes from Central Europe and *spaghetti* comes from Italy).

Key Points

❶ Adverbs add meaning to verbs. Adverbs often end in 'ly'—but not always.

Examples: here, soon, yesterday, later, hard
Adverbs can be made from nouns and adjectives.

Examples: scholar ➔ scholarly (adverbs from nouns), bright ➔ brightly (adverbs from adjectives)
Adding 'ly' to form adverbs follows the basic rules for adding suffixes (see Week 2 Day 3, p 42).

When the adjective ends in a consonant simply add 'ly': *sudden ➔ suddenly*.

When the adjective ends in consonant + **y**, change the **y** to **i** then add 'ly': *noisy ➔ noisily*.

When the adjective ends in **e** drop the **e** and add 'ly': *true ➔ truly*.

When the adjective ends in 'ful' simply add 'ly': *hopeful ➔ hopefully*.

❷ Adding the suffix 'ful'
Use the 'ful' spelling for words that mean 'full of'.

Examples: careful (full of care), useful (full of use), hateful (full of hate)
If the word ends with a consonant + **y**, the **y** is changed to **i** before 'ful' is added.

Examples: beauty ➔ beautiful, plenty ➔ plentiful

❸ 'ie' and 'ei' words
Usually **i** comes before **e** when the sound is 'ee'.

Examples: piece, niece, sieve, field, diesel, shield
In words where the sound is not 'ee' the **e** usually comes before the **i**.

Examples: height, neighbour, eight, eighty, feint, vein, reign, heir

Test Your Skills

Learn the words below. A common method of self-testing is the **LOOK, SAY, COVER, WRITE, CHECK** method. Any mistakes should be rewritten three times correctly and immediately. By rewriting the word correctly you become familiar with the correct spelling. If the word is particularly troublesome, rewrite it several more times or keep a list of words that you can check regularly.

friendly _____	quietly _____	family _____
receive _____	sharing _____	thankful _____
worried _____	wasteful _____	community _____
carefully _____	business _____	beautiful _____
neighbour _____	people _____	nephew _____
their _____	welcome _____	niece _____

Write any troublesome words three times: _____

Real Test

15 MIN

Please ask your parent or teacher to read to you the spelling words on page 209.
Write the correct spelling of each word in the box.

1 The children spoke _____ on the night of the awards.

2 The new boy in our class felt _____ .

3 We are all _____ that the floods don't come into our street.

4 Angela _____ all night when she had a sore throat.

5 It was a _____ result. We lost without scoring!

6 My torch shone _____ in the dark shed.

Each line has one word that is incorrect. Write the correct spelling of the underlined word in the box.

7 Soft drink <u>fizes</u> when you shake the bottle.

8 "Watch the two <u>aircrafts</u> do a loop as they dive," said Dad.

9 Most humans have two <u>kidnies</u> to help purify the blood.

10 The town's <u>greif</u> was shown on local television.

11 The judge was <u>mercyful</u> because the man was sorry for his actions.

12 Do you keep fruit and vegetables down in your <u>seller</u>?

Each sentence has a spelling mistake. Write the correct spelling of that word in the box.
There is only one mistake in each line.

13 That sum is too complecks for me to understand!

14 Cameron spoke quikly to the new neighbour.

15 The garden is colorful but it takes a lot of my time.

16 We found a revue of the games in an old magazine.

17 There were four resques of stranded motorists during the floods.

18 "Why did you stop so suddenly?" the driver asked fiercly.

☞ **Answers and explanations on pages 177-178**

GRAMMAR AND PUNCTUATION
Verbs, tense and use of commas

15 min

Key Points

1
a **Verbs are often called doing words or action words.**

Doing verbs include action, thinking and speaking verbs.

Examples: called, swam, collect, study, think, prepare, digest, compete

b There is a small group of words that are not 'actions'. These are often called **having** or **being** verbs. They do not involve actions or behaviour.

Examples: is, are, am, was, were

Sometimes these verbs combine with other verbs to make two-word verbs.

Examples: was running, is eating

2 Verbs can tell us when an action **is**, **was** or **will be**. This is called **tense**. Tense can be **past**, **present** or **future**. The form of the verb will change depending on when the action happens.

Examples: Yesterday I <u>kicked</u> the ball. I <u>am kicking</u> the ball now. I <u>will kick</u> the ball soon.

Most verbs in English form their past tense by adding 'ed' (e.g. he walked). Irregular verbs do not form their past tense this way.

Examples: say → said, keep → kept, blow → blew, write → wrote, have → had

In sentences singular subjects (nouns) need **singular verbs**; plural subjects (nouns) need **plural verbs**. Singular verbs end in *s*.

Examples: One boy <u>runs</u>. Josh <u>lives</u> in town. Plural verbs don't take an *s*.

3 **More on commas** In Week 2, you learned that commas can be used for a pause. Commas are used where the reader should pause in longer sentences.

Example: You expect me to help you, but you know I have to leave shortly.
Commas are also used after introductory words.

Examples: Look, it's not very useful to say that. Trudy, get off the bed!

4 **Troublesome words: *of*, *have* and *off***

There is often confusion as to when to use these three words. When speaking, words like *could've* or *should've* can sound like 'could of' or 'should of'. This is never right. It should be *could have* and *should have*. *Off* is a preposition indicating a movement down and away from something.

Test Your Skills

1 Write the correct word in each of the spaces.

a Jon could _____ checked the water level!

(of, off, have)

b Jill took a book _____ the display stand! (of, off)

2 Underline the four verbs in this sentence. Jacki was seen at the shop checking prices when she slipped and twisted her ankle.

3 Write the tense (past, present or future) of each of these sentences.

a Jim lost the car keys. _____

b I am ready to go to school. _____

c Raj will go to India soon. _____

4 Write the correct present-tense form of **sing** in each of the spaces.

In the concert Cindy _____ a solo

but her brothers _____ a duet.

5 What is the past tense of **dig**? _____

6 Add commas to these sentences.

a At the beach we played on the sand for a while then on the rocks we looked for starfish.

b Come here I want to show you something.

Real Test

GRAMMAR AND PUNCTUATION
Verbs, tense and use of commas

15 min

1 Choose the letter to show where the missing comma (**,**) should go.

Hey there do you want to play tennis?

A   B   C   D

2 Which of the following correctly completes the second sentence?
Charlie is a good writer. She is ▓▓▓▓▓ than some real novelists.
A gooder   B more good   C better   D best   E more better

3 Which of the following correctly completes this sentence?
Dad ▓▓▓▓▓ a cheque for the new car.
A writ   B writted   C writed   D wrote

4 Which of the following correctly completes this sentence?
We went down Richmond ▓▓▓▓▓ until we came to the street where you live.
A Rd   B Rd.   C rd   D rd.

5 Which word is the verb in this sentence?
The drivers store their tools in a space under the cabin.

Write your answer in the box.

6 Brackets are required in this sentence.
Which part should be enclosed in brackets?
Australia's <u>first</u> automatic teller machine <u>ATM</u> was installed <u>in Brisbane</u> <u>in 1977</u>.

A   B   C   D

7 Which of the following correctly completes this sentence?
Today, Sandy and Rocky ▓▓▓▓▓ in a band called the Mossy Stones.
A plays   B playing   C player   D play

8 Choose the word that is **not** required in this sentence.

The teacher said my facts were incorrect and I should refer back to my textbook.
A my   B and   C refer   D back

9 Which of the following correctly completes this sentence?
Bonny didn't want mustard ▓▓▓▓▓ was hot, ▓▓▓▓▓ she had tomato sauce.
A what—and   B what—but   C which—but   D that—or

10 Choose the word that has the apostrophe (**'**) used correctly.

A   B   C   D

As Reggie picked up his father's shoe's he saw the hole's in the sole's.

☞ **Answers and explanations on pages 178-179**

Real Test

GRAMMAR AND PUNCTUATION
Verbs, tense and use of commas

(continued)

11 Which of the following correctly completes this sentence?

Gems ▮▮▮▮▮ sparkle often make people gasp.

A what   **B** that   **C** which   **D** when

12 Which of the following correctly completes this sentence?

"Look at this mess!" cried the teacher. " ▮▮▮▮▮ responsible?"

A Whose   **B** Whoes   **C** Who's   **D** Who'se

13 Choose the option that is a sentence.

A Maybe, Jan and Mike.   **B** Qantas, the Australian airline.
C Sara laughs too much.   **D** The old car in the back lane.

14 Phil was surprised that his brother was late.

Which sentence shows this?

A "You've been in hospital!"   **B** "You've been in hospital?"
C "You've been in hospital."   **D** "You've been in hospital,"

15 Write the correct verb in the space to complete this sentence

A kit of tools [   ] removed from the garage this morning.

16 Which word or words should begin with a capital letter?

the class has to read the book *vampire*, but some parents objected.

Use as many boxes as you need.

[   ]   [   ]   [   ]

17 Which option is correctly punctuated?

A "This is my brother," said the new player. "He wants to join the team."
B "This is my brother," said the new player, "He wants to join the team."
C "This is my brother," said the new player. "he wants to join the team."
D "This is my brother," said the new player. He wants to join the team.

18 Choose the option that is correctly punctuated.

A The tough little old lady demanded, to drive the van.
B The tough, little, old lady demanded to drive the van.
C The tough little, old lady demanded to drive the van.
D The tough little old, lady demanded to drive the van.

👉 **Answers and explanations on pages 178-179**

READING
Understanding descriptions

10 MIN

Descriptions are word pictures of people, places or things. They do not always rely on what can be seen. The other senses, such as taste, sound, feel and smell, can play an important part. It is important the reader can visualise and experience what the writer is describing.

Read the description *School days* and answer the questions.

1 **School days**

2 Dad thinks we are all softies nowadays. When he went to school things were
3 tough. He likes to tell us so whenever we start grumbling about our teachers.

4 He says he had a principal that was the meanest, scariest, nastiest person that
5 ever became a teacher. His name was bad enough—Mr Stark. He was long
6 and lanky and as bent as the bush poles they used to play Aussie Rules. He
7 was so tall he had to bend sideways to get into Dad's classroom. Then he'd
8 stand up tall and look down on the class—and the class teacher—and make
9 his announcement, which usually meant new rules and how to obey them.

10 Mr Stark wore grey or fawn clothes every day. He wore a cardigan under his
11 coat, regardless of the weather. And this, according to Dad, was before anyone
12 had thought about air conditioning, especially for bush schools. Dad said that
13 had an effect on his smell, particularly in the last term of the
14 year—just before they broke up for the summer holidays. Sometimes the kids
15 would call him Stinky, being very, very careful they weren't heard.

16 Of course, he smoked. Everyone did then. That didn't help matters. It might
17 have helped to explain why he was so skinny. It certainly helped to explain his
18 BO. He would often be seen sitting in his office 'dragging on a ciggie', and
19 looking towards the ceiling. Dad reckons he was probably dreaming up new
20 rules and devious ways to make the kids' school lives more miserable.

21 "You think you've got it tough," Dad would say, with a far-off look. "In my
22 day only the tough survived!"

1 According to the narrator's father, Mr Stark was both _____ and _____.

A unhappy   B fair-minded   C cunning
D spiteful   E devious   F lazy

2 Mr Stark's odour was caused by the type of clothes he wore and

A hot weather.
B his smoking habit.
C the colour of his clothes.
D the lack of school air conditioning.

3 Dad had a *far-off look*. This suggests that he

A really had fond memories of his school days.
B didn't want to talk about his school days any more.

C had difficulty remembering his school days.
D didn't think school had changed all that much.

4 Which word best describes how the pupils felt about Mr Stark?

A respectful   B tolerant
C relaxed   D cautious

5 The description of Mr Stark relies mostly on what was seen, but also what was

A smelt.   B heard.
C felt.   D tasted.

Answers: 1 D, E 2 B 3 A 4 D 5 A

☞ **Explanations on page 179**

Read the description *Careers* and answer the questions.

1 **Careers**

2 So you want to be a dog-trainer? Dogs can
3 be trained for many duties. They might be
4 trained to help soldiers find bombs, sniff for
5 drugs for immigration officers or as guides for
6 people with <u>impaired vision</u>.

7 Most people want a dog trained to be well-
8 behaved at home. These people can take their
9 dog to a boarding kennel where a dog trainer
10 will teach a dog special ways to behave over
11 several weeks. The most common training is
12 that of obedience, where dogs learn to accept
13 a leash and collar, walk by the trainer's side,
14 sit, stand, stay in one place and come when
15 called. They must be able to <u>master</u> these
16 skills before advanced training can begin.

HEEL BOY!

17 Training may have to cure a dog's bad habits, such as chasing cars, or barking too much.

18 To train dogs successfully, trainers must work with the dogs every day they are in their care.
19 The dogs are taught certain tasks by giving them rewards, such as small pieces of food. When
20 handling dogs, the trainer must never show fear or be impatient.

21 Part of the training might also be to teach owners how to handle their dogs. There is no point in
22 training a dog if the owner is going to respond to the dog in the same way he or she did before
23 sending the dog off to 'dog school'.

From an idea in *Job Scene*, Commonwealth Employment Service, 1988

1 This is a description of
A a guide dog.
B a boarding kennel.
C a dog trainer.
D an occupation.

2 How long does it take to train a dog?
A a day   B several days
C a week   D several weeks

3 *Impaired vision* is vision that is
A similar in both eyes.
B weak or damaged.
C no longer working.
D receiving treatment.

4 According to the text, what might make the training of a dog more difficult?
A bad habits the dog has learned
B the age of a dog

C how the dog is being trained
D the size of the dog

5 It is probable that the most dangerous thing for a trained dog to do is to
A chase cars.
B sniff for drugs.
C help soldiers.
D return to the owner's home.

6 To encourage a dog to be obedient it should be
A allowed to bark a lot.
B let off the leash.
C rewarded with food.
D sent to a boarding kennel.

7 Without changing the sentence's meaning, the word *master* could be replaced with
A do.   B obey.
C solve.   D attempt.

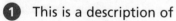 **Answers and explanations on pages 179-180**

Real Test

READING
Understanding recounts

10 MIN

A recount is the retelling of an event—it tells what happened. It usually retells events in the order the incidents happened. It is written in the past tense. A personal recount uses the personal pronoun *I*.

Read the recount *River meeting* and answer the questions.

---

1 **River meeting**

2 Many years ago a great chief arrived in Fiji with his
3 family. They landed on the coast at a place called
4 Vuda. They thought the island was <u>uninhabited</u>.

5 Roko, one of the chief's sons, decided to explore
6 the island. He wanted to find a good place for
7 the family to settle. He left early one morning,
8 promising to return as soon as he had been
9 successful.

10 After some days he came to a wide river. The young
11 man was hot and tired after his long walk along
12 beaches and then through thick jungle. He sat
13 down on the bank of the river and thought about
14 the family he had left behind.

15 While he was resting he was surprised to see some
16 women fishing in the river near the opposite bank.
17 He frowned and wondered who these people could
18 be, and where they could have come from.

19 He then noticed that they had canoes so he decided
20 to ask them for help to cross the river. Standing up,
21 he called out to the women but they could not hear
22 him. <u>Frustrated</u>, he decided to resume his journey
23 and follow the river to discover where it flowed into
24 the sea.

25 Before long he came across another group of
26 women fishing. This time they were on the same
27 bank as he was. Slowly he approached them,
28 hoping they could help him cross the river.

Source: *The Four Legends* by Bessie Kingdom, USP, Fiji, 1992

1 Roko began his journey of discovery
A from a river bank.
B entering a jungle.
C from a shoreline.
D by crossing a river.

2 Why was Roko surprised to see someone fishing?
Write your answer on the lines.

_____

_____

3 The word *uninhabited* has a similar meaning to
A forgotten.　　B lonely.
C deserted.　　D unpopulated.

4 What did Roko do when he first reached the river?
A He called out to women fishing on the opposite bank.
B He sat down and rested.
C He took a canoe to cross to the other side.
D He started walking along the river bank.

5 Roko felt *frustrated*. This means he was
A upset by his failure.
B annoyed by the women's behaviour.
C surprised he was ignored.
D relieved he wasn't heard.

6 Roko first saw women when he was
A exploring.　　B fishing.
C resting.　　D canoeing.

☞**Answers and explanations on page 180**

Real Test

10 MIN

Read the introduction to the poem *Possum* in Week 1, Day 4 (page 21).

Read the poem *The dog next door* by Elaine Horsfield and answer the questions.

1 **The dog next door**

2 There are many good reasons for owning a pet—
3 Puppies are cuddly and cute—
4 But the most common reason for those that I've met,
5 Seems just to annoy the neighbours!

6 The owners go off to work each day
7 Saying goodbye to their pets,
8 Who quickly get tired of their <u>solitary play</u>,
9 So they bark and annoy the neighbours!

10 They're supposed to guard and protect the house
11 Scaring intruders away.
12 But their yapping would hardly scare a mouse,
13 'though it certainly upsets the neighbours!

14 Some people have dogs that they know will bite—
15 Ferocious, prepared to attack.
16 And often they bark when a jogger's in sight,
17 But mostly it's just at the neighbours!

18 So if you have a dog, keep it under control
19 Take it walking, and teach it good manners
20 Let it bark at the thieves on their midnight patrol—
21 But don't let it bark at the neighbours!

① The poet feels the main reason people have a dog is to
A own a cuddly pet.
B annoy the neighbours.
C scare off joggers.
D take them for walks.

② The poet feels that neighbourhood dogs mainly bark because
A they don't like being on their own.
B there are intruders nearby.
C they want the owners to return.
D other dogs are barking.

③ *Solitary play* means playing
A without friends.
B and making a lot of noise.
C games that are difficult.
D while going for a walk.

④ Who is most upset by the noisy dogs?
A the dog owners
B thieves
C the neighbours
D joggers

⑤ The poet feels yapping dogs are
A cute.
B mice catchers.
C protective.
D of little use.

⑥ What does the poet suggest might be a way of stopping a dog from barking?
A Get it a friend.
B Teach it some manners.
C Stay home with it.
D Take it to work.

☞ **Answers and explanations on page 180**

Real Test

10 MIN

A timetable is a chart that shows arrival and departure times of services or a sequence of events.

Read the *Indian-Pacific train timetable* and answer the questions.

1 **Indian Pacific train timetable**

2 The *Indian Pacific*, which travels between the west coast and east
3 coast on a three-day, 4352-km trek across Australia, is said to be
4 one of the world's great train journeys. The three-day trip takes
5 passengers through a wide variety of Australian landscapes—and
6 gives a real indication of how vast Australia really is.

7 The train departs Sydney every Wednesday and Saturday. The
8 return journeys from Perth depart Saturdays and Wednesdays.
9 Passengers must be at the station at least one hour before the
10 train departs.

11 **Wednesday departures**

	Station	Arrival time	Departure time	Duration
13	Sydney (Central station), NSW		2:25 pm Wednesday	
14	Broken Hill, NSW	6:40 am Thursday	8:20 am Thursday	1 h 40 min
15	Adelaide, SA	3:05 pm Thursday	6:40 pm Thursday	3 h 35 min
16	Cook (SA ghost town)	Friday	Refuelling stop	2 h
17	Kalgoorlie, WA	7:10 am Friday	10:40 pm Friday	3 h 30 min
18	Perth, WA	9:10 Saturday		

1 The trip from Sydney to Perth on the *Indian Pacific* occurs

A overnight.
C over a week.
B over three days.
D over four days.

2 How many states does the *Indian Pacific* pass through?

Write your answer in the box. ☐

3 The *Indian Pacific* makes four stops on the trip from Sydney to Perth.
Write the numbers 1, 2, 3 and 4 in the boxes to show the order of the stops.

Broken Hill Kalgoorlie Cook Adelaide
☐ ☐ ☐ ☐

4 The word *landscapes* could be replaced with which word(s) with a similar meaning?

A countryside
C journeys
B ghost towns
D cities

5 The purpose of the map is to show

A how vast Australia is.
B the time spent at each stop.
C all the train stops.
D the route the train takes.

6 Why does the journey on the Indian Pacific take so long?

A The train stops for two hours at Cook to refuel.
B It is a great distance from Sydney to Perth.
C There is a one-hour wait before boarding the train.
D The stops at each station are over an hour.

7 How many trips between the cities of Perth and Sydney are made each week?

Write your answer in the box. ☐

☞**Answers and explanations on pages 180-181**

TIPS FOR WRITING RECOUNTS

A **recount** tells about events that have happened to you or other people. The purpose of a factual recount is to record a series of events in the order they happened and evaluate their importance in some way. A recount can also be fictitious. Whether the recount is factual or fictitious remember to tell who, what, when, where and why. There are many types of recount—diaries, newspaper reports, letters and biographies. Recounts can be the easiest texts to write if you are given the choice. They don't need much planning or organisation as they are a straightforward record of events.

When writing recounts it is best to keep these points in mind. They will help you get the best possible mark.

Before you start writing

- Read the question and check the stimulus material carefully. *Stimulus material* means the topic, title, picture, words, phrases or extract of writing you are given to base your writing on.
- Remember that a recount is usually told in the past tense because the events described have already happened.
- Write about something you know. Don't try to write about something way outside your experience.
- Use a setting you are familiar with, e.g. home, school, sport, holiday place or shopping centre.
- When you have chosen your topic it might be helpful to jot down a few ideas quickly on paper so you don't forget them. Make up your mind quickly if you are writing a first-person recount (using *I* as the main character) or a third-person recount. If it is a personal recount, try to avoid too many sentences beginning with *I*.

The introduction

- A striking title gives impact to a recount. Newspaper reports do this well.

The body

- Use conjunctions and connectives, e.g. *when, then, first* or *next*. Because recounts can record either events that happen over a short period or events that happen over a lifetime, you need conjunctions and connectives to link and order the events.
- Correctly paragraph your writing. You need a new paragraph when there is a change in time or place, or a new idea. You may want to comment on the events as you write about them.
- Include personal comments, e.g. about your feelings, your opinions and your reactions, but only include comments that add to your recount. 'Waffle' and unnecessary detail don't improve a recount. It is better to stick to the facts without getting sidetracked.
- Use language imaginatively so that the recount is interesting, but don't try to fill it with weird or disgusting events.

The conclusion

- Include a conclusion. This tells how the experience ended. You may give your opinion about what happened and some thoughts you may have had about it. This final comment on the events or experiences is a way to wrap up your recount.

When you have finished writing give yourself a few moments to read through your recount. Quickly check spelling and punctuation, and insert words that have been accidentally left out.

Vocabulary

- Adverbs and adjectives are well chosen.
- Good verbs are included.
- Personal pronouns (e.g. *we, I, me*) are correctly used and keep the recount flowing.

Sentence structure

- The narrator uses a variety of sentence beginnings including 'time' adverbs (connectives) suitably selected.
- The narrator has used a variety of sentence types and sentence lengths.
- There is a controlled use of *I* as a sentence starter.

Ideas

- The narrator includes senses other than sight (e.g. *backache*).
- A rhetorical question adds to the sense of fun.
- An exclamation is used appropriately.

Punctuation

- Punctuation is well handled. A short sentence is used effectively to conclude the recount.
- Capital letters for proper nouns and sentence beginnings are correctly applied.

Spelling

- There are no spelling mistakes in common or unusual words.

(a sample answer to the question on page 84)

Helping out

It was the first Saturday of the school holidays and I had just finished breakfast and was thinking I had all day to do whatever I wanted. That's when Dad strolled in from outside. He had a pair of plant clippers in his hand. What's he want?

Dad looked straight at me and grinned. I knew what was coming. "How about you help me clean up the garden seeing as you don't have any schoolwork?"

I couldn't refuse. I simply nodded and followed Dad into the front garden. The first thing I saw was all the bits he had cut off the bushes.

I went to the garden shed and found the small wheelbarrow and picked up the clippings. I put each barrowload into the green-lidded bin for the council to collect on Tuesday.

Then we were onto pulling out weeds around the petunias and pansies. We had to squat down to do this and Dad soon got a backache. He stood up wearily and rubbed his back.

"Think it's time for a change of jobs," he groaned. "Get the hoses Talyah. We can cool off and water where we have weeded."

We have two outdoor taps with hoses connected. I pulled one down for Dad and I used the other one. I played with the hose nozzle until I got a fine misty spray. Watering the garden is quite relaxing.

After that Dad got his sprays for the insects and grubs that attack the flowers. I didn't have to help. Dad wore a white facemask and protective glasses.

While he washed his hands I put the spray back on the high shelf in the shed.

Later Dad said we had done such a good job with the flowerbeds we could do the vegetable garden on Sunday. I think I'd rather do schoolwork!

Audience

- The title informs readers of the subject to be recounted.
- A home situation is firmly established in the first paragraph.
- Past tense is used.
- The use of the pronoun *I* indicates that this is a personal recount.

Character and setting

- The *who, where* and *when* are established quickly.
- The writer is recounting a familiar subject.

Text structure

- Events happen in order using adverbs of time.
- Precise words are used for details. The reader is made aware of the conditions at the time.
- Direct speech is used correctly.
- The narrator has used a casual, informative style.

Paragraphing

- New paragraphs start with changes in time.
- Personal reactions and opinions are included.

Cohesion

- A personal comment is used to round off the recount. The final sentence refers to the opening sentences.

Real Test

WRITING
Recount 1

42 min

Before you start, read the **General Writing Tips** on pages 23–24 and the **Tips for Writing Recounts** on page 82.

A recount is the retelling of an event. It usually retells the events in the order the incidents happened. A personal recount uses the personal pronoun 'I'.

Choose one of the following events and write several paragraphs, with a conclusion based on your opinion of the event.

- The day I lost my money (it could be lunch money, pocket money, money for a fare)
- The day I lost my homework sheet
- The day I lost my way home
- The day for helping out

Before you start to write, think about:
- where your personal recount takes place
- the events that take place in your personal recount and the problems that have to be resolved
- how you and others felt about the event—you may comment on the events as you write about them.

Remember to:
- plan your personal recount before you start writing
- write in correctly formed sentences and take care with paragraphing
- pay attention to the words you use, your spelling and punctuation
- write neatly but don't waste time
- quickly check your personal recount once you have finished.

Start writing here or type in your answer on a tablet or computer.

_____

_____

_____

_____

_____

☞ **Go to page 83 to see a sample answer to this question.**

☞ **Marking guide on page 181**

Real Test

WRITING
Recount 2

42 min

Before you start, read the **General Writing Tips** on pages 23–24 and the **Tips for Writing Recounts** on page 82.

Recounts can also recall historical (real) events, the lives of interesting people and events the writer may not be directly involved in. Such recounts are written from an impersonal point of view.

Choose one of the following events and write several paragraphs, with a conclusion based on an opinion of or comment on the event.

- The visit of a famous person (e.g. a movie star or prime minister) to your school.
- A group's visit to Luna Park (or a similar fun place such as Water World)
- Another person's visit to a sporting event that was exciting or special in some way

Before you start to write, think about:
- where your impersonal recount takes place
- the events that take place in your impersonal recount and the problems that have to be resolved
- how you and others felt about the event—you may comment on the events as you write about them.

Remember to:
- plan your recount before you start writing—list interesting events as you determine they have happened
- write in correctly formed sentences and take care with paragraphing
- pay attention to the words you use, your spelling and punctuation
- write neatly but don't waste time
- quickly check your recount once you have finished.

Start writing here or type in your answer on a tablet or computer.

_____

_____

_____

_____

_____

☞ **Marking guide on pages 181-182**

TIPS FOR WRITING DESCRIPTIONS

Descriptions function as pictures in words of people, places or things. In a description you aim to give the reader a clear and vivid picture of what you are describing. After reading your description the reader should be able to close his or her eyes and picture the subject.

Descriptions are seldom written to stand alone in the same way as, say, narratives or recounts. Descriptions are often part of another kind of writing; they help to make other text types interesting.

When writing descriptions, it is best to keep the following points in mind. They will help you get the best possible mark.

Before you start writing

- Read the question and check the stimulus material carefully. *Stimulus material* means the topic, title, picture, words, phrases or extract of writing you are given to base your writing on.
- Decide how you are going to present your description. It could be in the first person or third person. Take care when using the first person not to overuse the pronoun *I*.
- Decide on the tense you are going to use. Descriptions are usually written in the present tense but feel free to use past or future tenses if this suits your purpose.

The introduction

- Introduce the subject early in your writing. The title should put the subject in focus.

The body

- Always include some facts. Descriptions in an information report may consist entirely of facts.
- Don't just focus on what can be seen. Enhance your writing by adding 'imagined' sounds and smells—you can even describe how something feels.
- Make full use of adjectives and adverbs. Use a short series of adjectives to paint a vivid picture.
- Use action verbs to describe behaviour. This adds interest to your description.
- Use figurative language such as similes and metaphors to make your description clear and interesting. Avoid clichés.

The conclusion

The final paragraph may include some brief personal opinions in your description—the best place for this is often in the form of a concluding comment.

When you have finished writing give yourself a few minutes to read through your description. Quickly check spelling and punctuation, and insert any words that have been accidentally left out.

Real Test

Before you start, read the **General Writing Tips** on pages 23–24 and the **Tips for Writing Descriptions** on page 86.

The aim of a description is to give the reader a clear and vivid word picture of a person, thing, place or scene. Descriptions of scenes are often important in narratives. They help create different moods and atmosphere.

Pretend you are lost in a strange place and you sit down and look around. Describe what you see (you can include what you smell or hear).

You may be lost in an amusement park, an unknown street, a shopping centre or in the bush.

Before you start to write, think about:
- the general setting—what you are describing
- special features of your surroundings
- how you (or others) may feel or react in the setting—you may comment on each aspect as you write about it.

Remember to:
- plan your description before you start writing—list interesting points you might describe
- write in correctly formed sentences and take care with paragraphing
- choose your words carefully (especially adjectives and adverbs) and pay attention to your spelling and punctuation
- write neatly but don't waste time
- quickly check your description once you have finished.

Start writing here or type in your answer on a tablet or computer.

_____

_____

_____

_____

_____

☞ **Marking guide on page 182**

WRITING
Description 2

42 min

Before you start, read the **General Writing Tips** on pages 23–24 and the **Tips for Writing Descriptions** on page 86.

The aim of a description is to give the reader a clear and vivid word picture of a person, thing, place or scene. Descriptions of scenes are often important in narratives. They help create different moods and atmosphere.

Describe a snowman or a scarecrow. This picture may give you some ideas. You may want to add extra details of your own.

Before you start to write, think about:
- the subject and its setting—what you are describing
- special features of your subject
- how you and others feel about the subject—you may comment on each aspect as you write about it.

Remember to:
- plan your description before you start writing—list interesting points you might describe
- write in correctly formed sentences and take care with paragraphing
- choose your words carefully (especially adjectives and adverbs) and pay attention to your spelling and punctuation
- write neatly but don't waste time
- quickly check your description once you have finished.

Start writing here or type in your answer on a tablet or computer.

_____

_____

_____

_____

☞ **Marking guide on page 183**

Only one week to go!

Week 4

This is what we cover this week:

Day 1   **Measurement and Geometry:** ◎ Location, transformations and geometric reasoning

Day 2   **Statistics and Probability:** ◎ Chance and data

Day 3   **Spelling:** ◎ Adding suffixes to words ending in *y*; homonyms and demons

            Grammar and Punctuation: ◎ Pronouns, prepositions and adverbs; apostrophes and commas

Day 4   **Reading:** ◎ Understanding legends
                    ◎ Understanding procedures
                    ◎ Understanding explanations
                    ◎ Understanding recounts

Day 5   **Writing:** ◎ Procedures
            Writing: ◎ Explanations

Test Your Skills

MEASUREMENT AND GEOMETRY
Location, transformations and geometric reasoning

30 MIN

This plan shows the desks in three classrooms.

Classroom A		
Teacher		
1	2	3
4	5	6
7	8	9
10	11	12
13	14	15

Classroom B		
Sal		
	Dan	
Fi	Jye	Col
May	Ali	Jo
Ben	Kim	Ann

Classroom C		
		Ami
Mia		
		Jan
Ira		
	Sue	

Jan sits at desk C9. Which desks do these students sit at?

1 Col [ ]   **2** Ami [ ]   **3** Ira [ ]

Who sits at these desks?

4 B5 [ ]   **5** B12 [ ]   **6** C4 [ ]

The students sit in the classrooms facing the teacher's desk. Who sits

7 in front of Jye? [ ]   **8** behind Jo? [ ]

9 between Ben and Ann? [ ]   **10** on Ali's left? [ ]

Here is a grid.

Draw the shape that is found at

11 C3. [ ]

12 F4. [ ]

13 B2. [ ]

5				◆		
4		☺			○	
3	●		△		✪	
2		□				
1						♥
	A	B	C	D	E	F	G

Where will you find each of these?

14 ♥ [ ]   **15** ◆ [ ]   **16** ● [ ]

17 ☺ moves 1 square to the right. Where will it move to? [ ]

18 ✪ moved 2 squares to the left and 2 squares down. Where is it now? [ ]

Draw the result when these shapes are flipped over the dotted line.

19 ◤

20 ◤

MEASUREMENT AND GEOMETRY
Location, transformations and geometric reasoning

(continued)

Draw the result when this arrow ➡ is turned.

21 a half turn

22 a quarter turn clockwise

This is a map of Riverton.

Legend

➕ Hospital   ✉ Post Office

▨ Police Station   ▓ Park

F Fire Station   [P] Car Park

Ⓢ School   ✈ Airport

ⓘ Information Centre   [L] Library

Scale
⊢——⊣
100 m
Ⓝ

23 What does the symbol, **F**, mean?

24 What symbol is used to show a hospital?

25 The airport is at the corner of River St and what other street?

26 What is found at the intersection of Castle St and Brown St?

27 At the intersection of which two streets will you find the police station?

28 About how far is it from the post office to the library?

29 Jed walks along John St from the school to the park.
What does he pass on his right?

30 What building is found one block south of the post office?

31 Complete the other half of this pattern by colouring
in some of the squares so that the finished pattern
is symmetrical.

91

MEASUREMENT AND GEOMETRY
Location, transformations and geometric reasoning

1 **A plan can show us a pattern that has been followed**.

Example: In this plan the desks are numbered in Classroom A. We know that the same pattern is used in Classroom B and Classroom C because we are told that Jan sits at desk C9.

Classroom A		
Teacher		
1	2	3
4	5	6
7	8	**9**
10	11	12
13	14	15

Classroom B		
Sal		
	Dan	
Fi	Jye	Col
May	Ali	Jo
Ben	Kim	Ann

Classroom C		
		Ami
Mia		
		Jan
Ira		
	Sue	

Col is also in seat 9 but in Classroom B. So Col sits at desk B9.

Ami is in Classroom C. She is in seat 3.

So Ami's desk is C3. Ira's desk is C10.

To find the student who sits at B5 we first look at Classroom A to find the position of desk 5. It is in the middle of the second row. So looking at the same position in Classroom B we can see that Dan sits at desk B5.

Classroom A		
Teacher		
1	2	3
4	**5**	6
7	8	9
10	11	12
13	14	15

Classroom B		
Sal		
	Dan	
Fi	Jye	Col
May	Ali	Jo
Ben	Kim	Ann

Classroom C		
		Ami
Mia		
		Jan
Ira		
	Sue	

At desk B12 is Jo and at desk C4 is Mia.

The students sit in the classrooms facing their teacher's desk. So Dan sits in front of Jye.

FRONT

LEFT

Classroom A		
Teacher		
1	2	3
4	5	6
7	8	9
10	11	12
13	14	15

Classroom B		
Sal		
	Dan	
Fi	Jye	Col
May	Ali	Jo
Ben	Kim	Ann

Classroom C		
		Ami
Mia		
		Jan
Ira		
	Sue	

RIGHT

BACK

Ann sits behind Jo and Kim sits between Ben and Ann.

May sits on Ali's left.

2 **On a grid, letters and numbers are often used to show positions**. The letters are usually found along the bottom (or top) of the grid and the numbers go up (or down) the side.

We always put the letter (or number) that is found going across the bottom (or top) before the number (or letter) that goes at the side.

MEASUREMENT AND GEOMETRY
Location, transformations and geometric reasoning

(continued)

Example: On this grid to find the position C3 we look for C at the bottom and 3 on the side.

So the shape that is found at C3 is △.

To find the shape at F4 look for F along the bottom of the grid and 4 at the side.

So the shape that is found at F4 is ○. The shape that is found at B2 is □.

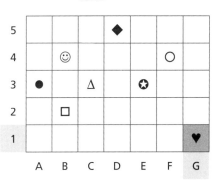

To give the position of a shape, find the letter below it and the number at the side.

So ♥ is found at G1.

◆ is found at D5 and ● is found at A3.

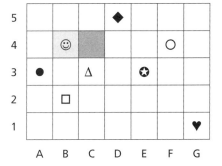

③ **Under a transformation, a figure might be translated (slid), rotated (turned) or reflected (flipped).**

④ **A shape on a grid might undergo a slide or translation.**
It might move to the right or to the left and up or down.
☺ is at B4.
If it moves 1 square to the right (➜) it will move to C4.
✪ is at E3. If it moves 2 squares to the left (⬅) and 2 squares down (⬇), it will move to C1.

⑤ **When a figure is flipped, it will face in a different direction.** The figure will not change in size or shape.

Example: Here is the result when the two arrows are flipped over the dotted lines.

⑥ **When an object is turned, it too will face in a different direction unless turned a full turn.**
Turns can be made either clockwise ↻ or anticlockwise ↺. If an object is turned through half a turn it will be turned upside down.

➜ turned through a half turn is ⬅.

➜ turned through a quarter turn in a clockwise direction is ⬇.

7 **The legend on a map shows us where to find certain places.**

Example:

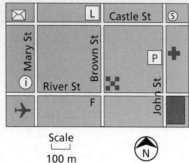

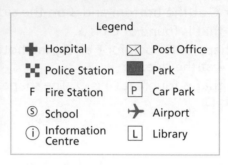

So on this map we can see from the legend that the symbol '**F**' means a fire station.

The legend also shows us that ✚ is used to show a hospital.

The symbol for an airport is a plane. This can be seen on the map at the corner of River St and Mary Street.

At the intersection of Castle St and Brown St this symbol, L̄, is found. The legend tells us that it is the symbol for a library. So a library is found at the intersection of Castle St and Brown St.

From the legend we can see that the symbol for a police station is ▨. This symbol is found on the map at the corner where Brown St meets River St. So the police station is at the intersection of Brown St and River St.

8 **The scale on a map tells us what the real distances would be.**
This map has a scale that shows us this distance ⌐⌐ is 100 metres.

Now, using the legend we find the post office and the library. On the map we can see that about 4 of those lengths are needed to reach from the post office to the library. So it is about 400 metres from the post office to the library.

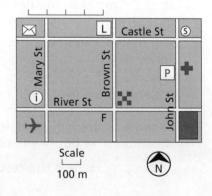

9 When we consider the path someone takes on a map, right and left might not be our right and left. For example, as Jed walks along John St from the school to the park the hospital is on his left. On his right he passes the car park.

10 **The four main directions are north, south, east and west.** If we face north, south will be behind us, east on the right and west on the left. So if we know where north is we can find all the other directions. For example, on this map the building one block south of the post office is the information centre.

11 **If a shape or pattern is symmetrical it means it could be folded along a line of symmetry and the two halves would match exactly.**
For example, this pattern is symmetrical.

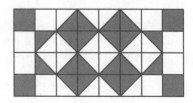

Real Test

MEASUREMENT AND GEOMETRY
Location, transformations and geometric reasoning

20 min

1 Which of these shapes have no line of symmetry? Select **all** possible answers.

A   B   C   D   E

2 There is a counter at C3. Polly moves the counter left one square and up two squares. Where does the counter move to?

A A4

B B5

C D1

D D5

5
4
3 ●
2
1
A B C D E

3 This shape is to be rotated a quarter of a turn clockwise. What will it look like after the turn?

A   B   C   D

4 What is second from the right in the top row?

A staples

B nuts

C screws

D washers

pins staples nuts bolts
nails screws washers bits

5 What will this shape look like if flipped over the dotted line?

A   B   C   D

Real Test

MEASUREMENT AND GEOMETRY
Location, transformations and geometric reasoning

(continued)

6 At a motel Bill comes up the stairs to his room, which is the second on the left. Which is Bill's room?

A 303

B 304

C 307

D 308

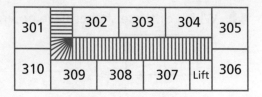

7 This is a plan's of Jo's home. What is west of the house?

A pool

B shed

C vegetable patch

D seating area

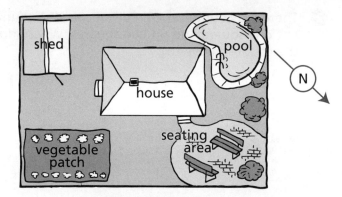

8 This is a map of Ourtown. Which two roads meet in square E3?

A River Rd and Mill Rd

B Mill Rd and Wattle Rd

C River Rd and Bunyip Rd

D Wattle Rd and Bunyip Rd

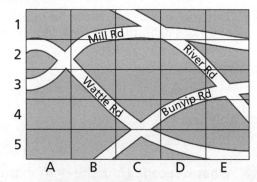

9 Sara has coloured half of a pattern. When completed, the dotted line will be an axis of symmetry.

How should Sara colour the square marked by an X?

A

B

C

D

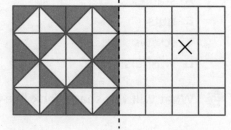

10 A customer in the shop wants directions to the post office.

Which directions are correct?

A Go right from the shop, left at Bay Rd.

B Go right from the shop, right at Bay Rd.

C Go left from the shop, left at Bay Rd.

D Go left from the shop, right at Bay Rd.

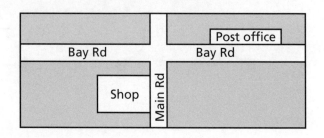

☞ **Answers and explanations on pages 183-184**

Test Your Skills

STATISTICS AND PROBABILITY
Chance and data

30 min

Each student in a class voted for their favourite vegetable.

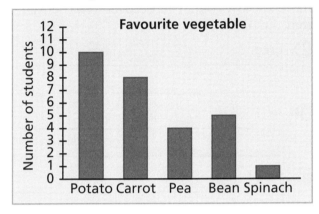

Favourite vegetable

Number of students

Potato Carrot Pea Bean Spinach

1 How many students voted for bean?

2 Exactly 8 students voted for one vegetable. What vegetable was that?

3 How many more students voted for potato than for pea and spinach together?

4 How many students voted altogether?

Some boys played two games of Darto.

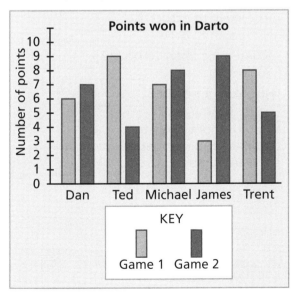

Points won in Darto

Number of points

Dan Ted Michael James Trent

KEY

Game 1   Game 2

5 How many points did Dan score in Game 1?

6 How many points did Trent score in Game 2?

7 Who scored the same number of points in Game 2 as Michael did in Game 1?

8 One boy scored 12 points altogether. Who was that?

9 Who scored the most points altogether?

In Greentown some students ride bikes to school.

Bicycles ridden to school

Year 2

Year 3

Year 4

Year 5

Year 6

Key = 2 students

10 How many students in Year 4 ride bikes?

11 In what year did 4 students ride bikes?

12 How many more students in Year 5 ride bikes than in Years 2 and 3 together?

Test Your Skills

STATISTICS AND PROBABILITY
Chance and data

(continued)

Some students did a maths quiz. The table shows their scores out of 10 for adding, subtracting, multiplying and dividing.

Name	+	−	×	÷
Rose	8	7	10	7
Anna	9	7	6	5
Max	7	6	9	8
Bill	8	8	7	6
Kumar	7	5	8	9

13 What did Max score in subtracting?

14 Who scored 9 in dividing?

15 Who scored the best mark and what for?

16 What is the total of Anna's scores?

Some friends counted fish at the beach.

Name	Tally
Joe	卌 II
Ali	IIII
Meg	卌
Sam	卌 卌

17 How many fish did Meg count?

18 Who counted 7 fish?

19 How many more fish did Sam count than Ali?

A bag contains 6 red, 1 green and 2 yellow balls. Without looking, one ball is taken from the bag. How could you describe the chance that the ball is

20 green?

21 red?

22 blue?

23 red or green or yellow?

If this spinner is spun, what number is

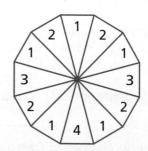

24 most likely to occur?

25 second most likely to occur?

26 least likely to occur?

27 Which is more likely to occur, an odd number or an even number?

Key Points

STATISTICS AND PROBABILITY
Chance and data

1 **A graph is a display of information.** Every graph should have a heading that tells us what it is about. There are different types of graphs. One type is a **column graph**.

Example: This graph shows the results when some students were asked to choose their favourite vegetable.

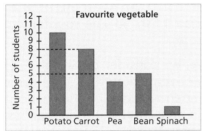

■ From the graph we can see that the top of the column for bean is level with the 5 on the vertical axis. So 5 students voted for bean.

■ To find the vegetable that 8 students voted for, we find 8 on the vertical axis and go across until we meet the top of a column. So the vegetable that 8 students voted for was carrot.

■ From the graph we can see that 10 students voted for potato. We can also see that 4 voted for pea and 1 for spinach. So 5 voted for pea and spinach.
Now 10 − 5 = 5.
So 5 more students voted for potato than for pea and spinach together.

■ To find the total number of students we need to add together all the votes.
10 + 8 + 4 + 5 + 1 = 28
So 28 students voted for their favourite vegetable.

2 **Sometimes a column graph can show more than one piece of information**.

Example:

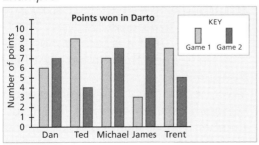

■ In this graph the points won for both Game 1 and Game 2 can be seen. The key is important because it helps us to understand what is happening.

■ For example, Dan scored 6 points in Game 1. He scored 7 points in Game 2. Adding those points we can see that Dan scored a total of 13 points in the two games.

■ In Game 2 Trent scored 5 points.

■ In Game 1 Michael scored 7 points. Dan scored 7 points in Game 2. So Dan is the person who scored the same number of points in Game 2 as Michael did in Game 1.

■ James scored 3 points in Game 1 and 9 points in Game 2. Now 3 + 9 = 12. So James is the person who scored 12 points altogether.

■ To find the person who scored the most points altogether, we add the points for Game 1 to the points for Game 2 for each person. Michael scored 7 points for Game 1 and 8 points for Game 2.
7 + 8 = 15. This is more than for any of the other boys. So Michael is the boy who scored the most points altogether.

■ A graph helps us see information easily. For example, we can see straight away that Michael scored more points than Dan because both of Michael's columns are taller than Dan's columns.

3 **Another type of graph is a picture graph**. Sometimes called a pictograph, this **uses symbols or pictures to show information**. This type of graph should have a key that tells what each symbol represents.

Example:

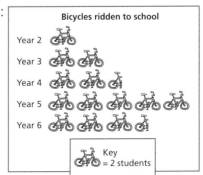

Excel Revise in a Month Year 4 NAPLAN*-style Tests

Key Points

STATISTICS AND PROBABILITY
Chance and data

(continued)

- This graph shows the number of bicycles ridden to school by students in different years. The key tells us that each bicycle symbol represents 2 students. This means that 1 student would be represented by half a symbol.
- Year 2 has one symbol and so 2 students in Year 2 rode bikes to school.
- In Year 4 there are 2 whole symbols and half a symbol, so 5 students in Year 4 rode bikes to school.
- 4 students means 2 symbols, so Year 3 had 4 students riding bicycles.
- In Year 5 there are 5 symbols. This means 10 students. 2 students in Year 2 and 4 in Year 3 rode bikes so that means 6 students altogether. So there are 4 more bike riders in Year 5 than in Years 2 and 3 together.

4 **A table is another way of displaying information. Data will be shown in rows and columns.**

Example:
In this table we can see the marks for 4 different maths tests for each of 5 people.

Name	+	−	×	÷
Rose	8	7	10	7
Anna	9	7	6	5
Max	7	6	9	8
Bill	8	8	7	6
Kumar	7	5	8	9

- By looking for Max in the column under Name, and the heading for subtracting, we can see that Max scored 6 in subtracting.
- Looking under the heading for dividing we can see that the score of 9 belongs to Kumar.
- The best mark is 10. This was scored by Rose in multiplying.
- Anna scored 9 in adding, 7 in subtracting, 6 in multiplying and 5 in dividing.
  Now 9 + 7 + 6 + 5 = 27.
  So the total of Anna's marks is 27.

5 **Tally marks are used to keep track of scores as they happen. They are arranged in groups of 5.** Four tally marks are vertical

Name	Tally
Joe	⊞ II
Ali	IIII
Meg	⊞
Sam	⊞ ⊞

and the fifth tally mark goes diagonally across to show a group of 5.

Example: So Meg has a tally that is a group of 5. This means that Meg counted 5 fish.

- A score of 7 means one group of 5 plus 2 more tally marks. This is the tally for Joe. So Joe is the person who counted 7 fish.
- Sam counted 10 fish (2 groups of 5) and Ali counted 4 fish. So Sam counted 6 more fish than Ali.

6 **In chance, we consider the likelihood of particular events occurring.** If an event must happen we describe the chance as **certain**. If an event cannot happen we describe the chance as **impossible**. If an event is more likely to happen than not happen we describe the chance as **likely**. If an event is less likely to happen than not happen, we describe the chance as **unlikely**.

Example: So if a ball is taken from a bag containing 6 red, 1 green, and 2 yellow balls, then the chance of getting a green ball can be described as unlikely. The chance of getting a red ball can be described as likely and the chance of getting a blue ball is impossible. We could be certain of getting a ball that is either red, green or yellow.

7 **A spinner is usually divided into sectors.** A spinner is most likely to stop on a sector that is largest or on a number that occurs the most.

Example: On this spinner there are five sectors showing 1, four sectors showing 2, two sectors showing 3 and one sector showing 4. It is most likely to stop on 1.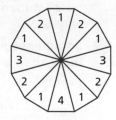
The number that it is second most likely to stop on is 2 and the number least likely to be spun is 4.
Seven sectors have odd numbers and five sectors have even numbers. So an odd number is more likely to occur than an even number.

Real Test

STATISTICS AND PROBABILITY
Chance and data

1 The colours of the eyes of students in a class were noted.

Colour	Tally
Blue	卌 II
Brown	卌 IIII
Green	IIII
Other	II

How many of the students had brown eyes?

A 4   **B** 7   **C** 8   **D** 9

2 A packet contains 8 red, 5 white and 7 blue balloons. Which colour is it impossible to take from the packet?

A blue   **B** green   **C** white   **D** red

3 The table shows the numbers of animals some farmers have.

	Cows	Sheep	Goats
Sandy	265	10	2
Ben	116	512	40
Nelly	12	0	78

How many more sheep than goats does Ben have? [ ]

4 Some students were asked which of four movies was their favourite.

How many students chose *Mattie*?

[ ]

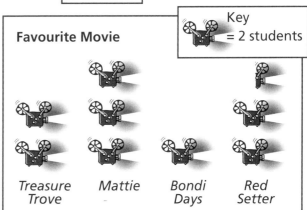

Favourite Movie

Key = 2 students

Treasure Trove   Mattie   Bondi Days   Red Setter

5 Which spinner is most likely to stop on red?

A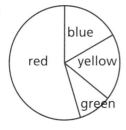
B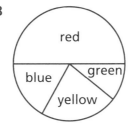
C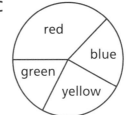
D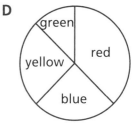

☞ **Answers and explanations on pages 184-185**

6 There are four jellybeans in a dish. Two of the jellybeans are red, one is black and one is white. Frances takes a red jellybean from the dish and eats it. Then Alex takes a jellybean. How could you describe the chance that Alex's jellybean is red?

A impossible   **B** unlikely   **C** likely   **D** certain

7 The graph shows the number of wickets five boys each took in a cricket competition.

Who took 3 more wickets than John?

A James

B Ray

C Dean

D Boyd

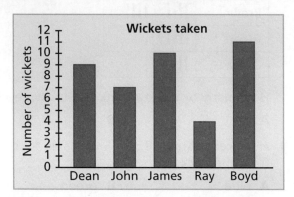

8 Tom rolls a normal dice 3 times. It shows 6 each time.
Tom rolls the dice a fourth time. Which of these statements are true?

A The dice is certain to show 6.

B The dice is certain not to show 6.

C The dice is unlikely to show 6.

D The dice is likely to show 6.

9 This graph shows the number of badges won by some students.
Which of these statements are true?
Select **all** the correct answers.

A Emily won more badges than Rose.

B Max won more badges than Emily.

C Dan won fewer badges than Emily.

D Rose won fewer badges than Dan.

E Dan won more badges than Max.

10 Jenny has 4 boxes of tiles.

She takes one tile from each box. Which could be the tiles Jenny takes?

A   **B**    **C**    **D**

☞ **Answers and explanations on pages 184-185**

 With most spelling rules there are exceptions. English words have varied origins (e.g. *siesta* comes from Spain and *kayak* is an Inuit word from North America).

Key Points

1 **Add suffixes to words ending with a consonant and *y*** by changing the *y* to *i* before adding the suffix. Some common suffixes are 'ly', 'less', 'ness', 'est' and 'er'.

Examples: happiness, happily, tidily, penniless, dizziness, laziest, angrily

An exception to this rule is when adding 'ing' there is no need to drop the *y*.

Examples: bully → bullying, carry → carrying

2 **Add suffixes to words ending with a vowel and *y*** by simply adding the suffix. There are a few common examples: *greyness, joyless.*

3 You need to be able to use **common homonyms** (words that sound the same but which have different spellings) in the correct context.

Examples: bye, by, buy; four, for; hear, here; wear, where

4 A **silent *k*** often comes before an *n*.

Examples: knife, knew, knock, kneel, knock

5 **Demon words** are words commonly misspelled. It is wise to know the spelling of these words. Here are twenty-five typical examples.

often	Tuesday	burglar	science	library
always	Wednesday	February	woollen	wooden
film	cough	safety	meant	women
they're	business	heard	forty	surprise
truly	legend	ache	colour	umbrella

Test Your Skills

Learn the words below. A common method of self-testing is the **LOOK, SAY, COVER, WRITE, CHECK** method. Any mistakes should be rewritten three times correctly and immediately. By rewriting the word correctly you become familiar with the correct spelling. If the word is particularly troublesome, rewrite it several more times or keep a list of words that you can check regularly.

rough _____	filming _____	break _____
laziness _____	happiest _____	weekly _____
restless _____	relaxing _____	luckiest _____
holiday _____	Saturday _____	forty _____
savings _____	sickness _____	knees _____

Write any troublesome words three times: _____

Real Test

SPELLING
Common misspellings

15 MIN

Please ask your parent or teacher to read to you the spelling words on page 209.
Write the correct spelling of each word in the box.

1 Did you wear your school _____ to school this week?

2 Lindy's blouse was _____ .

3 We are all _____ to keep the carpet clean in wet weather.

4 Angela put a _____ on her bedroom door.

5 It was a _____ match. We lost by one point.

6 There are _____ days in two weeks.

Each line has one word that is incorrect. Write the correct spelling of the underlined word in the box.

7 "Come <u>hear</u>, right now," demanded the squad leader.

8 Hurrah! We go on holidays <u>tomorow</u>!

9 Traffic clogged the <u>hiway</u> at the turn-off to the beach.

10 Dad bit into the <u>pair</u> and juice ran down his arm.

11 Did you get that problem <u>write</u> or was it too hard?

12 The days were <u>sonny</u> but the nights were frosty.

Each sentence has a spelling mistake. Write the correct spelling of that word in the box.
There is only one mistake in each line.

13 I know verbs are called doing words and nowns are the name words.

14 We watched the vampire filum right through to the end!

15 The girls at our school can wear either a chunic or trousers in winter.

16 Roger started glueing in his pictures before we were told to start.

17 The heat of the summer day made my throte sore.

18 "Witch way to the petrol pumps?" the driver asked.

☞**Answers and explanations on page 185**

GRAMMAR AND PUNCTUATION
Pronouns, prepositions and adverbs; apostrophes and commas

15 MIN

Key Points

1 **Pronouns are words that take the place of nouns.**

Examples: John gave the ball to Jill. <u>He</u> gave it to <u>her</u>. (*He* and *her* are pronouns.) Some common pronouns are *I, we, me, us, you, they, them, he, she, him, her* and *it*.

2 **Prepositions show the relationship between a noun or pronoun and another word.** They show the position (pre**position**).

Examples: at, above, among, under, off, until, into, up, upon, beside, between

3 **Adverbs help verbs.** They add extra meaning to the verbs. They tell how, when or where something happened.

Examples: quickly, lately, silently, patiently, roughly, soon

4 **Apostrophes** have two uses.

a To indicate **contractions** (shortened words). When letters are left out of a word, an apostrophe is put in their place.

Examples: cannot ➜ can't; she will ➜ she'll; we are ➜ we're; I am ➜ I'm; it is ➜ it's

b To show **ownership**. When something belongs to someone (or something) ownership is shown with **'s**.

Examples: Rob's nose, dog's collar, Ford's badge, doctor's fee, shop's window
Note: Commonly confused words are *it's* and *its*. The word **it's** stands for **it is**. **Its**, without an apostrophe, is a pronoun as is *hers, his* and *their*. (The dog wagged <u>its</u> tail.)

5 **More on commas.** Look at this sentence: *"We are going to see Santa,"* Dad said. See the comma after *Santa*. It indicates a pause. It is <u>inside</u> the speech marks.

Written another way the sentence becomes: *Dad said, "We are going to see Santa."* The pause and comma come after *said*.

Test Your Skills

1 In this passage underline the pronouns and **circle** the prepositions.

Lassie dashed under a bush when she heard the truck coming up the drive. The truck crunched to a stop beside the shed. Lassie watched Dan get out with something in his arms. It was the new pup. Slowly Lassie came out from her cover to meet her new companion.

2 Underline the adverbs in this passage. Singing sweetly Margie watched the judges. When she stopped singing she nodded briefly, then quickly left the stage. Soon the judges would loudly announce her score.

3 Add the missing comma into this sentence. "I will put the cream in the fridge" said Grandma.

4 Write these words in shortened form.

we will _____

there is _____ I will _____

you have _____

she is _____ I am _____

they are _____

cannot _____

5 Write suitable adverbs in the spaces.

Tammy crept _____ towards the creek that was gushing _____ over the fall.

Real
Test

GRAMMAR AND PUNCTUATION

Pronouns, prepositions and adverbs; apostrophes and commas

15 MIN

1 Choose the letter to show where the missing comma (,) should go.

"We won't get to the concert (A) on time (B) " (C) moaned my big (D) sister.

2 Which option has all pronouns?

A brightly, mostly, happily, lightly
B silly, very, destroy, valley
C car, caravan, van, trailer
D her, mine, our, it

3 Which of the following correctly completes this sentence?

I thought ______ have to go to the dentist next year, but maybe I got that wrong.

A we'd
B weed
C we'ed
D w'ed

4 Which of the following correctly completes this sentence?

Gerry ran ______ across the school grounds when he was told to be quick.

A slowly
B slow
C slowing
D slowest

5 Which word or words are common nouns in this sentence?

I looked at Gaylene and guessed she was making a joke.

Use as many boxes as you need.

6 Which of the following correctly completes this sentence?

______ brother and I have a game to play in Windsor.

A He's
B Hes
C His
D H'es

7 Omar always ______ the paint while Nayev cleans the walls.

A mix
B mixing
C mixes
D mixed

8 Choose the word that is **not** required in this sentence.

I heard the wet rain on the roof during the storm last night.

Write your answer in the box.

9 Choose the letter to show where the missing apostrophe (') should go.

It belong (A) s to the student (B) s in the class two door (C) s down but it (D) s in our room!

10 Read this sentence.

We work purposely and cheerfully on painting projects but never on a Sunday.

Write any adverbs from the sentences in the boxes. Use as many boxes as you need.

☞ Answers and explanations on pages 185–186

Real Test

GRAMMAR AND PUNCTUATION
Pronouns, prepositions and adverbs; apostrophes and commas

(continued)

11 Choose the words *it* refers to in this sentence.

Our new car has leather seats, automatic windows, a stereo system and cruise control. It is better than I expected!

A our new car

B leather seats

C stereo system

D cruise control

12 Which of the following correctly completes this sentence?

I know ▨▨▨▨ not getting a second chance!

A whose

B who'se

C who's

D whoser

13 Which sentence should have a question mark (**?**)?

A How you do it is not my worry

B How was the mystery solved

C How I love jellybeans

D How to set a table is easy

14 Choose the letter to show where the missing comma (**,**) should go.

The group leader stated " This time I will go first."

⬆ Ⓐ   ⬆ⒷⒸ   ⬆ Ⓓ

15 Which of the following would best end with a exclamation mark (**!**)?

A I want you to sweep the floor

B Please give a hand

C How far did it go

D That's crazy

16 Which of the following correctly completes the sentence?

The twins in our class ▨▨▨▨ us with lots of laughs.

A provide

B provides

C providing

D providers

17 Which sentence is correct?

A The reason why the machine has stopped because it ran out of coins.

B Why the machine has stopped is because it ran out of coins

C The machine stopped because it ran out of coins.

D Because the reason it ran out of coins the machine stopped.

18 Which of the following correctly completes the sentence?

The princess was ready to start the race. ▨▨▨▨ raised the flag.

A Her

B It

C They

D She

☞ **Answers and explanations on pages 185-186**

Test Your Skills

READING
Understanding legends

10 min

A legend is a form of narrative and part of an oral storytelling tradition. It is an attempt to explain a significant situation or historical event.

Read *The story of Muyim* and answer the questions.

1   **The story of Muyim**

2   A long time ago there
3   was a young man and a
4   young woman. They had
5   planned to get married.

6   The young woman was
7   very beautiful. She would
8   often go and sit by
9   the still waters
10 of a billabong.
11 She didn't know
12 that an evil spirit
13 lived there who
14 became very jealous
15 of the young man the
16 woman loved. The evil
17 spirit decided to take
18 the woman for himself.

19 He took her from the bank of the billabong
20 and turned her into a blue flowering
21 waterlily called Muyim. Keeping her this way
22 he would always be reminded of her beauty.

23 The young man felt great <u>heartache</u> at the
24 loss of his companion. He knew she loved
25 to wander the banks of the billabong so he
26 spent many days searching along the water's
27 edge and through the bushes and reeds that
28 grew there.

29 The evil spirit, seeing the <u>forlorn</u> young man
30 searching day after day for his companion,
31 finally felt sorry for him. But he was not
32 about to return Muyim to her world. Instead
33 he took the young man and changed him
34 into a bulrush, which is a tall grass-like
35 plant that grows in and near water. It is
36 called Yimbun.

37 In this way the couple could live and grow
38 close to each other. And when a breeze
39 blows over the surface of the billabong the
40 tall Yimbin can bend in the gentle wind
41 and be even closer to his companion, the
42 blue waterlily.

Adapted from *Australia's unwritten history: More legends of our land* by Oodgeroo Noonuccal, HBJ, 1992

1   This legend is a way of
    A   warning people to avoid places where evil spirits live.
    B   providing an explanation for something that can be observed.
    C   alerting people to the danger of wandering around billabongs.
    D   supplying evidence for why something happened.

2   Why did the evil spirit take the young woman?
    A   He wanted to have a blue waterlily in the billabong.
    B   He didn't want her sitting on the bank of the billabong.
    C   He was afraid she might leave and never return.
    D   He was jealous of the young man's good fortune.

3   According to the text what does a bulrush do in the breeze?
    Write your answer on the lines.

    _____

    _____

4   *Heartache* could be replaced with which word that has a similar meaning?
    A   grief   B   guilt
    C   shame   D   envy

5   The evil spirit turned the young woman into a waterlily so he could
    A   always be near her.
    B   admire her beauty.
    C   make the young man jealous.
    D   punish her for sitting on the bank.

6   A suitable synonym for *forlorn* would be
    A   tired.   B   fearful.
    C   forgotten.   D   sad.

Answers: 1 B 2 D 3 it bends 4 A 5 B 6 D

☞ **Explanations on page 186**

Real Test

READING
Understanding legends

`10 MIN`

Read *The legend of Devota* and answer the questions.

1 **The legend of Devota**

2 In the very early fourth century (more than
3 1600 years ago) the island of Corsica, off the
4 coast of France, was under the control of the
5 Roman governor Diocletian. He <u>persecuted</u>
6 the Christians because of their faith.

7 A young Christian woman, Devota, was
8 arrested, imprisoned and tortured. She died
9 without giving up her faith. The governor
10 ordered that her body be burnt, but the
11 Christians saved her body and placed it on a
12 boat bound for Africa, where they believed
13 she would receive a proper Christian burial.

14 Unfortunately, a storm overtook the boat. Then, a dove flew out from Devota's mouth and guided
15 the boat to Monaco on the French coast where it ran aground on a day which is close to the
16 present 27 January. Devota's body was discovered by local fishermen.

16 In her honour a chapel was built in a nearby valley. Sailors started going there to meditate.
17 Since then a number of miracles have been said to have occurred. Devota became the patron
18 saint of Monaco.

19 Each year, on 27 January, the people celebrate with religious ceremonies, feasts and flowers.
20 The royal family burns a fishing boat from which a white dove is released.

From an idea in *Principality of Monaco* by Oliver Marcel and Michel Mathis, 2010

1 Devota was tortured because she
   A tried to escape in a boat.
   B didn't like the Roman governor.
   C was arrested and imprisoned.
   D would not give up her beliefs.

2 What does the royal family do on
27 January each year?
   A catch doves   B burn a boat
   C go fishing   D leave for a holiday

3 Devota's body ended up in Monaco because
   A her boat was blown off course.
   B a dove led the boat the wrong way.
   C there was a suitable chapel there.
   D no-one knew the way to Africa.

4 In the text, a *persecuted* person is a
person who
   A receives unfair treatment because of
      their beliefs.

   B lived in the ancient Roman Empire.
   C is buried in a foreign country.
   D goes on a final sea journey.

5 Twenty-seventh of January is important
because it
   A means the people of Monaco burn
      their boats.
   B is the day doves escape from the
      mouths of saints.
   C celebrates the day Devota's body
      arrived in Monaco.
   D is when sailors go to a chapel to
      meditate.

6 Devota's boat was
   A sunk.   B stranded.
   C burnt.   D lost.

☞ Answers and explanations on page 187

Real Test

READING
Understanding procedures

10 MIN

A procedure is a set of instructions on how to do something. These are often called 'steps'. Procedures will often include the materials and tools needed and helpful hints. A recipe is a common form of procedure.

Read this recipe *How to make a spaghetti pie* and answer the questions.

---

1   **How to make a spaghetti pie**
2   This is a very easy and delicious <u>dish</u> to make. You can eat it hot or cold.

3   **Things you'll need**
4   500 g spaghetti
5   1 can (or tub) of pasta sauce
6   5 eggs
7   ¼ cup of parsley
8   ¾ cup of grated cheese
9   2 tablespoons of paprika
10   5 cups of water
11   2 tablespoons of olive oil

bowl and mixing spoon
frying pan
large dinner plate

¼ cup of tender parsley sprigs
(for decoration)

12   1   This is a fun way to use leftover spaghetti. No leftover spaghetti? Then you'll have to cook
13   spaghetti especially for this recipe.
14   2   Measure all of the ingredients (listed above), except the olive oil and parsley sprigs, into a
15   bowl, then carefully mix.
16   3   Add cooked spaghetti and thoroughly stir.
17   4   Heat the olive oil in the frying pan.
18   5   Pour the mixture into the oil in the pan. Cook on medium heat until the mixture turns golden
19   brown (about 5 minutes). Flip it over then cook this side until it's golden brown. This will absorb
20   all the oil.
21   6   Place a dinner plate over the top of the pan. Flip the pan over holding the plate in position.
22   Do not drop the plate!
23   7   Allow the spaghetti pie to stand for 20 minutes at room temperature. Decorate the pie with a
24   few sprigs of parsley, then cut it into wedges. Sprinkle it with salt and pepper and serve. This is
25   great as a snack or a meal.

Sources: http://www.ehow.com/how_2301389_make-spaghetti-pie.html
          http://www.food.com/recipe/spaghetti-pie-120972

---

1 The above text is an example of
A a narrative.
B an explanation.
C cooking directions.
D a factual recount.

2 The word *dish* as used in the first line refers to
A a bowl.
B a shape.
C serving food.
D prepared food.

3 There are four items listed separately in a box on the right. They are
A non-food items.
B the last things to be used.
C not required in the recipe.
D for cooking any extra spaghetti.

4 The olive oil is not part of the ingredients mixed in the bowl because it
A makes the pie oily.
B is used for cooking the mixture.
C is saved for serving the pie.
D makes the mixture go brown.

5 Which words are meant as a warning?
A Do not drop the plate!
B Heat the olive oil in the frying pan.
C No leftover spaghetti?
D Measure all of the ingredients.

6 How does the writer feel about the spaghetti pie recipe?
A unimpressed
B nervous
C fascinated
D enthusiastic

☞ **Answers and explanations on page 187**

Real Test

READING
Understanding explanations

10 min

Read the introduction to the explanation *What are mantis shrimps?* in Week 2, Day 4 (page 51).

Read the explanation *How does a match work?* and answer the questions.

1 **How does a match work?**

2 Rub your hands together quickly. What do you feel? You feel the
3 warmth that the rubbing makes. The rubbing of two surfaces
4 against each other causes friction. This creates energy which creates
5 heat. Knowing this will help you understand how the <u>two different</u>
6 <u>types of matches work—safety matches and 'strike anywhere'</u>
7 <u>matches</u>.

8 A safety match can only <u>ignite</u> when it is struck against the striking
9 surface on the side of a matchbox. The striking surface is made of
10 sand, glass powder and a chemical called red phosphorus. The head of
11 a safety match contains sulphur, glass powder and an oxide-forming
12 agent, such as oxygen.

13 When a match is struck on the striking surface of its box, the
14 friction caused by the glass powder on both surfaces produces
15 enough heat to turn a very small amount of the red phosphorus into white phosphorus. This
16 catches fire on air.

17 This small amount of heat is enough to start a chemical reaction that produces oxygen gas. The
18 heat and oxygen gas then cause the sulphur to burst into flame. The matchwood quickly catches
19 on fire. Striking a match starts a chemical reaction.

20 A 'strike anywhere' match can be lit by striking the match on anything solid. It uses a different set
21 of chemicals to do the same thing.

Source: http://www.pa.msu.edu/sciencet/ask_st/092596.html

1 The word *ignite* means
A catch on fire.   B explode.
C detonate.   D get hot.

2 What is on both the match head and the striking surface of the box?
Write your answer on the line.

_____

3 What would be the main reason for using sand and glass in match production?
A to make the match flame last longer
B They are the only chemicals that can create fire.
C to make it easy to see which surfaces should be struck
D They make rough surfaces to create more friction.

4 Safety matches catch light when rubbed
A against each other.
B between two hands.

C against anything solid.
D along the striking side of the box.

5 What is the last thing to catch on fire after striking a match?
A white phosphorus
B glass powder
C the wooden matchstick
D oxygen

6 A dash is a literary device used by writers.
… two different types of matches work—safety matches and 'strike anywhere' matches.
The writer uses the dash (—) in this sentence to
A introduce an unknown fact.
B add a point not thought of earlier.
C name the two match types.
D express two similar ideas.

☞ **Answers and explanations on page 188**

Real Test

10 min

Read the introduction to the recount *River meeting* in Week 3, Day 4 (page 79).

Read the recount *Tricia's report* and answer the questions.

After a school holiday, Class 5T had to write a report on something they did during the break. This is what Tricia wrote.

---

1 **Tricia's report**

2 Because it was school holidays and Dad had to go to France,
3 the family got to stay a few days in the seaside town of
4 Nice. One day Mum decided to take us to see the Colline du
5 Chateau (Castle Hill). Strangely there is no castle there, just
6 some remains in a huge park. It is the best place to get a
7 view of Nice and the houses of the old city.

8 The park is on top of a hill—over 200 steps from the bottom
9 to the top. We took the lift.

10 Once on top we were soon in an area of grassy, shady parks
11 and a playground where we had a play. Then we discovered the castle ruins.
12 We explored them and took photos. Then it was time to buy a cool drink at the nearby cafe.

13 After a rest we found the cemeteries for Jews, Catholics and Protestants near a wall. Mum laughed
14 and said <u>the people there had the best views</u> of anybody!

15 We decided we could walk down the steps back to the shops. Imagine my surprise when we
16 discovered a huge waterfall. A noticeboard stated it was artificial. It was built when the hill was
17 converted into a park at the end of the 19th century.

18 I'd love to come back in the evening and see the waterfall flooded in light, but we didn't do that.

Photo © Alan Horsfield

---

1 To get to the top of the hill Tricia's family
   A took a lift.   **B** rode in a bus.   **C** climbed steps.   **D** walked through a park.

2 What was the one thing Tricia's family did **not** do?
   A take photographs   **B** see the waterfall at night
   C play in a playground   **D** walk down steps

3 How did the family spend their time visiting Castle Hill? Write the numbers 1, 2, 3 and 4 in the boxes to show the order in which they did things.
   visited a cemetery   played in a playground   looked at castle ruins   found a waterfall
   □   □   □   □

4 Tricia and her mother found the waterfall
   A by deliberately searching for it.   **B** following instructions on signposts.
   C as a result of a fortuitous accident.   **D** while exploring near the ruins.

5 The family's visit to Colline du Chateau could best be described as
   A exciting.   **B** disappointing.   **C** dull.   **D** enjoyable.

6 Mum laughed when she said *the people there had the best views* because
   A they were dead people.   **B** the cemetery was behind a wall.
   C they weren't looking at it.   **D** park trees blocked their view.

☞**Answers and explanations on page 188**

TIPS FOR WRITING PROCEDURES

Procedures tell us how to do something. This might include instructions on how to carry out a task or play a game. More complicated procedures involve several phases, directions for getting to a place or rules to be followed.

The purpose of a procedure is to provide instructions. Written procedures aim to tell the reader how to make or do something. Procedures usually have two main parts:

- the materials and tools needed (these are often called *requirements* or, in recipes, *ingredients*)
- the steps to be followed.

When writing procedures, it is best to keep the following points in mind. They will help you get the best possible mark.

Before you start writing

- Read the question and check the stimulus material carefully. *Stimulus material* means the topic, title, picture, words, phrases or extract of writing you are given to base your writing on.
- Write about something you know. Don't pick a complicated topic. Even the steps in a simple everyday procedure can be difficult to explain simply and precisely.

The introduction

- Start by stating what will happen in the end—the goal of the activity. This is often contained in the title.

The body

- You may add personal opinions and comments to brighten up the largely impersonal language used in procedures.
- Follow the structure of procedures. The materials and tools required are listed first, followed by short, concise sentences describing the steps in chronological order. The steps may be numbered.
- Correctly paragraph your writing. This is important: put each step in a separate paragraph.
- Lay out your instructions clearly. The reader must be able to follow the steps easily in order.
- Add diagrams. These can be very useful, as they can often clearly illustrate a step that would take many words to explain.
- Include additional material such as safety notes and explanations.
- Use precise terms such as *lukewarm, spread evenly, hold for two minutes* or *sharp turn right*.
- Use command sentences. These are sentences starting with infinitive verbs without *to*, such as *put, place* and *allow*. This is known as the imperative mood.
- Use sequencing words, such as *then, after* and *while*, that establish the sequence of steps clearly.
- Include optional stages as necessary, such as explaining reasons, providing alternative steps, giving warnings or mentioning possible consequences.

The conclusion

- The final paragraph may include a comment on what will have been achieved by following the steps.

When you have finished writing give yourself a few minutes to read through your procedure. Quickly check spelling and punctuation, and insert any words that have been accidentally left out.

Year 4 Sample Writing
(a sample answer to the question on page 116)

How to wash your hair

These instructions are for people who have enough hair to wash. Most people wash their hair once or twice a week, depending on what they have been doing. If you've been swimming then a quick rinse-off under an outside shower will do to remove the salt or chlorine.

Before you enter the shower have the shampoo and conditioner close at hand. It is wise to have a bathroom mat in place for when you step out of the shower and a dry towel nearby. No one likes walking on a wet bathroom floor.

Step into the shower and adjust the temperature to your preferred heat. Let the water flow over your head so that your hair is thoroughly wet.

Open the cap of the shampoo bottle and squeeze a dollop into your hand. Massage the shampoo into your wet hair to produce a lather. Do not rinse off immediately. Let the shampoo penetrate right through your hair.

After a half a minute or so, rinse the hair thoroughly. Some people prefer to shut their eyes to stop shampoo irritating their eyes.

Open the cap of the conditioner bottle and squeeze a dollop into your hand. Massage the conditioner into your wet, clean hair from the hair tips to the roots. Do not rinse off immediately.

Rinse off most of the conditioner. It doesn't matter if a little conditioner remains on the hair as this will keep the hair soft for a few days.

Turn off the shower. Let excess water drain from the body. Step out of the shower onto the bathroom mat and gently dry your hair on the towel.

Depending on how much hair you have, washing your hair should take five to ten minutes.

Language and ideas

Vocabulary
- Adverbs and adjectives are well chosen.
- Precise verbs and nouns are included. Verbs are used to begin the steps.
- The correct use of personal pronouns (e.g. *you, your*) keeps the recount flowing.

Sentence structure
- The writer uses a variety of sentence beginnings. Short commands keep the instructions clear and easy to follow.
- Care is taken not to overuse a particular word as a sentence starter.

Ideas
- The writer includes senses other than sight (e.g. *heat, gently dry*).
- Some suggestions for the consideration of others are included.
- Optional steps are provided.

Punctuation
- Punctuation is well handled including commas and apostrophes.
- Capital letters correctly begin sentences.

Spelling
- There are no spelling mistakes in common or unusual words.

Structure

Audience
- The title informs readers of the goal of the instructions.
- Who the instructions apply to is firmly established in the first paragraph.
- Present tense is used.
- The use of the pronoun *you* indicates that the instructions may apply to the reader.

Character and setting
- The *who, where* and *when* are established quickly.
- The writer is describing a familiar procedure.
- Requirements are listed early in the text

Text structure
- Steps are in sequence using some adverbs of time.
- Precise words are used for details.
- The writer has used a casual, informative style.

Paragraphing
- New paragraphs start with changes in time and for each step.
- Personal suggestions and opinions are included.

Cohesion
- The final sentence refers to a factor that may be important to the reader.

This text is beyond what would be expected of a typical Year 4 student. It is provided here as a model. The assessment comments are based on the marking criteria used to assess the NAPLAN Writing Test.

Real Test

WRITING
Procedure 1

42 min

Before you start, read the **General Writing Tips** on pages 23–24 and the **Tips for Writing Procedures** on page 113.

In a procedure the aim is to describe to a reader how to do or make something.

Choose one of the following topics and tell the reader exactly what to do.

- How to make a sandwich with only one filling (e.g. peanut butter)
- How to clean your teeth
- How to put a battery in a toy or a household item (e.g. kitchen scales)
- How to go from the front door to the back door (inside or outside) of your home

TO BACK DOOR

YOU ARE HERE

Before you start to write, think about:
- the things you might need before you start
- what you have to do—get the order (steps) right
- what you achieve by following the instructions
- any safety hints
- any problems that might need some extra explaining.

Remember to:
- plan your procedure before you start writing
- make a list of the materials (if any) needed
- use command-type sentences in your instructions
- choose your words carefully and pay attention to your spelling and punctuation
- write neatly but don't waste time
- quickly check your procedure once you have finished.

Start writing here or type in your answer on a tablet or computer.

Title: _____

_____

_____

_____

_____

_____

☞ **Marking Guide on pages 188-189**

Real Test

WRITING
Procedure 2

42 min

Before you start, read the **General Writing Tips** on pages 23–24 and the **Tips for Writing Procedures** on page 113.

In a procedure the aim is to describe to a reader how to do or make something.

Choose one of the following topics and tell the reader exactly what to do.

- How to borrow a library book
- How to wash your hair
- How to get to a friend's home about a block away
- How to grow a plant in a pot

Before you start to write, think about:
- the things you might need before you start
- what you have to do—get the order (steps) right
- what you achieve by following the instructions
- any safety hints
- any problems that might need some extra explaining.

Remember to:
- plan your procedure before you start writing
- make a list of the materials (if any) needed
- use command-type sentences in your instructions
- choose your words carefully and pay attention to your spelling and punctuation
- write neatly but don't waste time
- quickly check your procedure once you have finished.

Start writing here or type in your answer on a tablet or computer.

Title: _____

_____

_____

_____

_____

☞ Go to page 114 to see a sample answer to this question.

☞ **Marking Guide on page 189**

TIPS FOR WRITING EXPLANATIONS

An **explanation** is a text that tells why things occur in scientific and technical fields. They are used in all the arts and sciences. Explanations are designed to help readers understand a topic. All explanations are not necessarily serious.

Keep these points in mind. They will help you get the best possible mark.

■ Write about a topic you know. Don't try to write about something outside your experience.

■ When you have chosen your topic, it might be helpful to jot a few ideas quickly on paper so you don't forget them.

■ Inform your reader early of the topic of your explanation. The title can be in the form of a question. The first few sentences or first paragraph may expand on this idea—a statement about what is to be explained.

■ Once you have introduced your topic, use a sequence of paragraphs to explain how your subject works, operates, grow or performs—the how and why part.

■ If possible, include simple definitions of any scientific or technical words you use. Definitions include the meaning of the word, a description of selected features and an example. Avoid common words that carry little or no meaning, such as *good*.

■ Only add information that helps the reader to better understand the subject of the explanation. 'Waffle' and unnecessary detail don't improve an explanation. Detail must be selected carefully.

■ Many explanations are in the simple present tense and passive voice.

■ Paragraphing is important. Take care not to include too much information in each paragraph. Separate paragraphs work well even for small points. Paragraphing may explain where, when and how. Cause and effect can be part of an explanation.

■ Explanations may include diagrams and pictures.

■ Many explanations end with a short comment. It is a way to round off your writing.

■ Make your writing interesting and informative by using words and phrases precisely.

■ Give yourself a few moments at the end to read through your explanation. Quickly check spelling and punctuation, and add words that have been accidentally left out. Use more difficult and technical words and have a go at the correct spelling.

Direct speech is not a feature of an explanation. Indirect speech (reported speech) does not have speech marks (' ').

Remember: Writing explanations requires some expert knowledge, so bear this in mind if you are given a choice of text.

Real Test

WRITING
Explanation 1

42 min

Before you start, read the **General Writing Tips** on pages 23–24 and the **Tips for Writing Explanations** on page 117.

An explanation tells **how** and **why** something happens or works.

Explanations are often about scientific, technical or natural phenomena.

The importance of the subject matter is stated.

Write an explanation of one of these topics:

- baseball cap
- flippers (for swimming)
- sunglasses.

Before you start to write, think about:
- what you are explaining
- special or unusual features of the item
- the value or benefit of the item for the wearer
- any safety hints.

Remember to:
- plan your explanation before you start writing
- write in correctly formed sentences and take care with paragraphing
- choose your words carefully and pay attention to your spelling and punctuation
- write neatly but don't waste time
- quickly check your explanation once you have finished.

Start writing here or type in your answer on a tablet or computer.

_____

_____

_____

_____

_____

_____

☞ **Marking Guide on pages 189-190**

Real Test

WRITING
Explanation 2

42 MIN

Before you start, read the **General Writing Tips** on pages 23–24 and the **Tips for Writing Explanations** on page 117.

An explanation tells **how** and **why** something happens or works.

Explanations are often about scientific or technical or natural phenomena.

The importance of the subject matter is stated.

Write an explanation of one of these topics:
- photo album
- vase
- doorbell/chime (electric or otherwise).

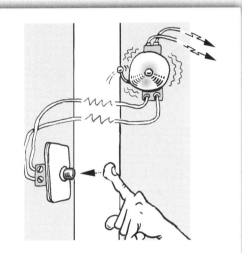

Before you start to write, think about:
- what you are explaining
- special or unusual features of the item
- the value or benefit of the item
- any safety hints.

Remember to:
- plan your explanation before you start writing
- write in correctly formed sentences and take care with paragraphing
- choose your words carefully and pay attention to your spelling and punctuation
- write neatly but don't waste time
- quickly check your explanation once you have finished.

Start writing here or type in your answer on a tablet or computer.

_____

_____

_____

_____

_____

_____

_____

_____

☞ **Marking Guide on page 190**

Sample NAPLAN Online-style tests

DIFFERENT TEST LEVELS

- There are eight tests for students to complete in this section. These sample tests have been classified as either Intermediate or Advanced according to the level of the majority of questions. This will broadly reflect the NAPLAN Online tailored testing experience where students are guided into answering questions that match their ability.
- The following tests are included in this section:
  - one Intermediate-level Test for each of Reading, Conventions of Language and Numeracy
  - one Advanced-level Test for each of Reading, Conventions of Language and Numeracy
  - two Writing Tests.

CHECKS

- The NAPLAN Online Reading, Conventions of Language and Numeracy tests will be divided into different sections.
- Students will have one last opportunity to check their answers in each section when they have reached the end of that section.
- Once they have moved onto a new section, they will not be able to go back and check their work again.
- We have included reminders for students to check their work at specific points in the Sample Tests so they become familiar with this process before they take the NAPLAN Online tests.

EXCEL TEST ZONE

- After students have consolidated their topic knowledge by completing this book, we recommend they practise NAPLAN Online–style questions on our website at www.exceltestzone.com.au.
- Students will be able to gain valuable practice in digital skills such as dragging text across a screen, using an onscreen ruler, protractor and calculator to answer questions, or listening to an audio recording of a spelling word which they then type into a box.
- Students will also become confident in using a computer or tablet to complete NAPLAN Online–style tests so they will be fully prepared for the actual NAPLAN Online tests.

Today you are going to write a **narrative**. Your story will be called **The talking animal**. Your work will be judged on the structure of your story and how well you express your ideas.

Tell about an animal that can talk. Remember an animal is any living creature, from a butterfly to a dolphin to a bird. It might be a pet. You might be the only one that can hear it talk.

Your story can be amusing but you may want to be serious.

Before you start to write, think about:
- where your story takes place
- the characters and what they do in your story
- the events that take place in your story and the problems that have to be resolved
- how the story begins, what happens in your story and how your story ends.

Remember to:
- plan your story before you start writing
- write in correctly formed sentences and take care with paragraphing
- pay attention to the words you use, your spelling and punctuation
- write neatly but don't waste time
- quickly check your story once you have finished.

Start writing here or type your answer on a tablet or computer.

_____
_____
_____
_____
_____
_____
_____
_____
_____
_____

☞ **Marking guide on pages 191–194**

Read the extract adapted from *Alice in Wonderland* (1865) by Lewis Carroll and answer questions 1 to 7.

1 **Alice in Wonderland**

2 *Alice has just left three odd characters at a tea party.*
3 *Now read on.*

4 "At any rate I'll never go *there* again!" said Alice as she
5 picked her way through the wood. "It's the stupidest tea-
6 party I ever was at in all my life!"

7 Just as she said this, she noticed that one of the trees had
8 a door leading right into it. "That's very curious!" she
9 thought. "But everything's curious today. I think I may as
10 well go in at once." And in she went.

11 She found herself in the long hall, and close to the little
12 glass table. "Now, I'll manage better this time," she said
13 to herself, and began by taking the little golden key
14 from the table, and unlocking the door to a passage. She
15 walked down the passage into the beautiful garden with
16 bright flowerbeds and the cool fountains.

17 A large rose bush stood in the garden. The roses growing on it were white, but there were three
18 gardeners at it, busily painting them red. Alice thought this a very curious thing, and she went
19 nearer to watch them, and just as she came up to them she heard one of them say, "Look out
20 now! Don't go splashing paint over me like that!"

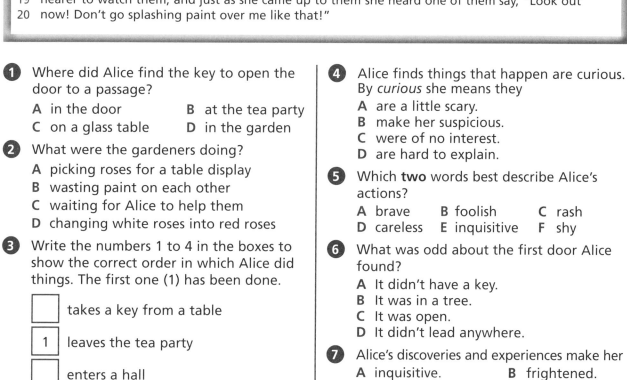

1 Where did Alice find the key to open the door to a passage?

A in the door
B at the tea party
C on a glass table
D in the garden

2 What were the gardeners doing?

A picking roses for a table display
B wasting paint on each other
C waiting for Alice to help them
D changing white roses into red roses

3 Write the numbers 1 to 4 in the boxes to show the correct order in which Alice did things. The first one (1) has been done.

[ ] takes a key from a table

[1] leaves the tea party

[ ] enters a hall

[ ] finds a door in a tree

4 Alice finds things that happen are curious. By *curious* she means they

A are a little scary.
B make her suspicious.
C were of no interest.
D are hard to explain.

5 Which **two** words best describe Alice's actions?

A brave
B foolish
C rash
D careless
E inquisitive
F shy

6 What was odd about the first door Alice found?

A It didn't have a key.
B It was in a tree.
C It was open.
D It didn't lead anywhere.

7 Alice's discoveries and experiences make her

A inquisitive.
B frightened.
C annoyed.
D careful.

☞ **Answers and explanations on pages 191-194**

Read *What are mountain devils?* and answer questions 8 to 13.

1 **What are mountain devils?**

2 The name makes a person think of mysterious, evil spirits that lurk in dark mountains. In fact they
3 are vivid red native Australian flowers.

4 The red and green buds are spectacular, providing a gleaming display as they unfold into flowers
5 which are 50 mm long. Each flower is actually a cluster of seven tubular flowers. Common names
6 include honey flower and honeysuckle because, when there is plenty of moisture around, the
7 tubes fill with a nectar which attracts ants and birds, especially honeyeaters.

8 Although it has a glorious vivid red flower, the mountain
9 devil (*Lambertia formosa*) is named after the shape of the
10 woody 'fruit' it bears—the seed capsule—which has a beak
11 and two horns, resembling a horned devil.

12 Pollinated by birds, a cluster of flowers usually produces
13 only one 'devil'. However it is not unusual for two or three
14 'devils' to emerge. The 'devils' become grey and harden
15 like the wood as they get older.

16 There is nothing evil about this native Australian.

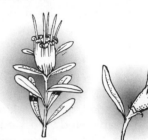

8 Complete this sentence. The name *mountain devil* comes from the

_____

9 The word *lurk* suggests that the mountain devils
A avoid getting caught. B lure their victims. C wait silently to attack. D look like real devils.

10 According to the text which statement is true?

A The seed capsules are red before they are green.

B Birds eat the seeds from the seed capsules.

C The mountain devils are not wicked at all.

D Birds are frightened by the devil shapes on the bush.

11 The words *Lambertia formosa* are in brackets because they are

A not very important.   B the plant's scientific name.
C the name of a devil.   D interesting information for readers.

12 Why are some birds attracted to the mountain devil bush?

A They are fascinated by the devil-shaped capsules.

B They see the vivid red flowers.

C They eat the ants that look for food on the bush.

D They feed on the nectar in the tubular flowers.

13 According to the text, what finally happens to the seed capsules?

A They split into two devil heads.   B They get horns and a beak.
C They turn green.   D They become woody and grey.

It would be a good idea to check your answers to questions
1 to 13 before moving on to the other questions.

☞ **Answers and explanations on pages 191-194**

Read *Bedroom scene* and answer questions 14 to 20.

1 **Bedroom scene**

2 Pippa's room was covered in pictures of animals. Above her
3 head hung a poster of two pandas feeding in a bamboo
4 clump. On the ceiling were photographs of dolphins diving
5 through the surf. On the window was a stained glass
6 picture of a rosella. The sliding doors of her wardrobe were
7 covered in pictures of African mammals: lions, giraffes,
8 gazelle, hippos and hyenas.

9 On her bookshelf were books of glossy photographs of
10 animals from all over the world. Next to them were DVDs
11 of her favourite animal shows. Some were documentaries,
12 including some by David Attenborough, but she also had
13 copies of animal films she really enjoyed.

14 Shoved in behind the bookcase were more posters and photographs. Their corners poked out at
15 various angles. These had been replaced by new pictures when Pippa discovered something that
16 took her eye. They would not be thrown out—could not be thrown out—no matter how faded and
17 worn they were. She simply stored them in an ever-thickening pile.

18 On a coffee table in the corner was her favourite display—a collection of cuddly Australian
19 animals. A kangaroo with a joey stood above all the rest.

14 This text could best be described as

A an explanation.
B a description.
C a report.
D a narrative.

15 How did Pippa's Australian collection differ from her other collections?

A It was a toy collection.
B It was stored behind the bookcase.
C It was faded and worn.
D It was displayed on the ceiling.

16 What hung above Pippa's head?

A a poster of pandas
B photographs of dolphins
C a picture of African lions
D a David Attenborough DVD

17 The text states something *took her eye*. It means something

A poked Pippa in the eye.
B hurt Pippa's eye.
C got Pippa's attention.
D caused Pippa to squint.

18 Choose an option from each column. Pippa could best be described as a

A photographer.   W explorer
B ranger.   X researcher
C reader.   Y cleaner
D collector.   Z artist

19 You are required to compare these texts: *What are mountain devils?* (page 124) and *Bedroom scene* (above).

For which purpose were these texts written? Tick **two** boxes for each text.

	What are mountain devils?	Bedroom scene
to describe	☐	☐
to inform	☐	☐
to amuse	☐	☐

20 What does Pippa do that suggests she could sometimes be an untidy person?

A She puts posters on the ceiling.
B She has pictures on her cupboard doors.
C She keeps books near her DVDs.
D She stores her old pictures behind her bookcase.

☞ **Answers and explanations on pages 191-194**

Online-
Style
Sample
Test

READING TEST 1
Intermediate level

(continued)

Read *Beautiful glass* and answer questions 21 to 27.

1 **Beautiful glass**

2 The common glass container in the home is made of simple materials: silica sand (often seen
3 as sand dunes), soda ash (a common type of mined salt) and crushed limestone (crushed from
4 limestone rock).

5 When used glass is crushed, it returns to its natural state. It can't
6 contaminate the environment even when put in landfill sites. But
7 glass containers need never become part of landfill when they can
8 be used over and over again.

9 Glass, as containers, is 100% recyclable—it can be recycled forever
10 to make new glass. The glass recycled in today's jam jar can
11 become a wine bottle, a coffee jar, a sauce bottle or a cooking oil
12 bottle. Perfect recycling! Crushed recycled glass is called 'cullet'.
13 Glass from other sources is collected separately.

14 We should be recycling all glass food and drink containers.
15 New glass would only be made if there were a need for *more* glass.

16 Glass is the ideal container for the environment. To make full use of recycled glass, recyclers
17 separate the clear glass from coloured glass. Only clear glass can be recycled to make new, clear
18 glass containers.

21 What impresses the writer most about glass?

A its many colours
B It is safe in landfill.
C It has many uses.
D It can be recycled many times.

22 What is crushed recycled glass called?
Write your answer in the box.

23 According to the text, clear glass is best

A used as landfill.
B reused after cleaning.
C separated from coloured glass.
D recycled for coloured glass.

24 The text is mainly concerned with glass

A used for food containers.
B from broken windows.
C in car windscreens.
D from light fittings.

25 The materials needed to make glass are

A scarce.   B costly.
C dangerous.   D readily available.

26 The writer refers to glass as [B]eautiful because

A most glass in anyone's home is coloured.
B he finds all glass pleasing to look at.
C he is trying to stress an important feature of glass.
D the shapes that can be made from glass are varied.

27 What would the writer like everyone to do?

A use more glass containers in the home
B recycle all glass food containers
C buy only clear glass containers
D separate clear glass from coloured glass

It would be a good idea to check your answers to questions 14 to 27 before moving on to the other questions.

☞ **Answers and explanations on pages 191-194**

Read *Pool rules!* and answer questions 28 to 34.

1   **Pool rules!**

2   At the beginning of summer I went down to our local pool.
3   The first thing I saw was a brand-new sign at the entrance
4   gate: Rules for the Pool.

5   I had to wait a couple of minutes to pay so I read the sign.
6   I was flabbergasted! There were over fifteen rules to obey
7   if you wanted to *enjoy* the pool.

8   Near the top of the list was this rule: Running, diving,
9   bombing, spitting, pushing, dunking, noisy behaviour and
10 ball games are not permitted. So what are you supposed
11 to do? Well, I suppose you can stand in the pool, sit on the
12 edge of the pool, swim lengths like someone training for the Olympics and have a really great time.

13 Obviously spitting in pools is Yuk! but the other rules take all the fun out of a pool visit. What's
14 wrong with a few kids having a sensible game of chasings?

15 The quickest way to get into a pool on a really hot day is to dive in or jump in. It is easy enough
16 to look before you jump or dive. It's commonsense. What's wrong with bombing if it's done
17 safely? It's great to feel the water gush over your body as you sink under the bubbling surface.
18 Instead you have to walk to the shallow end and enter the water carefully using the steps!

19 Little kids love to run around. This is banned! Try telling that to an excited four-year-old. What harm
20 does it do? These kids aren't going to knock someone over.

21 Pools are supposed to be fun places. Not any more! It's more fun running through a sprinkler. Pool
22 rules! Phooey!

Rule No.1
Obey all pool rules.

28 The writer learned about the rules for the pool when she
  A saw a sign inside the pool area.
  B arrived at the pool entrance.
  C was doing her training laps.
  D entered the water.

29 Which pool rule does the writer agree with?
  A No bombs into the pool
  B No ball games in the pool
  C No spitting in the pool
  D No running around the pool

30 When the writer says *Pool rules! Phooey!* she is expressing
  A disgust.   **B** delight.
  C spite.   **D** wickedness.

31 Which word best describes how the writer felt about the pool rules?
  A amused   **B** astounded
  C relaxed   **D** confused

32 The writer feels the rules
  A take the fun out of pool visits.
  B let more people enjoy the pool.
  C make the pool safer.
  D give ideas for pool activities.

33 Which pool rule does the writer feel is unfair on little children?
  A No diving into the pool
  B No ball games in the pool
  C No noisy pool behaviour
  D No running around the pool

34 You are required to compare these texts: *Beautiful glass* (page 126) and *Pool rules!* (above). For which purpose were these texts written? Tick two boxes for each text.

	Beautiful glass	*Pool rules!*
to entertain through ridicule	☐	☐
to explain	☐	☐
to expose foolishness	☐	☐
to persuade	☐	☐

☞ **Answers and explanations on pages 191-194**

Read *John Flynn* and answer questions 35 to 39.

1 **John Flynn**

2 John Flynn was born in a Victorian mining town, in 1880.
3 Flynn became a teacher but after five years decided to train
4 as a Presbyterian minister, paying for his studies by working
5 in missionary centres around Victoria.

6 After his graduation his church had him visit the outback and
7 report on the living conditions of the people. Flynn knew the
8 hardships of outback living. He had experienced the tough
9 conditions of the Northern Territory outback.

10 Because of his report and his concern for the isolated people
11 John was sent to a mission at Beltana, South Australia.

12 From Beltana, Flynn patrolled far and wide and his ideas for better services for the outback were
13 developed. Nursing homes were opened at remote inland towns, each home managed by two
14 Sisters who had some church work training. Flynn became known as 'Flynn of the Inland'.

15 Once his nursing homes were operating successfully Flynn started talking about an aero-medical
16 service for the outback people. Flynn's dream was to bring the doctor to the patient, rather than
17 taking the patient over tracks for days to the nearest hospital.

18 It seems strange that a mission established at Beltana in remote South Australia, over a century
19 ago, led to the birth of the Royal Flying Doctor Service.

Source: http://www.southaustralianhistory.com.au/royalflying.htm

Flynn's home—Beltana
Photo by Alan Horsfield

35 John Flynn's life shows that he was
  A strong and powerful.
  B brave and determined.
  C firm and skilled.
  D caring and understanding.

36 Flynn's early experience with mission work was in
  A Victoria.
  B Northern Territory.
  C South Australia.
  D Queensland.

37 In the text the word *patrolled* has the meaning of
  A guarding a place.
  B supplying protection.
  C gathering information.
  D touring a military base.

38 Write the numbers 1 to 4 in the boxes to show the correct order in which Flynn did things. The first one (1) has been done for you.

  [ ] trains as a Presbyterian minister

  [1] becomes a teacher

  [ ] goes to Beltana Mission

  [ ] sets up nursing homes in remote towns

39 The writer finds it strange that from Beltana Mission, Flynn got the idea for
  A the name 'Flynn of the Inland'.
  B missions in remote outback towns.
  C churches in isolated places.
  D a flying doctor service for outback people.

☞**Answers and explanations on pages 191-194**

1 Which article best completes this sentence? Write your answer in the box.

My dog is kept in our backyard. Last night it dug [   ] escape hole under a fence!

2 Which of the following correctly completes this sentence?
Misty is a poor debater. She is [   ] than some of the younger girls.

A worser   B worse   C worst   D more poorer   E badder

3 Which word is the noun in this sentence?

We will <u>soon</u> arrive and then we will find a <u>shady</u> <u>place</u> to <u>park</u>.

Ⓐ   Ⓑ   Ⓒ   Ⓓ

4 Which of the following correctly completes this sentence?
The girls [   ] in the creek while the boys climbed rocks.

A swim   B swum   C swam   D swimmed

5 Which of the following correctly completes this sentence?
The taxi turned into Mulga [   ] and stopped at the last house on the right.

A St.   B St   C st.   D street

6 Which sentence is a command? The punctuation marks have been left out.

A Please bring it here
C Hello there
B Hey, do you want to play
D I will give my work to Mum

The writing below has some gaps. Choose the best option to fill each gap.

Weather report

If you think 2011 and 2012 have been wet you are not wrong.

Australia has had [   ] wettest two-year

period on record. [   ] have been floods

in [   ] country towns. Water in some rivers

may take months to flow [   ] one town

to the next. What can residents [   ] Nothing

really, except wait [   ] hope the levee

banks hold the water back.

7	its	it's	Its	its'
	A	B	C	D
8	They're	there	their	There
	A	B	C	D
9	much	more	many	them
	A	B	C	D
10	on	through	at	from
	A	B	C	D
11	do.	do?	do!	do,
	A	B	C	D
12	and	as	although	but
	A	B	C	D

☞ **Answers and explanations on pages 194-196**

13 Choose the word (or words) that is **not** required in this sentence.
Write your answer in the box.

Dozens of branches dropped down from the old gum during the storm.

14 Which sentence has the correct punctuation?

A When do you think we should stop?

B When it rains dad watches television?

C When you ask silly questions I will refuse to answer?

D When we get there I will have a sleep?

15 Brackets are required in this sentence.
Which part should be enclosed in brackets?

Lionel Rose MBE 1948–2011 was the first Indigenous Australian to win a world boxing title.

$\underset{A}{\text{MBE}}$ $\underset{B}{\text{1948–2011}}$ $\underset{C}{\text{Indigenous}}$ $\underset{D}{\text{world}}$

16 Which of the following correctly completes the sentence?

Those few days ▆▆▆▆ the worst days of the whole camp. I'm glad we are home!

A is   **B** was   **C** are   **D** were

17 Which sentence is correctly punctuated?

A "We need to get milk for coffee," Dad said to Mum.

B "We need to get milk for coffee," Dad said "to Mum."

C "We need to get milk for coffee" Dad said. to Mum.

D "We need to get milk for coffee, Dad said" to Mum.

18 Which of the following correctly completes this sentence?

The train sped ▆▆▆▆ the tunnel and out into the clean air of the countryside.

A at   **B** in   **C** through   **D** inside

19 Choose the letter to show where the missing comma (**,**) should go.

Will you have tomato cheese or sliced ham on your lunch today?

$\underset{A}{\uparrow}$ $\underset{B}{\uparrow}$ $\underset{C}{\uparrow}$ $\underset{D}{\uparrow}$

20 Abby has many skills but her paintings are both artistic and striking.
Write any adjectives from the sentences in the boxes. Use as many boxes as you need.

☞ **Answers and explanations on pages 194-196**

21 Which of the following correctly completes this sentence?
Steve didn't want to watch the movie ▮▮▮▮ he had seen, ▮▮▮▮ he listened to his music!

A what—so **B** what—because **C** which—as **D** which—so

22 Choose the letter to show where the missing apostrophe (') should go.

(A) (B) (C) (D)

The mistakes were yours but it was Fays bad explanations that caused the problem.

23 Choose the word or words which *it* refers to below. Write your answer in the box.

In class Ian made a model truck with Lego blocks.
He was very proud of his effort because it looked
like the big rig his father drove.

24 Which of the following correctly completes this sentence?
Janice will still go to work, ▮▮▮▮ the fact that there is a bus strike!

A because **B** despite **C** regardless **D** even though

25 Choose the letter which shows where the missing comma (,) should go.
Hey Jack do you want to play cricket or soccer?

(A) (B) (C) (D)

It would be a good idea to check your answers to questions 1 to 25
before moving on to the other questions.

To the student
Ask your teacher or parent to read the spelling words for you. The words are listed on page 210. Write the spelling words on the lines below.

26 _____ **34** _____

27 _____ **35** _____

28 _____ **36** _____

29 _____ **37** _____

30 _____ **38** _____

31 _____ **39** _____

32 _____ **40** _____

33 _____

☞ **Answers and explanations on pages 194-196**

Read the sentences below. The spelling mistakes have been underlined. Write the correct spelling of the word in the box.

41 Craig <u>forght</u> with a big fish but it escaped when his line broke.

42 "Our biggest <u>enemmy</u> in the bush is the leech," said Greg.

43 A <u>rabbert</u> with a fluffy tail ran into a hollow log.

44 Dad is a <u>whelder</u> in a factory making spare parts for trucks.

45 "I forgot my purse. It had the <u>monny</u> for the battery," said Susie.

Read the lines below. Each line has a word that is incorrect. Write the correct spelling of the word in the box.

46 Dad helps Mum vaccume the carpets each weekend.

47 I'd like a muffine but you can have a coconut slice.

Gift shop

48 There are quiet a few gift shops in our village. I went into one that

49 had a splenderd view across the Hunter River. I was looking for

50 somethink special but I ended up buying a silver teaspoon!

☞ **Answers and explanations on pages 194-196**

1 This 3D object is a

   A cone.
   B cylinder.
   C prism.
   D pyramid.

2 Which number is three thousand and twenty-seven?

A 3027   **B** 3270   **C** 3207   **D** 300 027

3 Which shows the picture flipped over the dotted line?

  A   **B**   **C**   **D**

4 Which of these is used to measure time?

  A   **B**   **C**   **D**

5 Penny put some stamps on a grid.
Which stamp is at D2?

  A   **B** ★

  C ◎   **D** ♣

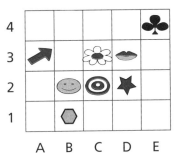

6 This shape is a trapezium.

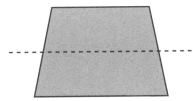

Ethan cuts the shape into two pieces along the dotted line. What shape are the two pieces?

A pentagons   **B** rectangles   **C** trapeziums   **D** hexagons

7 What time does this clock show?

A 6:07
B 6:30
C 6:50
D 7:06

8 How many faces does a triangular prism have?

A 3   B 4   C 5   D 6

9 Which shape has been cut into quarters?

A 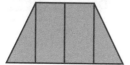   B   C   D

10 Mandy is third from the right.

Which is Mandy?

A   B   C   D

11 Which angle is the largest?

A   B 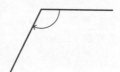   C   D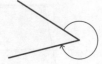

☞ **Answers and explanations on pages 196-199**

Online-
Style
Sample
Test

NUMERACY TEST 1
Intermediate level

(continued)

⓬ Some students at a school were asked to choose their favourite flower.

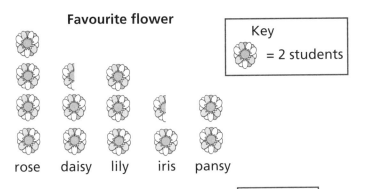

Favourite flower

Key

= 2 students

rose   daisy   lily   iris   pansy

How many students chose the lily? ⬚

⓭ Heath buys this book.

How much change does he get from $10.00?
A $7.25   B $7.35   C $8.25   D $8.75

⓮ Kel had these toy cars.

He gave 3 to Sam and 4 to David. How many cars did Kel have left?
A 3   B 4   C 5   D 7

It would be a good idea to check your answers to questions 1 to 14
before moving on to the other questions.

☞**Answers and explanations on pages 196–199**

15 Which shape has exactly two lines of symmetry?

A   B   C   D

16 6 rows of 4 cards is the same number of cards as 8 rows of ⬚ .

17 Which spinner is most likely to stop on 2?

A   1   2

B   3   2   1

C   4 1   2 3   3 2   1 4

D   3 4   1   2

18 Ned has these coins.

He buys an apple for 85 cents.
How much money does Ned have left? $ ⬚ . ⬚

19 Mervyn has 23 hectares of land. Alice has 18 hectares. Kelly has more land than Alice but not as much as Mervyn. How many hectares of land could Kelly have? Select **all** the possible answers.

A 19.5   B 17   C 31   D 25   E 22

20 Sally made this shape from 9 blocks.

What is the view from the top?

A   B   C   D

21 Isabel wrote a number pattern. She added 3 each time to get the next number.
Which could be Isabel's pattern? Select **all** possible answers.

A 3, 13, 23, 33, …   B 3, 6, 9, 12, …   C 5, 8, 11, 14, …   D 6, 9, 13, 18, …

22 Suzy puts her blocks into 5 rows of 6 blocks and she has 4 blocks left over.

How many blocks does Suzy have altogether? ⬚

23 Which two shapes cover the same area?

A   B   C   D

 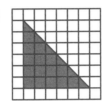

24 There are 5 blue, 6 green, 4 red and 2 yellow marbles in a box. Heath takes two marbles. Which is impossible?

A   a blue and a green   B   a red and a blue   C   two green   D   a yellow and a black

25 How long is this nail in millimetres?

A   57   B   52
C   67   D   62

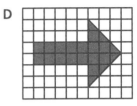

26 Stephanie looks at this calendar.

JULY						
S	M	T	W	T	F	S
			1	2	3	4
5	6	7	8	9	10	11
12	13	14	15	16	17	18
19	20	21	22	23	24	25
26	27	28	29	30	31	

"Today is the third Saturday in July," she said. "It is exactly two weeks to my birthday."

What is the date of Stephanie's birthday?

A   1 August
B   2 August
C   3 August
D   4 August

27   38 + 25 = ☐

28 A pattern is made with this arrow. The arrow is being turned a quarter turn in a clockwise direction each time.

What will the arrow look like here? - ↗

A   B   C   D

It would be a good idea to check your answers to questions 15 to 28 before moving on to the other questions.

☞ **Answers and explanations on pages 196-199**

29 Ruby leaves the post office and turns left into Main St. At the next intersection she turns right. Where might Ruby be going?

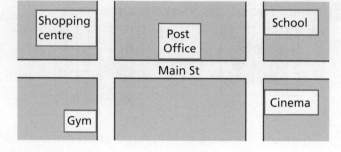

| Shopping centre | | Post Office | | School |

Main St

| | | | | Cinema |
| | Gym | | | |

A cinema

B gym

C shopping centre

D school

30 100, 99, 97, 94, 90, 85, ?

What is the next number in this pattern? ☐

31 James opens a bottle that contains one litre of orange juice. He fills this jug from the bottle.

600 mL

How many millilitres of juice remain in the bottle? ☐ millilitres

32 How many odd numbers are between 10 and 50?

A 40   B 30   C 25   D 20

33 The table shows the number of stickers some students have collected, but the names are missing. Ned collected the most stickers and Tom the least. Ramy collected more than Olivia but less than Mary. Write the names in the table.

Student					
Number of stickers	28	31	23	19	26

34 82 − 47 = ☐

☞**Answers and explanations on pages 196-199**

35 Mia made this pattern with sticks.

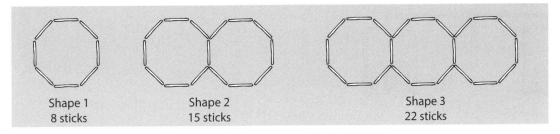

Shape 1
8 sticks

Shape 2
15 sticks

Shape 3
22 sticks

How many sticks will Mia need for Shape 5? ☐

36 Place the numbers 0.06, 0.4 and 0.15 in order from highest to lowest.

☐ ☐ ☐

highest **lowest**

37 Chris has 74 footy cards. Ali has 39 footy cards.

What is the difference between the number of footy cards that Chris and Ali have?

A 113   B 45   C 35   D 33

38 This tray holds 6 cakes.

How many trays will be needed for 42 cakes? ☐

39 Three boys share these marbles equally.

How many marbles does each boy get? ☐

☞ **Answers and explanations on pages 196–199**

40 This balance shows that 5 blocks balance 2 cans.

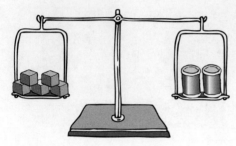

How many cans will balance 20 blocks?

41 Write a single number in each empty box to make this number sentence correct.

| 5 | | 1 | + | | 4 | 6 | = | 9 | 2 | |

42 This graph shows the number of students in some of the years at a small school.

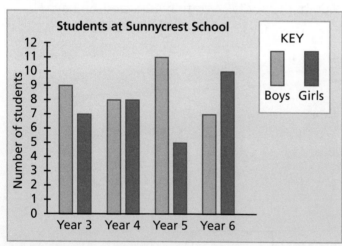

Which year has the most students?

A Year 3   B Year 4   C Year 5   D Year 6

☞ **Answers and explanations on pages 196-199**

Today you are going to write a **persuasive text**. You have learned that the council is going to allow a bowling club to be built in your local park. The bowling club will be for members only. Your teacher wants you and the other students in her class to express their opinions in writing.

She has provided the first sentence.

Before you start to write, think about:
- how you feel about the idea—are you for or against it?
- two or three clear 'arguments' supporting your opinion
- any examples of events that have happened that support why you feel the way you do
- a concluding paragraph briefly reminding the reader of how strongly you feel about the idea
- try to make your writing convincing.

Remember to:
- plan your writing before you begin
- write in correctly formed sentences and take care with paragraphing
- choose your words carefully and pay attention to your spelling and punctuation
- write neatly but don't waste time
- quickly check your work once you have finished.

Start writing here or type your answer on a tablet or computer.

The council wants to allow a bowling club in part of our public park. To me this (is / is not) a good idea.

(delete one)

_____

_____

_____

_____

_____

_____

_____

☞ **Marking guide on page 199**

Read *Happy Christmas for pets* and answer questions 1 to 7.

1 **Happy Christmas for pets**

2 Many people forget that pets are for life, not just for
3 Christmas. Many kids want a pet and Christmas seems the
4 perfect time for such a present. But getting a new puppy
5 or kitten is more than having a cuddly pet. Unfortunately
6 many families get tired of the new pet by the end of the
7 summer holidays and a sad puppy or kitten is given to
8 the pound.

9 What do new pet owners have to think about?

10 Firstly, there is the cost. Not just the food—the new pet
11 has to be registered, vaccinated and microchipped. It will
12 require medical care against parasites from ticks to worms.
13 Some worms can be fatal.

14 The house and the yard will have to be made suitable for the pet. Families must think about
15 protecting items that can be chewed or scratched. Fences and gates must be made secure. Roads
16 are dangerous. Neighbours won't want your pet.

17 The new pet needs exercise and to be toilet trained. This can be a frustrating task that requires
18 patience and a calm response to those little 'accidents'.

19 If you want a pet for Christmas, first think about the responsibilities, cost and time that go with
20 owning a pet. Make it a happy Christmas for a pet too!

1 The writer is concerned that many new pets are not

A vaccinated.
B exercised.
C toilet trained.
D loved for long.

2 The writer suggests that many people

A don't have enough money to keep a pet.
B don't know when to return the pet to the pound.
C get tired of caring for an untrained pet.
D only want a pet for the Christmas holidays.

3 Puppies and kittens put in the pound would feel

A relieved.
B unwanted.
C happy.
D excited.

4 The word *accidents* is written in inverted commas because

A it's a 'nice' word for wee and poo.
B no-one knows what the accidents will be.
C there are too many accidents to list them all.
D sometimes pets are really well behaved.

5 What is an important cost in owning a pet?

A giving it exercise
B getting it registered
C toilet training
D putting the pet in a pound

6 The information in this text is meant to be

A advice.   B a warning.
C a threat.   D a suggestion.

7 Gates should be kept secure because

A parasites will get in.
B the pet will go to the pound.
C neighbours might come in.
D pets might run onto a road.

☞ **Answers and explanations on pages 199-202**

Read *The swim* and answer questions 8 to 13.

1 **The swim**

2 *The Priest family have just taken over a remote farm. Now read on.*

3 Once we had settled in, Dad took Jenny and me down to the river for a swim. He had to check it
4 out. After leaving the farmhouse we arrived at a little rise overlooking a paddock of corn. A flock
5 of birds screeched up from the scraggly stalks.

6 "They're the crows and ravens I saw coming here!" said Jenny.

7 Dad pressed his lips together and shook his head. "Prettiest
8 crows and ravens I've ever seen! No Jen, just parrots!"

9 "What are they eating?" asked Jenny. I could have answered
10 that!

11 "They're into corncobs. Parrots love corn. They rip the cobs
12 open, then crack the yellow grains of corn."

13 "Why don't we eat it? I love corn," I said.

14 Dad thought for a minute. "Good idea Nigel! We can pick
15 some on the way back. I like fresh corn on the cob—with
16 plenty of butter."

17 "What if the parrots have eaten it all?" said Jenny.

18 "I'm sure we'll find enough for dinner tonight. Let's have that swim first." Dad was already
19 heading down to the riverbank.

20 The swim was fun. Dad let me jump off a rocky overhang after he had swum out to see how deep
21 the hole was. The water was cool and the riverbed was sandy.

8 What did the family have to pass before reaching the river?
   A rocks   **B** corn growing in a paddock   **C** a farmhouse
   D crows and ravens   **E** a waterhole   **F** a rocky overhang

9 The cornstalks are described as *scraggly*. This means they were
   A ripped about.   **B** bent over.   **C** lying on the ground.   **D** scrunched up.

10 Why did Nigel think *I could have answered that!* to Jenny's question?
   A He was acting cocky.   **B** He thought Jenny was stupid.
   C The answer was obvious.   **D** No-one else knew the answer.

11 After seeing parrots in the corn Nigel thought that
   A the crop was ruined.   **B** Jenny would stop talking
   C other birds were nearby.   **D** the family could have a food treat.

12 The family's farm explorations could best be described as
   A thrilling.   **B** peaceful.   **C** disappointing.   **D** tiring.

13 A good alternative title for the text would be
   A Corn pickers.   **B** Jenny's questions.   **C** Crows and ravens.   **D** Exploring the farm.

It would be a good idea to check your answers to questions 1 to 13 before moving on to the other questions.

☞**Answers and explanations on pages 199–202**

Look at this cartoon and answer questions 14 to 19.

14 What is the most likely time the action in the cartoon takes place?
Write your answer on the line. _____

15 What would be a suitable question for the grandmother's speech bubble?

A Is it time to feed the dog?
B Have you finished reading the news?
C Can dogs play computer games?
D Do you think it's time to retrain Fido?

16 What is the boy most likely thinking?

A Can I go now?   B Poor Fido.   C Here we go again!   D Old trick!

17 It is most likely the dog

A needs to go for a walk.
B wants to please its owner.
C is not very obedient.
D is not allowed in the home.

18 A suitable caption for the cartoon would be

A Plug it in!
B No news is good news.
C Sit Fido.
D Man's best friend!

19 According to the cartoon which statement is most likely correct?

A Fido used to fetch the paper each day.
B The grandfather is not interested in the daily news.
C Most people read the newspaper online.
D Dogs are learning to use computers.

☞ **Answers and explanations on pages 199–202**

Read *Who is Robbie Paul?* and answer questions 20 to 26.

1 ## Who is Robbie Paul?

2 Robert 'Robbie' Paul was born into a large Aboriginal and South
3 Sea Islander family in Bowen (Qld) and now lives in Townsville.
4 After working in the meat processing plant for 14 years, he
5 wanted to try something different. He took up art. He had always
6 had an interest in practising art at home as a hobby, painting
7 murals and exhibiting paintings.

8 Using acrylic paints he now designs quirky Christmas cards that have a real north Queensland
9 flavour. In this first card, Robbie has Santa waving to a group of outback kids. An old Holden is
10 in the background. The kangaroo has a really mischievous look on his face in the way he winks
11 at us!

12 Robbie says completing university studies not only improved his illustrations
13 but also introduced him to computer graphics. This card has been created
14 in the digital world of the computer. Here, an Indigenous Santa in thongs is
15 coming ashore from a fishing trip. He is being stalked by a croc. Robbie says
16 he put the croc on the card for a bit of north Queensland humour.

17 No snow-laden pine trees in these scenes!

18 Robbie has orders for his unusual Christmas cards from all around Australia.
19 Robbie is also a book illustrator.

Thanks to Robbie Paul and Black Ink Press for the information and graphics.

20 Robbie's cards are different from most other Christmas cards because they

A are painted with bright acrylic paints.
B have an Indigenous Santa dressed for Queensland conditions.
C do not include scenes of snow-covered trees.
D are not produced for sales.

21 Robbie's Christmas cards show

A the harshness of country living.
B the importance of getting presents to everyone.
C what Christmas is like without snow.
D that Robbie enjoys his culture and where he lives.

22 Robbie began using a computer for his artwork

A while at university.
B when working at a meatworks.
C when painting murals.
D during his time in Bowen.

23 Robbie's Christmas cards are intended to

A shock. B confuse. C amuse. D upset.

24 The name *Robbie* is in inverted commas ('Robbie'). This is to show it is

A his real name.
B the name he is known by.
C a meat worker's name.
D a name he no longer uses.

25 Which word would be a suitable replacement for *mischievous* as used in the text?

A cheeky   B rude
C naughty   D interesting

26 A picture that is *quirky* most likely includes something

A clever.   B pretty.
C unusual.   D serious.

It would be a good idea to check your answers to questions 14 to 26 before moving on to the other questions.

☞ Answers and explanations on pages 199–202

Read the poem *Snapshots* by Elaine Horsfield and answer questions 27 to 33.

1 **Snapshots**

2 It's Summer …
3 The weather's hot and so am I
4 The clouds are building in the sky
5 It looks as though it's going to rain
6 Perhaps we'll get a storm again
7 It's Summer …

8 It's Autumn …
9 The days are cooler, and the nights
10 When I get up I need the lights
11 The leaves are falling off the trees
12 They drift to earth upon a breeze
13 It's Autumn …

14 It's Winter …
15 I snuggle down inside my bed
16 The doona covers up my head
17 A chilly wind blows through the town
18 And much too soon the sun goes down
19 It's Winter …

20 It's Spring
21 The gardens start to come alive
22 The bees fly buzzing from their hive
23 The days are getting longer now
24 And blossom drifts down from the bough
25 It's Spring …
26 It's Summer …

27 This poem is mainly about
 A taking photos.
 B days and nights.
 C unpleasant weather.
 D the changing seasons.

28 You are required to compare these texts: *Who is Robbie Paul*? (page 145) and *Snapshots* (page 146). For which purpose were these texts written? Tick **two** boxes for each text.

	Who is Robbie Paul?	*Snapshots*
to describe	☐	☐
to outline differences	☐	☐
to entertain	☐	☐
to recount a life	☐	☐

29 The poem is called 'Snapshots'. This is because it is
 A a brief summary of the seasons.
 B made up of four short stanzas.
 C full of colourful descriptions.
 D a record of the poet's memories.

30 The leaves *drift* to earth. A synonym for *drift* as used in the poem is
 A drop. **B** float.
 C swirl. **D** plunge.

31 Which of the four stanzas describes the poet's seasonal preference? (Each new stanza begins with a season's name.)
 Write the name of the season in the box.
 It's _____

32 The clouds are *building* in the sky. In the poem *building* means the clouds are
 A getting bigger. **B** turning black.
 C being set up. **D** making rain.

33 The last line of two words starts a new unfinished stanza because the
 A reader is meant to add the next lines.
 B poet didn't finish the poem.
 C seasons are back to summer.
 D poet decided to take photos.

☞ **Answers and explanations on pages 199–202**

Read *The lollipop man* and answer questions 34 to 39.

1 **The lollipop man**

2 Meanwhile, up from the Sundale School, Mr Rhodes was
3 placing orange witchhat markers down the centre of Elm
4 Road. These markers were used to guide the traffic past
5 new and dangerous roadworks.

6 Mr Rhodes worked with the road crew for Sundale Council.
7 Mostly the road crew filled potholes, repainted road
8 markings and fixed signs. Mr Rhodes wore clothes with
9 bright orange markings and a hard hat. He had a very
10 responsible job to do. He controlled the traffic when the
11 road crew was working.

12 When he first joined the road crew he used to have a long
13 pole with a round sign on the top. The green side had (GO)
14 on it. The other side was red with the word (STOP). His sign
15 looked like a giant lollipop. Some people, for fun, had called
16 Mr Rhodes a lollipop man, but drivers knew by obeying the
17 signs they could pass safely.

18 Mr Rhodes would stand on the road and proudly turn the
19 sign one way, then the other, giving the cars and trucks turns when passing the crew at work.
20 He knew it was vital that there were no accidents.

21 The road crew had many different jobs to do for the new project to widen Elm Road. They had to
22 drive rollers, graders and a hot-bitumen truck. Mr Rhodes had to put out markers before the start
23 of work and collect them at the end of each day.

34 Where was Mr Rhodes putting out the orange traffic markers?

A in front of Sundale School
B along Elm Road
C behind the road machinery
D near Sundale Council office

35 What was the new project for the Sundale Council workers?

A build a new road
B put orange road markers on Elm Road
C widen Elm Road
D repaint road markings at the school

36 Mr Rhodes most likely felt his job was

A boring. B tiring.
C difficult. D important.

37 What did Mr Rhodes's traffic sign look like? Write your answer in the box.

38 You are required to compare these texts: *The swim* (page 143) and *The lollipop man* (above). Are the following details mentioned in both texts? Tick **two** boxes for each text.

	The swim	The lollipop man
a farming environment	☐	☐
a work environment	☐	☐
repairing roads	☐	☐
a relaxing activity	☐	☐

39 What was the last job to be done on the roadworks each day?

A collect the traffic markers
B fill in potholes
C fix road signs
D let the traffic pass

☞ **Answers and explanations on pages 199–202**

Online-Style Sample Test

CONVENTIONS OF LANGUAGE TEST 2
Advanced level

1 Choose the letter which shows where the missing comma (,) should go.

My teacher (A) stood up (B) and said (C) "You can all stop writing (D) now."

2 Read this sentence.
Dogs and cats make good pets but rats are pests.
Write any conjunctions from the sentences in the boxes. Use as many boxes as you need.

3 Which of the following correctly completes this sentence?
I know ______ feeling sick but you still have to drink water.

A you're B you've C your D you'r

4 Which of the following correctly completes this sentence?
The class did their work ______ and were given some free time.

A quick B more quick C quicker D quickly

5 Which sentence has all capital letters correctly in place?

A My uncle called, "It's about time you returned Peter's bat."
B My Uncle called, "It's about time you returned Peter's bat."
C My uncle called, "it's about time you returned Peter's bat."
D My Uncle called, "It's about time you returned Peter's Bat."

6 Which of the following correctly completes this sentence?
"This is not mine. It is ______!" snapped Toni.

A her's B hers C hers' D her

7 Oscar ______ all the way in the car.

A sleeped B slept C sleep D sleped

8 Choose the word or words that are **not** required in this sentence.
Write your answer in the box.

Lachlan was following behind his team when he slipped and fell off a rock.

9 Which sentence has the correct punctuation?

A Good morning, smiled the reporter, "I've come to see the coach."
B "Good morning, smiled the reporter, I've come to see the coach."
C "Good morning," smiled the reporter, I've come to see the coach.
D "Good morning," smiled the reporter, "I've come to see the coach."

☞ Answers and explanations on pages 202–204

10 Choose the letter to show where the missing apostrophe (') should go.

Ⓐ   Ⓑ   Ⓒ   Ⓓ

The boy s were on the swing s when a girl s bracelet was found in some weed s.

11 Which of the following correctly completes this sentence?

Lucy ▮▮▮▮▮▮ all her spelling and has started on her drawings.

A done   **B** have did   **C** has did   **D** has done

12 Brackets are required in this sentence. Which part should be enclosed in brackets?

The first Indigenous person to captain an Australian team was the rugby league player Arthur 'Artie' Beetson OAM 1945–2011.

A Indigenous   **B** Australian   **C** rugby league   **D** 1945–2011

13 Which pronoun best replaces *Mary's* in this statement?

We knew it was Mary's but there was no way to prove it.

A hers   **B** her   **C** she   **D** ours

14 Which word does *her* refer to in this sentence? Write your answer in the box.

Sara has two sisters, Meg and Kim, who are twins.
The twins go to pre-school with Ms Beatty but Sara
hasn't started school yet. Her birthday is not until next year.

15 Which of the following correctly completes this sentence?

Those ▮▮▮▮▮▮ names were called out should leave the room now.

A whose   **B** who'se   **C** who's   **D** how's

16 Which of the following correctly completes this sentence?

The bats in the cricket kit bag ▮▮▮▮▮▮ been damaged by vandals!

A have   **B** has   **C** are   **D** were

17 Which option is a statement and requires a full stop?

A Going up the steep hill on the left-hand side of the road
B While listening to the radio in bed I soon went to sleep
C Did you ever meet the people from across the park
D Hey you, clear off

18 Which of the following correctly completes this sentence?

Trevor had $30 to spend at the show ▮▮▮▮▮▮ he decided to save it for a party.

A and   **B** because   **C** but

D if   **E** whether   **F** also

19 Choose the letter that shows where the missing comma (**,**) should go.

Hey there you on the back of the truck!

Ⓐ   Ⓑ   Ⓒ   Ⓓ

☞**Answers and explanations on pages 202–204**

20 Basil didn't watch the news ▨▨▨ he found upsetting ▨▨▨ he went for a walk.

    A that—yet   **B** what—so   **C** who–as   **D** which—so

21 Which of the following correctly completes the sentence?
Everybody in our family ▨▨▨ glasses for reading.

    A wears   **B** wearing   **C** weared   **D** wear

22 Choose the sentence that is correct.

    A Despite the heavy rain, the reason why there was a trickle in the creeks.
    B Why there's a trickle in the creeks despite the heavy rain.
    C Although the rains were heavy, the creeks were nothing but a trickle.
    D The rain trickle in the creeks, was despite the heavy rain.

23 Which of the following correctly completes this sentence?
There are many pets in the pound, ▨▨▨ were taken there after January.

    A what   **B** that   **C** who   **D** which

24 Which of the following correctly completes the sentence?
Ingrid needed $2 so she borrowed it ▨▨▨ her sister.

    A off   **B** of   **C** from   **D** by

25 Which of the following correctly completes the sentence?
The gardener ▨▨▨ the leaves into a huge bag before another wind gust came.

    A sweeps   **B** swept   **C** sweeping   **D** sweeped

It would be a good idea to check your answers to questions 1 to 25 before moving on to the other questions.

To the student
Ask your teacher or parent to read the spelling words for you. The words are listed on page 210. Write the spelling words on the lines below.

26 _____   **34** _____

27 _____   **35** _____

28 _____   **36** _____

29 _____   **37** _____

30 _____   **38** _____

31 _____   **39** _____

32 _____   **40** _____

33 _____

☞ **Answers and explanations on pages 202-204**

Read the sentences below. The spelling mistakes have been underlined. Write the correct spelling of the word in the box.

41 You should always <u>chue</u> with your mouth fully shut!

42 Muddy water gushed down the <u>drane</u> and into the stream.

43 Did you know that <u>socker</u> is one of the world's great sports?

44 When the sun is setting I get a long <u>shadder</u>.

45 Who does the team play <u>againest</u> after the morning match?

Read the lines below. Each line has a word that is incorrect. Write the correct spelling of the word in the box.

46 On top of the muntain were blocks of ice and deep snowfields.

47 This pasta has a very cheesey, peppery taste.

48 The tribesmen took a heard of hairy goats up the rocky valley.

49 The valley was rough and narrer and too steep for vehicles.

50 Rebels were fleaing from the troops arriving from the city.

☞ **Answers and explanations on pages 202–204**

 50 min

1 Peter drew these shapes.

How many triangles did Peter draw?

A 3   **B** 4   **C** 5   **D** 6

2 Which is most like a cylinder?

A   **B**    **C**   **D**

3 Which number is three thousand and forty?

A 3400   **B** 3014   **C** 3040   **D** 300 040

4 What would this be used to measure?

A length
B mass
C capacity
D temperature

5 Justin used half a packet of buttons. These are the buttons that Justin has left.

How many buttons were in the packet? ☐

6 This is part of a map of Treeville.
What road crosses Rosewood River in B2 on the map?

A Wattle St
B Blackbutt Rd
C Cedar Lane
D Ironbark Rd
E Mahogany Street

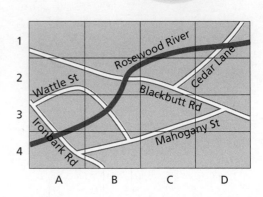

☞ **Answers and explanations on pages 204–207**

7 3 groups of 6 students is the same number of students as 2 groups of

A 4. **B** 6. **C** 8. **D** 9.

8 Which clock shows quarter to seven?

A 06:45 **B** 07:15 **C** 07:45 **D** 06:15

9 2 + 40 + 500 =

A 245 **B** 240 500 **C** 542 **D** 500 402

10 A packet holds iceblocks in four flavours. There are 7 lemonade, 4 orange, 5 lime and 8 raspberry iceblocks. Without looking, Claire takes an iceblock from the packet. Order the flavours from most likely to least likely to be taken.

most likely **least likely**

11 How long is a quarter of an hour?

A 15 seconds **B** 15 minutes **C** 25 seconds **D** 25 minutes

12 Rory has this piece of paper.

He folds the paper in half and cuts out a square.

fold

What does Rory's paper look like when he unfolds it?

A **B** **C** **D**

13 What number comes next in this pattern?

7, 11, 15, 19, ?

☞ **Answers and explanations on pages 204-207**

14 There is a sports day at school. This is the plan for Year 4 students.

Start time	Activity
9:00	Bus to swimming pool
9:15	Swimming
10:15	Bus back to school
10:30	Basketball
11:15	Morning tea
11:30	Cricket
12:45	Lunch
1:30	Walk
2:45	Awards presented

What will Year 4 students be doing at 11:00?

A basketball **B** morning tea **C** cricket **D** lunch

It would be a good idea to check your answers to questions
1 to 14 before moving on to the other questions.

15 Kylie is going to cut these oranges into quarters.

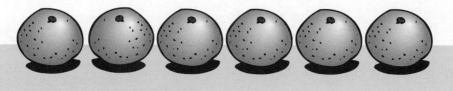

How many quarters will Kylie have? [   ]

16 37 + 18 has the same value as 40 + [   ]

17 Gemma draws a picture.
How many lines of symmetry does Gemma's picture have?

A 2
B 4
C 6
D 8

☞ **Answers and explanations on pages 204–207**

18 Toby left home at 5 am. He got home again at 8 pm. How long was Toby away from home?

    A 3 hours   **B** 7 hours   **C** 13 hours   **D** 15 hours

19 Jack is putting tiles on a floor.

How many tiles will fit
on the floor altogether? ▭

20 Write a number in the box to make this number sentence correct.

    43 − ▭ = 19

21 Jennifer is putting some beads on a string to make a necklace. The beads form a pattern.

Which bead comes next?

  A   **B**   **C**   **D**

22 Which has the same value as 17 + 9? Select **all** correct answers.

    A 9 + 17   **B** 20 + 6   **C** 16 + 10   **D** 14 + 14

23 Khaled has this money.

He buys a sandwich for $2.40.
How much money does Khaled have now?

    A $1.85

    B $1.95

    C $2.05

    D $2.15

☞**Answers and explanations on pages 204-207**

24 Tomorrow is Wednesday and Jean is leaving on an overseas holiday. She will be away for 3 weeks.

Which is certain?

A Jean will visit America.

B All overseas holidays last for 3 weeks.

C Yesterday was Monday.

D All holidays are overseas.

25 Students voted for their favourite colour.

How many students voted altogether?

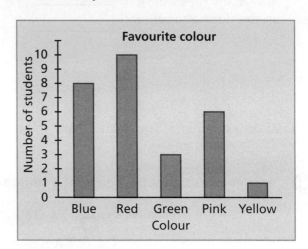

26 What number is at the position marked by the arrow?

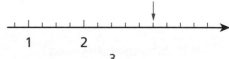

A $2\frac{3}{4}$

B 3

C $3\frac{1}{4}$

D $3\frac{3}{4}$

27 56 + 17 =

28 This is a map of Shark Island.
How many kilometres is it from Bowerville to Luton?

_____ km

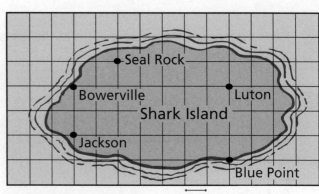

Scale: 1 unit = 5 km   1 unit

It would be a good idea to check your answers to questions 15 to 28 before moving on to the other questions.

☞ Answers and explanations on pages 204–207

29 Edward starts with an odd number. He adds 5 then divides by 2. Edward's answer is 7. What number did Edward start with?

A 3   B 5   C 7   D 9

30 A box holds yellow, red, blue, white and green marbles as shown in the picture. Billy takes 3 marbles from this box at the same time. Which is impossible?

A (B)(B)(B)   B (Y)(G)(G)

C (R)(B)(G)   D (R)(W)(W)

31 6 of the same drinks cost 12 dollars.

How many dollars does one of those drinks cost? [   ] dollars

What is the greatest number of those drinks that can be bought for 30 dollars? [   ]

32 These are the weights of four different packets of food from the pantry.

| 1.4 kg | 1 kg 80 g | 1200 g | 1.05 kg |

Place them in order from the least mass to the greatest mass.

[   ] [   ] [   ] [   ]

least mass   **most mass**

33 Bree has 37 points in a game. She needs 90 points to go to the next level.

How many more points does Bree need? [   ]

34 5 pens cost the same total amount as 7 pencils. Each pencil costs 50 cents.

How many cents does each pen cost? [   ] cents

☞ **Answers and explanations on pages 204–207**

35 This graph shows the number of books read by some students.

Key = 4 books

Sid   Jake   Jenna   Rachel   Milly

How many more books did Rachel read than Milly and Sid together? ☐

36 Which is the same as 0.17? Select **all** correct answers.

A $\frac{17}{10}$

B $\frac{1}{10} + \frac{7}{100}$

C $\frac{1}{100} + \frac{7}{10}$

D $\frac{17}{100}$

37 Sue made this pattern.

♥○♥☆♥□♥☆♥♥○♥☆♥□♥☆♥○♥☆♥□♥☆♥♥○♥☆♥□♥☆♥○♥☆♥□♥☆♥♥○♥☆♥□♥☆♥○♥☆♥□♥☆

How many ♥ are needed for each ○?

A 2   B 3   C 4   D 5

38 Four friends each built a rectangular prism with blocks.

Abi

Shae

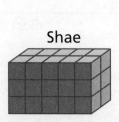

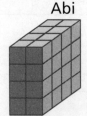

Jane

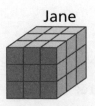

Pia

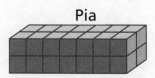

Place the girls in order from the one who used the most blocks to the one who used the least number of blocks.

☐   ☐   ☐   ☐

most blocks   **least blocks**

39 Mel has 40 eggs. She has 5 cartons. Mel puts 6 eggs in each carton.

How many eggs will Mel have left?

A 3   B 4
C 5   D 10

☞ **Answers and explanations on pages 204–207**

40 This cube was made from 27 unpainted blocks.
The finished cube was painted green.

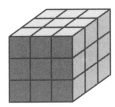

How many of the blocks have green paint on just one face? ☐

41 Molly looks in a mirror and sees this clock.
What is the time?

A 5 o'clock
B 7 o'clock
C half past 5
D half past 7

42 How many centimetres tall is John?

1 metre

0   ☐ cm

WEEK 1

1 C **2** 924 **3** C **4** B **5** A **6** D **7** 9812
8 1100 **9** B **10** D **11** 650 **12** 5049 **13** 6018
14 540 **15** 4 **16** B **17** A **18** C

EXPLANATIONS

1 687 is 6 hundreds, 8 tens and 7 ones.

So it is 600 + 80 + 7.

2 Nine hundred and twenty-four is 9 hundreds, 2 tens and 4 ones. It is 924.

3 Mary has 12 crayons. Isabel has more crayons than Mary so she has more than 12 crayons. James has 18 crayons. Isabel has fewer crayons than James so she has less than 18 crayons. So Isabel could have 13 or 14 or 15 or 16 or 17 crayons. Only one of these, 15, is an option. So Isabel could have 15 crayons.

4 32 is 3 tens and 2 ones. So there must be 3 groups of ten and 2 single blocks.

5 Of the options, the closest number to 90 is 88.

85 86 87 88 89 90 91 92 93 94 95 96 97 98 99

6 Seven thousand and forty-five is 7 thousands, 0 hundreds, 4 tens and 5 ones. It is 7045.

7 To make an even number with the four cards it would need to end in 2 or 8.

The largest card is 9, so the largest number will have 9 in the first (thousands) position.

The second largest card is 8, so 8 should be placed in the second (hundreds) position.

So to be even the number must end in 2.

The largest possible even number is 9812.

8 1099 + 1 = 1100

The next number after 1099 is 1100.

9 Odd numbers end in 1, 3, 5, 7 or 9.

The odd numbers between 40 and 64 are 41, 43, 45, 47, 49, 51, 53, 55, 57, 59, 61 and 63.

There are 12 odd numbers between 40 and 64.

10 6208 is 6 thousands, 2 hundreds, 0 tens and 8 ones.

6208 = 6 thousands + 2 hundreds + 8 ones

11 The number at the arrow is 650.

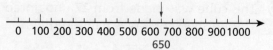

0 100 200 300 400 500 600 700 800 900 1000
                                    650

12 The closest number to 5000 will start with 5 or 4. The closest number to 5000 that starts with 4 is 4950. The closest number starting with 5 is 5049. 5049 is closer to 5000 than 4950. So the closest number is 5049.

13 Six thousand and eighteen is 6 thousands, 0 hundreds, 1 ten and 8 ones.

It is 6018.

14 The number halfway between 450 and 630 is 540.

450 470 490 510 530 550 570 590 610 630
                    540

15 Odd numbers end in 1 or 3. So Peter could make four odd numbers; 231, 321, 123 and 213.

16 The odd numbers in the list are 17, 35, 83, 207 and 333. There are five odd numbers.

17 9027 is 9 thousands, 0 hundreds, 2 tens and 7 ones. So it is nine thousand and twenty-seven.

18 7 + 60 + 500 = 500 + 60 + 7
= 567

1 19 **2** D **3** C, D **4** 6 **5** 12 **6** 16 **7** B **8** C **9** 5
10 A **11** C **12** A **13** C **14** 37 **15** B **16** 45

EXPLANATIONS

1 3, 7, 11, 15 …

Now 3 + 4 = 7; 7 + 4 = 11; 11 + 4 = 15

So the numbers are going up by 4 each time.

15 + 4 = 19

So the next number is 19.

2 There are ten symbols in the pattern before it begins to repeat. ✳︎⌘☺︎✧⌘✳︎✧☺︎⌘✳︎

The last symbol in the question

✳︎⌘☺︎✧⌘✳︎✧☺︎⌘✳︎✳︎⌘☺︎✧⌘✳︎✧☺︎⌘✳︎✳︎⌘☺︎✧⌘✳︎

is the sixth symbol in the pattern. So the symbols that come next are the seventh, eighth, ninth and tenth in the pattern. ✧☺︎⌘✳︎

3 Alice adds 6 each time.
Try each option.
6, 9, 12, 15, …
3 is being added each time so this is not Alice's pattern.
6, 12, 24, 48, …
The numbers are doubling each time so this is not Alice's pattern.
2, 8, 14, 20, …
2 + 6 = 8; 8 + 6 = 14; 14 + 6 = 20
6 is being added each time so this could be Alice's pattern.
5, 11, 17, 23, …
5 + 6 = 11; 11 + 6 = 17; 17 + 6 = 23
6 is being added each time so this could be Alice's pattern.
Alice's pattern could be 2, 8, 14, 20, … or 5, 11, 17, 23, …

4 9 + 6 = 15
So the number that must be added to 9 to give 15 is 6.

5 4, 8, ?, 16, 20, 24
4 + 4 = 8
16 + 4 = 20
20 + 4 = 24
So 4 is being added each time.
Now 8 + 4 = 12
and 12 + 4 = 16
So the missing number is 12.

6 From the pattern we can see that 3 is being added each time.

Shape 1	Shape 2	Shape 3
4 pins	4 + 3 = 7 pins	7 + 3 = 10 pins

So 10 + 3 or 13 pins will be needed for shape 4 and 13 + 3 or 16 pins will be needed for shape 5.

7 1, 2, 3, 6, 11, 20, ?
We know that each number is found by adding the 3 numbers before it.
Now 6 + 11 + 20 = 37.
So the next number is 37.

8 There are 4 shapes being repeated in the pattern.

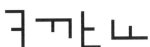

The shape that comes after is ⊢.

9 17 − 5 = 12
So the number that can be taken away from 17 to leave 12 is 5.

10 43, 36, 29, 22, 15, …
43 − 7 = 36; 36 − 7 = 29; 29 − 7 = 22
The pattern is counting backwards by 7.

11 There are 6 shapes repeating in the pattern:
✳ ⊕ ✳ ★ ✳ ○
So there are 3 ✳ for each ★.

12 William's answer is 15.
Before he added 7 the answer was 8 (because 8 + 7 = 15).
Now 8 is double 4, so 4 was the number that William started with.

13 The length of the spanners is going up by 2.5 cm each time.
Now 15 + 2.5 = 17.5.
So the length of Spanner 4 will be 17.5 cm.

14 In 3 years time Levi will be 10. His dad will be 10 × 4 = 40. So Levi's dad is 37 now. (40 − 3 = 37)

15 1, 2, 4, 7, 11, 16, 22, ?
1 + 1 = 2; 2 + 2 = 4; 4 + 3 = 7;
7 + 4 = 11; 11 + 5 = 16; 16 + 6 = 22
The differences between the numbers are going up by 1 then 2 then 3 then 4, and so on. The next difference will be 7.
Now 22 + 7 = 29.
The next number will be 29.

16 Each triangle shape like this △ uses 3 sticks.
Shape 1 has 1 triangle and 3 sticks.
Shape 2 has 1 + 2 or 3 triangles.
So it uses 3 × 3 = 9 sticks.
Shape 3 has 1 + 2 + 3 or 6 triangles.
It uses 6 × 3 = 18 sticks.
Shape 4 will have 1 + 2 + 3 + 4 or 10 triangles.
Shape 5 will have 1 + 2 + 3 + 4 + 5 or 15 triangles.
It will use 15 × 3 = 45 sticks.

SPELLING (Real Test)
Making singular verbs and plural nouns
Page 14

1 pianos **2** stresses **3** displays **4** thinks
5 branches **6** believes **7** mechanic **8** pliers
9 spanner **10** assemblies **11** gastric **12** right
13 complete **14** gravel **15** zebras **16** real
17 crosses **18** banana

EXPLANATIONS

1 *Pianos* is one of those nouns ending in **o** where the plural is not **oes**.

2 *One stress, many stresses*. The **es** suffix is used to change the single form of a noun that ends with **ss** to the plural form.

3 To make the plural of nouns that end with a vowel + **y**, simply add **s**.

4 To add the suffix **s** to words that end with a **k** simply add an **s**, not **es**.

5 Make sure you pronounce the word correctly. To make the plural of nouns that end with **ch** you add **es**, not **ers**.

6 *Beliefs* is a noun. *Believes* is the verb. Remember: For some nouns and singular verbs ending in **f** or **fe**, change the **f** to **v** and add **es**.

7 There is no **k** on the end of *mechanic*: **ic** is a common ending for many multisyllabic words ending with that sound (e.g. atomic, romantic) and some occupations (e.g. cleric).

8 *Pliers* is an '**i** before **e**' word. Pronounce it carefully to help you work out the correct spelling.

9 Think of *spanner* as **span** + the suffix **er**. To add the suffix you double the final consonant.

10 *One assembly, many assemblies*. When a word ends in a consonant + **y**, to make the plural you change the **y** to **i** and add **es**.

11 There is no **k** on the end of *gastric*: **ic** is a common ending for many multisyllabic words ending with that sound (e.g. atomic, romantic) and some occupations (e.g. mechanic).

12 *Right* in this sentence means 'on the right-hand side'. The word does not have a silent **w**. *Write* and *right* are homonyms—words that sound the same but which are spelt differently. *Wright* means 'builder' (e.g. shipwright).

13 Make sure you pronounce the word correctly. It is **complete**.

14 Most two-syllable words that end with **l** only have a single **l** (e.g. travel, formal).

15 *Zebras* has two syllables: **zeb–ras**. Make sure you pronounce the word correctly.

16 *Real* and *reel* are homonyms—words that sound the same but which are spelt differently. *Real* means 'actually exists'. A *reel* is a revolving device onto which something is wound (e.g. fishing line). Take care to use each word in its correct context.

17 *One cross, many crosses*. Add **es** to make the plural of words that end with **s** or double **s** (**ss**). Make sure you pronounce the word correctly.

18 Don't be tempted to double the **n** (**nn**).

GRAMMAR AND PUNCTUATION
(Real Test)   Pages 16–17
Types of sentences and articles

1 D **2** C **3** A **4** B **5** left **6** A **7** A **8** C
9 B **10** A **11** D **12** D **13** C **14** B **15** C
16 were **17** A **18** B

EXPLANATIONS

1 *The* is used because it refers to a particular fence: the back fence.

2 Remember *good, better* and *best* are used when describing items. *Good* is used when describing one item. *Better* is used when comparing two items. *Best* is used when judging more than two items. The comparison is between Leslie and the rest of the class as one group. 'More better' is incorrect. 'Gooder' is not a word.

3 *Keep* is an irregular verb. Most verbs in English form their past tense by adding **ed** (e.g. he walked). Irregular verbs do not form their past tense this way. The past tense of *keep* is the irregular verb *kept* (not 'keeped'). 'Keept' is not a real word.

4 If a title is shortened and still retains its last letter then no full stop is required.

5 *Left* is a verb (doing word) and the past tense of *leave*.

6 Prepositions put events in position in time or place. Use *into* to indicate that the cat is going towards and inside a building.

7 *A* is used because the reference is to any particular idea. It could be one of several.

8 *Or* links two or more alternatives. It is normally used only before the last alternative.

9 The correct punctuation is *community events, church programs or local markets*. Use a comma to separate the items in a series of three or more things (or for a pause). There is no comma where *or* is used in the series.

10 *Christmas* is one word. Proper nouns always begin with a capital letter. *Christmas* also has a capital letter because it is the first word in this sentence.

11 *Fireworks* is the last word in a statement and requires a full stop. The next word (*These*) has a capital letter and is the beginning of a new sentence.

12 This is a tense question. *Will* is future tense: *These will provide happy memories.*

13 Questions usually expect an answer. This question can be answered. Not all sentences that start with *How* are asking questions.

14 *Prof.* is a title and requires a capital letter. It also requires a full stop as *f* is not the last letter of *Professor*. *Friday* and *Sinclair* are proper nouns in this sentence.

15 *An* is correct because it come before the adjective *eight* which starts with a vowel sound.

16 Basic rule: Singular subjects (nouns) need singular verbs; plural subjects (nouns) need plural verbs. In this case *were* must be used because there are many frogs (even though there was only one cricket).

17 Only the actual words spoken are in speech marks (quotation marks). Mum asks a question so a question mark is required within the speech marks.

18 Use a comma to separate the items in a series of three or more things, or for a pause. There is no comma where *and* is used in the series: *school books, her pencils, a spare lunch box and a money purse.* Remember: Two or more words can make a single item (*spare lunch box*).

READING (Test Your Skills)
Understanding narratives
Page 18

Go to **page 206** for a guide to question types.

The tent

EXPLANATIONS

1 This is a **fact-finding type of question.** The answer is a fact in the text. You read that narratives are told in the first person and Megan says to the storyteller *"Come on Tracey, it was your idea!"* (see line 21). Megan is talking to the narrator of the passage, who is Tracey. Tracey refers to herself as *I*.

2 This is a **language type of question.** To find the answer you have to read the text carefully, especially the section that is quoted: *"Isn't this a bit <u>old hat</u>,"* offered Megan timidly. *"It's in the Stars every day in the paper…"* (see lines 28–29). Combine this comment with your own knowledge of how people talk about something that's been around for a long time. *Old hat* means 'old-fashioned'—like an old hat.

3 This is a **language type of question.** To find the answer you have to read the text carefully. You read that Megan speaks *timidly* (see line 28) and that when the other girls get a bit daring *Megan*

didn't say anything (see lines 19–20). *Cautious* is the best word to describe Megan. Megan is described as *timid*. She is quieter and not as forward as the other two girls.

4 This is an **inferring type of question.** To find the answer you have to 'read between the lines'. You read that the girls treat the whole idea of getting their fortunes read as a bit of *a lark* (see line 36). Then you read, *As I pulled back the flap of the tent and entered the eerie gloom a sinister voice said, "Welcome to your future Tracey." She knows my name!* (see line 37–39). Tracey was surprised the fortune-teller knew her name. There is no indication they have ever met before. The exclamation mark at the end of the final sentence is a clue.

5 This is a **fact-finding type of question.** The answer is a fact in the text. You read that two of the girls are egging each other on—daring one another— *"Let's give it a go?" said Angela* (see line 18). The reply was *"If you go first," I dared* (see line 19). The girls thought it would be a bit of excitement and fun to see what the fortune-teller had to say. Their plan is described as a *lark* (see line 36), implying they were treating the visit as a good-humoured prank.

6 This is an **inferring type of question.** To find the answer you have to 'read between the lines'. You read that the tent and the sign were a bit tatty. *We all looked at the lopsided sign on the side of an old tent, which was covered in stains and sun-bleached blotches* (see lines 2–7). This made the girls suspicious. The girls were also sceptical about star signs predictions. The girls thought the fortune-teller was a phoney. Angela is dismissive of claims of fortune-telling. The quality of the tent suggests that the fortune-teller doesn't have the ability to predict the future.

READING (Real Test)
Understanding narratives
Page 19

Alice's Adventures in Wonderland
1 B **2** D **3** It looked at its watch. **4** C **5** D
6 A **7** A

EXPLANATIONS

1 This is a **fact-finding type of question**. The answer is a fact in the text. You read *nor did Alice think it so very much out of the way to hear the Rabbit say to itself, "Oh dear! Oh dear! I shall be too late!"* (see lines 5–7). By reading the text carefully you will identify the correct order of events. The White Rabbit was complaining before it took its watch from its waistcoat-pocket.

Check Your Answers

ANSWERS
Week 1

2 This is a **language type of question.** To find the answer you have to read the text carefully, especially the section that is quoted: *Burning with curiosity, she [Alice] ran across the field after it, and was just in time to see it pop down a large rabbit-hole under the hedge (see lines 14–15).* Combine this with your own knowledge of language to work out that this metaphor is suggesting that if you are burning with curiosity you are so excited about finding out something it is 'consuming' all your thoughts. Nothing else matters.

3 This is an **inferring type of question.** To find the answer you have to 'read between the lines'. You read that *When the Rabbit actually took a watch out of its waistcoat-pocket, and looked at it, and then hurried on, Alice started to her feet (see lines 9–11).* Alice didn't really notice the White Rabbit talking to itself until *she thought it over afterwards* because *at the time it all seemed quite natural (see lines 7–9)* but she jumped to her feet when she realised it had a watch in its waistcoat-pocket.

4 This is a **synthesis type of question.** To find the answer you have to read the whole text. The text is about how Alice decides to follow the rabbit down a hole—Into the unknown. A good title is one that has something to do with an important part of the story. It does not focus on minor details.

5 This is a **judgement type of question.** You read that Alice followed the White Rabbit down a hole *never once considering how in the world she was to get out again (see lines 16–17).* This is being reckless. She *found herself falling down what seemed to be a very deep well (see lines 19–20).* She didn't know what dangers she might encounter.

6 This is an **inferring type of question.** To find the answer you have to 'read between the lines'. You read that as Alice fell she *had not a moment to think about stopping herself before she found herself falling down what seemed to be a very deep well (see lines 19–20).* Combine this with your own knowledge of falling a long way and you would expect Alice to be frightened. She was more aware of her surroundings than her predicament. She didn't do anything to show she was scared. She was not worried.

7 This is a **language type of question.** To find the answer you have to read the text carefully, especially the section that is quoted: *Alice started to her feet, for it flashed across her mind that she had never before seen a rabbit with either a waistcoat-pocket or a watch (see lines 11–13).* Combine this with the context in which the word is used. *Started* in this passage means 'to stand up suddenly as if startled'.

READING (Real Test)
Understanding narratives   Page 20

Clean-up

1 C   **2** B   **3** C   **4** A   **5** D   **6** B   **7** A

EXPLANATIONS

1 This is an **inferring type of question.** To find the answer you have to 'read between the lines'. You read that Ms Green said to her class *"Now we are settled I want you to look at the playground. Turn and have a good look! That's right. What do you see?" (see lines 13–15).* She wanted the playground cleaned up. She could see the mess from the classroom landing.

2 This is a **language type of question.** To find the answer you have to read the text carefully, especially the section that states: *Ms Green stood on the small classroom landing (see lines 2–3).* Then *she descended the steps (see line 19).* Combine this with your own knowledge of landings. Pete Morgan was standing and his eyes were *level with Ms Green's feet (see line 6).* Landings are raised platforms above steps. *Descended* means 'move down'. Ms Green came down the steps.

3 This is an **inferring type of question.** To find the answer you have to 'read between the lines'. You read that when Ms Green sends the class off to collect litter she says *"Not you Bob. You get a carton from the classroom and bring it here. That's a good boy!" (see lines 20–21).* Ms Green regarded Bob as reliable. He was sent inside to get a carton.

4 This is an **inferring type of question.** To find the answer you have to 'read between the lines'. You read that, *Pete Morgan (called Morgue behind his back) was first in the boys' line (see lines 5–6).* Combine this with your own knowledge of how some people make comments about people without that person hearing them. People only call a person a name behind their back because they don't want to be heard. Maybe they are afraid that person will be very annoyed and react in some way. It's usually not a nice thing to do.

5 This is a **fact-finding type of question.** The answer is a fact in the text. You read Anna said *"We always have to wait for Smudger" (see line 10).* Anna's complaint was they had to wait for Smudger to line up because he was always late.

6 This is a **synthesis type of question.** To find the answer you have to read the whole text. In the text Smudger is always speaking out and making defensive comments: *"Smudger's okay," growled Smudger (see line 12)* and *"Not true," brayed Smudger. "My scraps are in the bin!" (see line 18).* Smudger also litters. Combine this information about his behaviour with your own knowledge to realise the sort of person Smudger is. He is bold.

He talks loudly and roughly. He doesn't wait to be asked to speak.

7 This is an **inferring type of question.** To find the answer you have to 'read between the lines'. You read that *Ms Green stood on the small classroom landing, her hands on her hips, her whistle in her mouth. She tapped her foot (see lines 2–4).* Combine this information with your own knowledge of people who are impatient. They often put their hands on their hips and tap their feet. Ms Green is impatient: she has her whistle in her mouth ready to blow, waiting for her class to assemble.

READING (Real Test)
Understanding poetry
Page 21

Possum

1 D   **2** *Clean-up* A, C; *Possum* B, C   **3** A   **4** D
5 A   **6** C

EXPLANATIONS

1 This is an **inferring type of question.** To find the answer you have to 'read between the lines'. You read that the possum *wakes up the whole house (see line 9)* and *You should have heard the noise they made (see line 16).* The possum often gets into possum fights. You can work out that these descriptions are of a problem—the problem is the noisy possum in the roof space.

2 This is a **synthesis type of question.** To find the answer you have to read both texts. The *Clean-up* text is intended to be read for enjoyment: to **entertain** the reader. It is a **narrative** of a fictional incident. The *Possum* poem is to entertain: to be read for enjoyment. It is written in **first person.** It is told from the narrator's point of view. The personal pronoun *I* is used.

3 This is a **language type of question.** To find the answer you have to read the text carefully, especially the section that states *He clomps around the rafters (see line 10).* Then you combine it with your own knowledge of words when used in their context. *Stomps* and *clomps* are synonyms.

4 This is a **fact-finding type of question.** The answer is a fact in the text. You read that the narrator's father said *we'll get a possum house / And put it near the shed (see lines 18–19).*

5 This is a **fact-finding type of question.** The answer is a fact in the text. You read that the possum *leaps into the tree outside / The window by my bed (see lines 12–13).*

6 This is an **inferring type of question.** The answer is a fact in the text. To find the answer you have to 'read between the lines'. You read *You should have heard the noise they made— / It ended in a fight (see lines 16–17).* The possum makes a lot of noise but he made the most noise when partying one night and the party ended in a fight.

READING (Real Test)
Understanding information reports
Page 22

Border towns

1 B   **2** D   **3** C   **4** South Australia   **5** A   **6** D   **7** B

EXPLANATIONS

1 This is an **inferring type of question.** To find the answer you have to 'read between the lines'. You read that Mungindi *is the only border town in the southern hemisphere with the same name on both sides of the border (see lines 15–16)* and *Some residents have a NSW address and phone number but live in Queensland (see lines 18–19).* Combine this with the information provided about other border towns and you will conclude that the writer is *most* interested in Mungindi as a border town.

2 This is a **fact-finding type of question.** The answer is a fact in the text. You read that *Some residents have a NSW address and phone number but live in Queensland (see lines 18–19).* The residents in Mungindi, Queensland, have a NSW address.

3 This is an **inferring type of question.** To find the answer you have to 'read between the lines'. You read that in Tweed Heads and Coolangatta *you can change time zones simply by crossing the street (see lines 11–12).* The other two listed 'twin' border towns are separated by rivers. *The twin towns of Albury–Wodonga sit on opposite sides of the Murray River (see lines 3–5)* and for the two parts of Mungundi the border is the Barwon River which separated two states.

4 This is a **fact-finding type of question.** The answer is a fact in the text. You read that *Bordertown (5268) in South Australia (see line 20).*

5 This is a **language type of question.** To find the answer you have to read the text carefully, especially the section that states *Tweed Heads, NSW (2485), is next to the Queensland border, adjacent to the 'Twin Town' of Coolangatta (4225) on the Gold Coast (see lines 8–10).* You also read that *you can change time zones simply by crossing the street (see lines 11–12).* Combine this information with your own knowledge of word meanings to work out that *adjacent* means 'next (to) or very close by'.

6 This is a **fact-finding type of question.** The answer is a fact in the text. You read that *Bordertown (5268) in South Australia is 20 km west of the border. There is no twin town over the border (see lines 20–21).* It is not on the border.

7 This is an **inferring type of question.** To find the answer you have to 'read between the lines'. The

clue is in the first paragraph where the postcodes of Albury and Wodonga are given: *New South Wales (postcode 2640) and Victoria (postcode 3689) (see lines 6–7)*. The number (5268) is a postcode.

WRITING (Real Test)
Narrative 1   Page 27

Tick each correct point.
Read the writer's work through once to get an overall view of their response.

Focus on general points
☐ Did it make sense?
☐ Did it flow?
☐ Did the story arouse any feeling?
☐ Did you want to read on? Did the story create any suspense?
☐ Was the handwriting readable?

Now focus on the detail. Read the following points and find out whether the writer's work has these features.

Focus on content
☐ Did the opening sentence(s) 'grab' your interest?
☐ Was the setting established (i.e. when and where the action took place)?
☐ Was it apparent who the main character(s) is? (It can be the narrator, using *I*.)
☐ Was there a 'problem' to be 'solved' early in the writing?
☐ Was a complication or unusual event introduced?
☐ Did descriptions make reference to any of the senses (e.g. cold nose, warm coat)?
☐ Was there a climax (a more exciting part near the end)?
☐ Was there a conclusion (resolution of the problem) and was it 'believable'?

Focus on structure, vocabulary, grammar, spelling, punctuation
☐ Was there variation in sentence length and beginnings?
☐ Was a new paragraph started for changes in time, place or action?
☐ In conversations or speaking were there separate paragraphs for each change of speaker?
☐ Were adjectives used to improve descriptions (e.g. *careful* movements)?
☐ Were adverbs used to make 'actions' more interesting (e.g. tail wagged *joyfully*)?
☐ Were capital letters where they should have been?
☐ Was punctuation correct?
☐ Was the spelling of words correct?

Marker's suggestions (optional)

WRITING (Real Test)
Narrative 2   Page 28

Tick each correct point.
Read the writer's work through once to get an overall view of their response.

Focus on general points
☐ Did it make sense?
☐ Did it flow?
☐ Did the story arouse any feeling?
☐ Did you want to read on? Did the story create any suspense?
☐ Was the handwriting readable?

Now focus on the detail. Read the following points and find out whether the writer's work has these features.

Focus on content
☐ Did the opening sentence(s) 'grab' your interest?
☐ Was the setting established (i.e. when and where the action took place)?
☐ Was it apparent who the main character(s) is? (It can be the narrator, using *I*.)
☐ Was there a 'problem' to be 'solved' early in the writing?
☐ Was a complication or unusual event introduced?
☐ Did descriptions make reference to any of the senses (e.g. cold nose, warm coat)?
☐ Was there a climax (a more exciting part near the end)?
☐ Was there a conclusion (resolution of the problem) and was it 'believable'?

Focus on structure, vocabulary, grammar, spelling, punctuation
☐ Was there variation in sentence length and beginnings?
☐ Was a new paragraph started for changes in time, place or action?
☐ In conversations or speaking were there separate paragraphs for each change of speaker?
☐ Were adjectives used to improve descriptions (e.g. *careful* movements)?
☐ Were adverbs used to make 'actions' more interesting (e.g. tail wagged *joyfully*)?
☐ Were capital letters where they should have been?
☐ Was punctuation correct?
☐ Was the spelling of words correct?

Marker's suggestions (optional)

WRITING (Real Test)
Narrative 3   Page 29

Tick each correct point.
Read the writer's work through once to get an overall view of their response.

Focus on general points
- ☐ Did it make sense?
- ☐ Did it flow?
- ☐ Did the story arouse any feeling?
- ☐ Did you want to read on? Did the story create any suspense?
- ☐ Was the handwriting readable?

Now focus on the detail. Read the following points and find out whether the writer's work has these features.

Focus on content
- ☐ Did the opening sentence(s) 'grab' your interest?
- ☐ Was the setting established (i.e. when and where the action took place)?
- ☐ Was it apparent who the main character(s) is? (It can be the narrator, using *I*.)
- ☐ Was there a 'problem' to be 'solved' early in the writing?
- ☐ Was a complication or unusual event introduced?
- ☐ Did descriptions make reference to any of the senses (e.g. cold nose, warm coat)?
- ☐ Was there a climax (a more exciting part near the end)?
- ☐ Was there a conclusion (resolution of the problem) and was it 'believable'?

Focus on structure, vocabulary, grammar, spelling, punctuation
- ☐ Was there variation in sentence length and beginnings?
- ☐ Was a new paragraph started for changes in time, place or action?
- ☐ In conversations or speaking were there separate paragraphs for each change of speaker?
- ☐ Were adjectives used to improve descriptions (e.g. *careful* movements)?
- ☐ Were adverbs used to make 'actions' more interesting (e.g. tail wagged *joyfully*)?
- ☐ Were capital letters where they should have been?
- ☐ Was punctuation correct?
- ☐ Was the spelling of words correct?

Marker's suggestions (optional)

WRITING (Real Test)
Narrative 4   Page 30

Tick each correct point.
Read the writer's work through once to get an overall view of their response.

Focus on general points
- ☐ Did it make sense?
- ☐ Did it flow?
- ☐ Did the story arouse any feeling?
- ☐ Did you want to read on? Did the story create any suspense?
- ☐ Was the handwriting readable?

Now focus on the detail. Read the following points and find out whether the writer's work has these features.

Focus on content
- ☐ Did the opening sentence(s) 'grab' your interest?
- ☐ Was the setting established (i.e. when and where the action took place)?
- ☐ Was it apparent who the main character(s) is? (It can be the narrator, using *I*.)
- ☐ Was there a 'problem' to be 'solved' early in the writing?
- ☐ Was a complication or unusual event introduced?
- ☐ Did descriptions make reference to any of the senses (e.g. cold nose, warm coat)?
- ☐ Was there a climax (a more exciting part near the end)?
- ☐ Was there a conclusion (resolution of the problem) and was it 'believable'?

Focus on structure, vocabulary, grammar, spelling, punctuation
- ☐ Was there variation in sentence length and beginnings?
- ☐ Was a new paragraph started for changes in time, place or action?
- ☐ In conversations or speaking were there separate paragraphs for each change of speaker?
- ☐ Were adjectives used to improve descriptions (e.g. *careful* movements)?
- ☐ Were adverbs used to make 'actions' more interesting (e.g. tail wagged *joyfully*)?
- ☐ Were capital letters where they should have been?
- ☐ Was punctuation correct?
- ☐ Was the spelling of words correct?

Marker's suggestions (optional)

WEEK 2

NUMBER AND ALGEBRA
(Real Test)   Page 35
*Adding, subtracting, multiplying
and dividing*

1 10 **2** A **3** C **4** 161 **5** D **6** 10 **7** 13 **8** 32
9 36 **10** 312 × 4 **11** 11 **12** 10 **13** 3, 36 **14** 29
15 9 **16** B

EXPLANATIONS

1 25 − 7 = 18
So after giving 7 to Francis, Joel had 18 cards left.
Now 18 − 8 = 10.
So after giving 8 cards to Harry, Joel had
10 cards left.

2 There are 20 groups and 5 strawberries in
each group.
20 × 5 = 100
There are 100 strawberries altogether.

3 Each packet has 100 ear tags.
So there are 200 ear tags in 2 packets and that is
not enough.
Beth would need 3 packets.

4 76 + 85 = 161
Altogether, Kylie and Ella have 161 books.

5 Sally needs to divide the 30 cans into groups of 6.
This means she needs to find 30 ÷ 6.

6 There are 24 children altogether.
There are 4 more boys than girls.
Now 24 − 4 = 20.
So if there were the same number of boys as girls,
there would be 20 children.
Now half of 20 is 10.
So there would be 10 boys and 10 girls.
There are 10 girls in kindergarten (and 14 boys).

7 37 + 28 = 35 + 30 = 65
So Thomas has 65 cars and trucks altogether.
Oliver must also have 65 cars and trucks altogether.
He has 52 cars.
Now 65 − 52 = 13.
So Oliver must have 13 trucks.

8 17 + 35 = 17 + 3 + 32 = 20 + 32

9 Ryan has 9 marbles.
Billy has 5 × 9 = 45 marbles.
Difference = 45 − 9
            = 36

10 Divide 1248 by each of the numbers on the cards.
1248 ÷ 1 = 1248
1248 ÷ 2 = 624
1248 ÷ 3 = 416
1248 ÷ 4 = 312
Of these answers only 312 can be made with
the cards.
So 312 × 4 = 1248

11 The 3 girls share 32 stickers, but they don't share
them evenly.
Now 30 ÷ 3 = 10.
So they will have around 10 stickers each.
Suppose Daisy had 10 stickers.
Then Jenna would have 6 stickers (10 − 4) and
Lucy would have 13 (10 + 3).
Now 10 + 6 + 13 = 29
But there were 32 stickers altogether. This is 3 more
stickers. So each girl will have one more sticker.
Daisy will have 11 stickers.

12 6 × 5 = 30
Now 10 × 3 = 30
So the missing number is 10.

13 There are 3 cartons of eggs and 12 eggs in each
carton.
So to find the number of eggs we must multiply
3 by 12.
Now 3 × 12 = 36 so this is the correct number
sentence.

14 116 balloons were divided into lots of 4.
Now 116 ÷ 4 = 29
So there were 29 children in the group.

15 3 × 7 = 21
12 + 9 = 21
So the missing number is 9.

16 Altogether there are 145 photos.
Suppose Ken had 4 albums with 30 photos in each.
Now 4 × 30 = 120.
Ken has more than 120 photos. Some of the
albums would need to have more than 30 photos.
So this is not the answer.
Suppose Ken had 5 albums.
Now 5 × 30 = 150
This number is 5 more than the number of
photos Ken has. One of the 5 albums could have
25 photos and the others all have 30. Or all five
albums could have 29 photos in them.
Ken could have 5 albums.
Suppose Ken had 6 albums with 25 photos in each.

Now $6 \times 25 = 150$.

This is more photos than Ken has, so some of the albums would need to have less than 25 photos. This is not the answer.

If Ken had 7 albums each album would need to have even fewer photos, so he could not have 7 albums.

Ken must have 5 albums.

NUMBER AND ALGEBRA (Real Test)
Fractions, decimals and money
Pages 40–41

1 9 **2** A **3** D **4** D **5** $8.70 **6** B **7** D
8 0.03, 0.103, 0.13, 0.3 **9** C **10** $1.10 **11** C **12** C
13 B **14** B **15** D

EXPLANATIONS

1 Ben had 18 pencils.
He divides them into 2 equal parts.
Half of 18 is 9.
So Ben gave 9 pencils to Casey.
He has 9 pencils left.

2 Angus could use these coins to buy the drink.

He would have these coins left.

So Angus has $1.25 left.

3 One apple can be cut into 4 quarters.
So three apples can be cut into 3×4 or 12 quarters.
Half an apple can be cut into 2 quarters.
So altogether there are 14 quarters.

4 Imagine the number line between 0 and 1 divided into 10 parts.

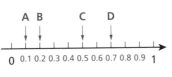

The position of 0.75 is halfway between 0.7 and 0.8. So D is the arrow closest to 0.75.

5 The truck costs 25 cents more than $8.45.
Adding the cents: $25 + 45 = 70$
So the truck costs $8.70.

6 The calves eat half a bale of hay every day. So in two days they eat one bale. Now two weeks is 2 lots of 7 days. This is the same as 7 lots of 2 days. So the calves will eat 7 bales of hay.

7 There are 2 halves in each sandwich.
There are 4 sandwiches.
So the number of halves is 4×2 or 8.

8 0.3 has 3 tenths.
0.03 has no tenths.
0.13 has 1 tenth (and 3 hundredths).
0.103 has 1 tenth (and 0 hundredths) and 3 thousandths.
So 0.3 is the largest because it has the most tenths.
0.03 is the smallest because it has the least tenths.
0.13 is larger than 0.103 because it has more hundredths.
[Or write them all with 3 numbers after the decimal point: 0.300, 0.030, 0.130, 0.103.]
In order from smallest to largest the numbers are 0.03, 0.103, 0.13 and 0.3.

9 Two out of 8 triangles are shaded. This means that one out of every four are shaded. So $\frac{1}{4}$ of the shape is shaded.

10 $2.25 + $1.65 = $3.90
Now $5.00 − $3.90 = $1.10.
The correct change is $1.10.

11 12 people share 3 pizzas.
Now $12 \div 3 = 4$.
So 4 people share each pizza.
This means that each pizza is divided into 4 parts or quarters.
So each person will get $\frac{1}{4}$ of a pizza.

12 6 tens, 8 ones and 3 hundredths.
There are no tenths.
So the number is 68.03..

13 $\frac{1}{5}$ is 1 of 5 equal parts.

So the number line needs to be divided into 5 equal parts.

This means that arrow B points to $\frac{1}{5}$.

14 $4.35 + $1.65 = $6.00
So Jack must have given the shopkeeper $6.00.

15 $\frac{1}{3}$ is one of three equal parts.

This shape has one out of every three parts shaded, so it is the shape that has one-third shaded.

SPELLING (Real Test)
Adding 'ing' or 'ed' to verbs and 'er' and 'est' to adjectives Page 43

1 afternoon 2 captain 3 meat 4 almonds
5 boiled 6 bulbs 7 climate 8 juicy
9 Where 10 decision 11 wonder 12 citrus
13 lifetime 14 wasp 15 harbour 16 daisies
17 nurse 18 wound

EXPLANATIONS

1 *Afternoon* is a compound word: *after + noon.*

2 The letter combinations *ane* and *ain* both make the same sound. Learn to recognise words with a similar spelling (e.g. train, explain, insane, humane). Sometimes there are homonyms that can be tricky (e.g. plain, plane).

3 *Mete* is a word rarely used in everyday language. *Meet* and *meat* are homonyms—words that sound the same but which are spelt differently. *Meat* is the flesh of an animal. *Meet* is to encounter somebody at a particular point. Learn when to use each word in its correct context.

4 *Almond* has a silent *l*. A silent *l* often comes before an *m* in many words (e.g. calm).

5 When a word ends with two vowels and a consonant (e.g. boil) you do not double the last letter to add a suffix beginning with a vowel.

6 *Bulb* ends with two consonants. To make the plural noun simply add an *s*.

7 Pronounce the word correctly. *Ate* is a common ending in English (e.g educate, relate). The *arte* ending is most uncommon.

8 When a word ends with a consonant + *e*, drop the *e* before adding the suffix *y* (e.g. taste → tasty).

9 The common words beginning with *wh* can be tricky. 'Whear' is not a word and not to be confused with *wear* (put on clothes). *Where* is about place.

10 Think of *decision* in parts: *de–cision*. *Cision* is a part of a number of words (e.g. incision, precision).

11 *Wander* (walk around) and *wonder* (think about) sound very similar. Make sure you pronounce them very carefully.

12 *Citrus* has two syllables: *cit–rus*. You should notice it begins with a *c*, not an *s*. Make sure you pronounce *citrus* correctly.

13 *Lifetime* is a compound word: *life + time*. *Life* belongs to a family of *ife* words (e.g. wife, strife, knife).

14 A silent *h* often follows a *w* (e.g. what, why) but this is not an example of that pattern.

15 You may often see *harbour* spelt as *harbor*. This is an American spelling and not acceptable in Australia.

16 One *daisy*, many *daisies*. When a word ends in consonant + *y*, to make the plural form you change the *y* to *i* and add *es*.

17 The letter combinations *er*, *ir* and *ur* can make the same sound. Learn to recognise groups of words that use the same combinations (e.g. purse, curse). Often you will have to simply learn and remember these words.

18 *Wound* is a tricky word. It doesn't rhyme with other *ound* words (e.g. sound, found). It is a word you will have to learn and remember.

GRAMMAR AND PUNCTUATION (Real Test)
Types of nouns and adjectives and use of commas and brackets Pages 45–46

1 B 2 C 3 D 4 C 5 team 6 C 7 A 8 B
9 A 10 D 11 Bret 12 B 13 D 14 C 15 A
16 C 17 A 18 A

EXPLANATIONS

1 A comma is used to indicate a pause when some additional information is added to a sentence.

2 Remember: *fast, faster* and *fastest* for comparative adjectives. *Fast* is used when describing one person. *Faster* is used when comparing two people. *Fastest* is used when comparing more than two people. The comparison is between Chad and his other brothers as a single group.

3 *Bite* is an irregular verb. Most verbs in English form their past tense by adding *ed* (e.g. he walked). Irregular verbs do not form their past tense this way. The past tense of *bite* is the irregular verb *bitten* (not 'bitted'). *Bitten* needs another verb to help it—*was*.

4 If a title is shortened and still retains its last letter then no full stop is required.

5 *Team* is a collective noun. It refers to a single group of players—probably eleven players, in this example.

6 The year dates are additional information that the writer may feel the reader would appreciate.

7 *Door* is the last word of a statement. The next word is *The* (with a capital letter). It is the beginning of a new sentence.

8 *Together* is unnecessary. It is a redundant word. People that intend to *meet* will come *together*. No meaning is lost by omitting *together*.

9 *Which* is a pronoun used to refer to things. *So* is a conjunction indicating a reason for a decision.

10 This apostrophe indicates possession or ownership; it is his dad's desk. *His* is a possessive pronoun, *tests* is the plural of *test*, and *atlas* is the name of a type of book.

11 Pronouns, such as *who* (and *he*), are located close to the person that they stand for: *he* was the one *who* …

12 Make sure you read the question carefully. In this case *of* cannot follow *despite* or *even though*. The exclamation mark implies that the person is not going *because* of the weather.

13 Questions usually expect an answer. This question can be answered. Not all sentences that start with *What* are asking questions.

14 The response: *"I didn't know you'd be so late"* carries the implication that Eni expected Greg to meet her but at an earlier time.

15 *An* is correct because it comes before the noun *hour* which has a silent *h*. This means *hour* starts with a vowel sound.

16 Basic rule: Singular subjects (nouns) need singular verbs; plural subjects (nouns) need plural verbs. In this case *was* must be used because there is only one band even though it has two drummers. *The band* is the subject of the sentence. Think of the sentence as: *The band … was belting out rock songs all night*. It is in the past tense.

17 Only the actual words spoken are in speech marks (quotation marks). The words spoken are broken by *warned the bus driver*, which is not included in the words spoken.

18 Use a comma to separate the items in a series of three or more things (or for a pause). There is no comma where *and* is used in the series.

READING (Test Your Skills)
Understanding persuasive texts
Page 47

Go to   page 208   for a guide to question types.

Dogs in towns

EXPLANATIONS

1 This is a **fact-finding type of question.** The answer is a fact in the text. You are asked *Have you tried doing homework or sleeping when next door's pet won't be quiet? (see lines 15–16).* The writer also complains that it is *amazing how many dogs run along fences barking at people for simply using public footpaths.*

Many don't stop well after you have passed by. It's a form of harassment (see lines 8–11). The writer is most upset by dogs that bark and yap all the time.

2 This is a **judgement type of question.** You can find the answer to the question by reading the whole text carefully and then working out the answer. You will have to combine the facts that you read with your own knowledge. You have to make a judgement about the information provided, in order to work out the final answer. The writer is *indignant* about the noise and disturbance dogs create. *Indignant* means 'annoyed at something that seems unfair or unreasonable'. The language the writer uses confirms this point: *If something stirs it up at night, a yap, yap, yapping mutt will carry on for ages! (see lines 14–15).*

3 This is an **inferring type of question.** To find the answer you have to 'read between the lines'. You read that the writer believes *most dogs in town and cities should be banned (see lines 2–3)* because many are in *poky little flats, many floors from the ground (see lines 6–7).* The writer feels many dogs are *imprisoned (see line 6).* The writer's language is quite strong.

4 This is a **language type of question.** To find the answer you have to read the text carefully, especially the section that states *The big ones with bared teeth look as if they could climb over any flimsy fence and attack at the first chance (see lines 11–13).* Then you combine it with your own knowledge of how big some dogs grow and how protective some fences look. The word *flimsy* means 'weak and easily broken'. A flimsy fence might not stop a big dog from getting out.

5 This is a **language type of question.** To find the answer you have to read the text carefully, especially the section that states *small yards or poky little flats (see lines 6–7).* Then you combine it with your own knowledge of how small some flats are, especially for a dog that needs exercise. The word *poky* means 'small and cramped'.

6 This is a **language type of question.** To find the answer you have to read the text carefully, especially the section that states *a yap, yap, yapping mutt will carry on for ages! (see lines 14–15).* Repeating a word is a literary technique to make a point. The writer repeats the word *yap* to emphasise how much yapping some dogs do.

7 This is a **fact-finding type of question.** The answer is a fact in the text. You read that the writer excludes farm dogs because they *help farmers (see line 4).* The following listed dogs in the next sentence also help people. The writer understands that some dogs perform an important service. These include guide dogs who help people who cannot see.

Pet cemeteries

1 C **2** B **3** B **4** A **5** C **6** D **7** B

EXPLANATIONS

1 This is a **fact-finding type of question**. The answer is a fact in the text. You read that the writer asks that *[e]veryone should contact their local council and ask them to provide public pet cemeteries (see lines 18–20)*.

2 This is a **fact-finding type of question**. The answer is a fact in the text. You read *A cemetery doesn't have to be in the city. Country councils could make money out of providing space for pet cemeteries (see lines 9–11)*.

3 This is a **language type of question**. To find the answer you have to read the text carefully, especially the section that states *For pets there are few private cemeteries and even fewer public cemeteries. I think there should be more (see lines 2–3)*. The writer has thought about the issue and has an interest in improving the situation. Combine this with your own knowledge of how people think about issues. The language used by the writer indicates a concern about the lack of public pet cemeteries. *Concerned* suggests it is something the writer thinks seriously about.

4 This is an **inferring type of question**. To find the answer you have to 'read between the lines'. You read that the writer states: *Pets are more than farm animals (see line 18)*. The writer wouldn't expect a pet cemetery to be used for a calf as it is a farm animal—not really a pet like a cat or budgie.

5 This is a **language type of question**. To find the answer you have to read the text carefully, especially the section that states *Lonely or single people find pets give them an easy way to interact with neighbours (see lines 5–6)*. From this sentence and your own knowledge of what people do with neighbours you can work out that the word *interact* means 'to become involved in a conversation or other social activity'.

6 This is a **fact-finding type of question**. The answer is a fact in the text. You read that the writer states *For pets there are few private cemeteries and even fewer public cemeteries. I think there should be more (see lines 2–3)*.

7 This is a **fact-finding type of question**. The answer is a fact in the text. You read that *Pets are more than something to own like a car or a TV (see line 7)*.

Australia Day poster

1 D **2** 1:00/1 o'clock **3** A **4** A **5** B **6** C

EXPLANATIONS

1 This is an **inferring type of question**. To find the answer you have to 'read between the lines'. You read that the event is a *FAMILY DAY OF FUN (see line 2)* and people are invited to *enjoy an Aussie barbecue (see line 5)*. There are fun activities planned. Combine this with your own knowledge of family events and you will conclude that the poster is trying to persuade people to join in the fun that has been organised to celebrate Australia Day.

2 This is a **fact-finding type of question**. The answer is a fact on the poster. You read *Come along and enjoy an Aussie barbecue lunch (see line 5)* and *1:00 Barbecue (see line 13)*.

3

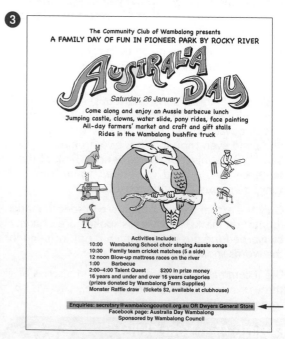

This is a **fact-finding type of question**. The answer is a fact on the poster. You read *Enquiries: secretary@wambalongcouncil.org.au OR Dwyers General Store (see line 18)*.

4 This is an **inferring type of question**. To find the answer you have to 'read between the lines'. You read *FAMILY DAY OF FUN (see line 2)*, *Family team cricket matches (5 a side) (see line 11)* and *Blow-up mattress races on the river (see line 12)*. The sporting events are not serious; they are meant to be fun for the players and entertaining for the spectators.

5 This is a **language type of question.** To find the answer you have to read the poster carefully, especially the section that is quoted: *Sponsored by Wambalong Council (see line 20).* Then you combine it with your own knowledge of how events like this are paid for. A *sponsor* is a person (or organisation) that pays in part or full for the cost of running an event. Wambalong Council sponsored the Fun Day.

6 This is a **fact-finding type of question.** The answer is a fact on the poster. You read *Blow-up mattress races on the river (see line 12).*

READING (Real Test) Understanding cartoons
Page 50

Cartoon
1 B **2** over a year **3** C **4** D **5** B **6** A **7** D
EXPLANATIONS

1 This is a **judgement type of question.** You can see the conditions the men are living in. They would have sent the note to get help but instead all the teacher was concerned with was spelling mistakes. You can work out the answer. This is not serious. This is a cartoon intended to make the reader smile.

2 This is an **inferring type of question.** To find the answer you have to 'read between the lines'. You see the state of their clothes and the fish bone on the sand which show they have been on the island a long time. You also read *It's a reply to my message I sent a year ago (see lines 1–3).* You can work out the men have been on the island for over a year.

3 This is an **inferring type of question.** To find the answer you have to 'read between the lines' and look at the cartoon carefully. The man reading the note is disbelieving. The look on his face and his comment with exclamation mark confirms this. The ex-teacher is more concerned with correct spelling than rescuing the men!

4 This is a **synthesis type of question.** To find the answer you have to look at the whole cartoon. The cartoon shows two men wanting to be rescued from a small island. Combine this observation with your understanding of being marooned. A suitable caption for the cartoon would be 'A spell on a desert island'. There is a pun on the word 'spell'. It can mean using letters correctly in a word (spelling) or it can mean a brief stay. In this case the stay on the island has been anything but brief!

5 This is an **inferring type of question.** To find the answer you have to 'read between the lines'. You read that the reader says the returned note *was found by my old Year 4 teacher! (see lines 4–5).* The once Year 4 student is now a man. It is most likely

the Year 4 teacher has a long memory. It must be many years since the note writer was at school.

6 This is an **inferring type of question.** To find the answer you have to 'read between the lines'. You look at the expression on the face of the man on the right. This is a tricky question. The look is not obvious but he seems to have a slight smile. Combine this with your own understanding of the cartoon's situation to work out the man is slightly amused by the teacher's response. It is not a reply he would expect.

7 This is a **judgement type of question.** You can find the answer to the question by looking carefully at the picture, combining your observation with your own knowledge and then working out the answer. You have to make a judgement about the information provided. It is most likely the men will have to think about food. The island is very small with just one coconut tree. The fish bone suggests that food has been scarce. The men look undernourished.

READING (Real Test) Understanding explanations
Page 51

What are mantis shrimps?
1 D **2** B **3** C **4** A **5** B **6** 2 **7** C
EXPLANATIONS

1 This is a **language type of question.** To find the answer you have to read the text carefully, especially the section that is quoted: *Mantis shrimps are lightning-fast predators (see line 9).* Then you combine it with your own knowledge of how quick a lightning flash is. If something is lightning-fast it is very quick. It is supposed to have the speed of a lightning strike. This is a figurative expression and not meant to be taken literally.

2 This is a **fact-finding type of question.** The answer is a fact in the text. You read that *They are either 'spearers' … or 'smashers' that possess club-like limbs (see lines 9–13).* Mantis shrimps have two methods of catching prey: spearing and clubbing.

3 This is a **synthesis type of question.** To find the answer you have to read the whole paragraph. The first paragraph describes the mantis shrimp's unusual eyes: *They have the most complex eyes in the animal kingdom (see lines 3–4).* The paragraph also lists the different colours the shrimps can see.

4 This is an **inferring type of question.** To find the answer you have to 'read between the lines'. You read that mantis shrimps have *forelimbs with numerous barbs to capture soft-bodied prey like fish (see lines 10–11).* Combine this information with your own knowledge of how barbs are used on

such weapons as spears or even fish hooks. The barbs on the mantis shrimp's forelimbs are used to hold or secure their prey and make it difficult for prey to slip off the 'spear' point.

5 This is a **fact-finding type of question.** The answer is a fact in the text. You read that *They can see colours other animals cannot see. They can see ultraviolet, visible and infra-red light* (*see lines 4–6*). Ultraviolet is a colour. It is included in a sentence with other colours.

6 This is a **synthesis-type of question.** You have to read the whole of both paragraphs to get the answer. Paragraph 2 tells the reader that the shrimp is a predator (*line 9*) and the following sentences contain facts about their methods. They spear and club and can deliver blows (*lines 14, 15*) with the force of a rifle bullet.

7 This is a **judgement type of question.** You can find the answer to the question by reading the whole text very carefully then working out the answer. You have to make a judgement about the information provided in order to work out the final answer. Someone with an interest in how sea creatures adapt most likely wrote the text. The mantis shrimp is a particularly unusual marine creature.

WRITING (Real Test)
Persuasive text 1
Page 54

Tick each correct point.
Read the writer's work through once to get an overall view of their response.

Focus on general points
- ☐ Did it make sense?
- ☐ Did it flow?
- ☐ Did the opinions expressed arouse any feeling/ reaction?
- ☐ Did you want to read on to understand/appreciate the writer's point of view?
- ☐ Was the handwriting readable?

Now focus on the detail. Read the following points and find out whether the writer's work has these features.

Focus on content
- ☐ Was the purpose of the writing clearly introduced?
- ☐ Was there a clear statement of the writer's opinion?
- ☐ Were possible objections to the writer's opinion stated and refuted by logical argument or observations?
- ☐ Were the opinions expressed objectively?
- ☐ Was the original opinion clearly repeated? (optional)

Focus on structure, vocabulary, grammar, spelling and punctuation
- ☐ Was there a variation in sentence length and beginnings?
- ☐ Were there clear paragraphs to separate various arguments or points (maybe a line space)?
- ☐ Were adjectives used to highlight a point (e.g. *dangerous* game)?
- ☐ Were capital letters where they should have been?
- ☐ Was punctuation correct?
- ☐ Was the spelling of words correct?
- ☐ Did the speech open with an appropriate greeting?

Practical suggestion: Ask yourself if you were convinced by the argument raised.

Marker's suggestions (optional)

WRITING (Real Test)
Persuasive text 2
Page 55

Tick each correct point.
Read the writer's work through once to get an overall view of their response.

Focus on general points
- ☐ Did it make sense?
- ☐ Did it flow?
- ☐ Did the opinions expressed arouse any feeling/ reaction?
- ☐ Did you want to read on to understand/appreciate the writer's point of view?
- ☐ Was the handwriting readable?

Now focus on the detail. Read the following points and find out whether the writer's work has these features.

Focus on content
- ☐ Was the purpose of the writing clearly introduced?
- ☐ Was there a clear statement of the writer's opinion?
- ☐ Were possible objections to the writer's opinion stated and refuted by logical argument or observations?
- ☐ Were the opinions expressed objectively?
- ☐ Was the original opinion clearly repeated? (optional)

Focus on structure, vocabulary, grammar, spelling and punctuation
- ☐ Were letter-writing conventions followed?
- ☐ Was there a variation in sentence length and beginnings?
- ☐ Were there clear paragraphs to separate various arguments or points (maybe a line space)?

☐ Were adjectives used to highlight a point
(e.g. *dangerous* game)?
☐ Were capital letters where they should have been?
☐ Was punctuation correct?
☐ Was the spelling of words correct?

Practical suggestion: Ask yourself if you were convinced by the argument raised.

Marker's suggestions (optional)

WRITING (Real Test)
Persuasive text 3   Page 56

Tick each correct point.
Read the writer's work through once to get an overall view of their response.

Focus on general points
☐ Did it make sense?
☐ Did it flow?
☐ Did the opinions expressed arouse any feeling/reaction?
☐ Did you want to read on to understand/appreciate the writer's point of view?
☐ Was the handwriting readable?

Now focus on the detail. Read the following points and find out whether the writer's work has these features.

Focus on content
☐ Was the purpose of the writing clearly introduced?
☐ Was there a clear statement of the writer's opinion?
☐ Were possible objections to the writer's opinion stated and refuted by logical argument or observations?
☐ Were the opinions expressed objectively?
☐ Was the original opinion clearly repeated? (optional)

Focus on structure, vocabulary, grammar, spelling and punctuation
☐ Was there a variation in sentence length and beginnings?
☐ Were there clear paragraphs to separate various arguments or points (maybe a line space)?
☐ Were adjectives used to highlight a point (e.g. *dangerous* game)?
☐ Were capital letters where they should have been?
☐ Was punctuation correct?
☐ Was the spelling of words correct?
☐ Did the speech open with an appropriate greeting?

Practical suggestion: Ask yourself if you were convinced by the argument raised.

Marker's suggestions (optional)

WRITING (Real Test)
Persuasive text 4   Page 57

Tick each correct point.
Read the writer's work through once to get an overall view of their response.

Focus on general points
☐ Did it make sense?
☐ Did it flow?
☐ Did the opinions expressed arouse any feeling/reaction?
☐ Did you want to read on to understand/appreciate the writer's point of view?
☐ Was the handwriting readable?

Now focus on the detail. Read the following points and find out whether the writer's work has these features.

Focus on content
☐ Was the purpose of the writing clearly introduced?
☐ Was there a clear statement of the writer's opinion?
☐ Were possible objections to the writer's opinion stated and refuted by logical argument or observations?
☐ Were the opinions expressed objectively?
☐ Was the original opinion clearly repeated? (optional)

Focus on structure, vocabulary, grammar, spelling and punctuation
☐ Was there a variation in sentence length and beginnings?
☐ Were there clear paragraphs to separate various arguments or points (maybe a line space)?
☐ Were adjectives used to highlight a point (e.g. *dangerous* game)?
☐ Were capital letters where they should have been?
☐ Was punctuation correct?
☐ Was the spelling of words correct?
☐ Did the speech open with an appropriate greeting?

Practical suggestion: Ask yourself if you were convinced by the argument raised.

Marker's suggestions (optional)

WEEK 3

MEASUREMENT AND GEOMETRY
(Real Test)   Pages 64–65
Units of measurement

1 A **2** 26 **3** B **4** C **5** C **6** A **7** D **8** C **9** Kim, Mia, Meg, Nora **10** B **11** D **12** B **13** D **14** 1250

EXPLANATIONS

1 From 3:35 until 4:00 is 25 minutes, because $60 - 35 = 25$.
From 4:00 until 4:04 is another 4 minutes.
$25 + 4 = 29$
So altogether Liz was on the train for 29 minutes.

2 The temperature shown is 26 degrees.

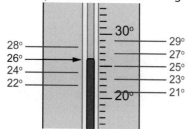

3 $100 \text{ cm} = 1 \text{ m}$
so $600 \text{ cm} = 6 \text{ m}$

4 3 October is a Thursday.

OCTOBER						
Sun	Mon	Tue	Wed	Thu	Fri	Sat
		1	2	3	4	5
6	7	8	9	10	11	12
13	14	15	16	17	18	19
20	21	22	23	24	25	26
27	28	29	30	31		

So we can fill in the days on the calendar.
26 October is a Saturday.

5 Mass is measured in kilograms. [Length is measured in metres, capacity in litres and time in seconds.]

6 The minute hand is pointing to 9 so it is 45 minutes after the hour. The hour hand is after 4. So the time is 4:45.

7 The end of the pencil is at 1 cm, which is the same as 10 mm. The tip of the pencil is at 88 mm. Now $88 - 10 = 78$.
So the pencil is 78 mm long.

8 One hour after 6:30 pm is 7:30 pm. A quarter of an hour, or 15 minutes, after that is 7:45 pm. So the movie finished at 7:45 pm.

9 Meg's ribbon is the longest, so Meg is the third girl. Kim's ribbon is longer than both Mia's and Nora's ribbons. So Kim is the first girl.
Mia has the shortest ribbon so she is second.

Kim   Mia   Meg   Nora

10 One minute is 60 seconds. So half a minute is 30 seconds.

11 These objects all appear as the lighter of two masses at one time. So the remaining object ⬭ must have the greatest mass. [In order from least to greatest mass the objects are ▱ ▭ ⬡ ⬭.]

12 A cup holds around 200 mL.

13 Some measurements are missing from the yard. The missing side measurement is $(3 + 6)$ metres or 9 metres.

The missing top measurement is $(12 - 7)$ metres or 5 metres.

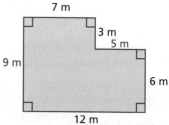

Now $7 + 3 + 5 + 6 + 12 + 9 = 42$
So the fence is 42 metres long.

14 2 litres is 2000 millilitres.
Now $2000 - 750 = 1250$
So 1250 millilitres remain in the bottle.

MEASUREMENT AND GEOMETRY
(Real Test)   Pages 70–71
Shape and angles

1 A **2** C **3** 18 **4** A **5** 120 **6** C **7** B
8 E, I, F, X, L **9** 18 **10** 40 **11** B **12** B

EXPLANATIONS

1 This is a cone.

2 The tiles could each have eight sides.
The tiles could have been octagons.

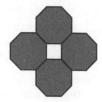

3 There would be 3 more rows of stickers and 6 stickers in each of those rows.
Now $3 \times 6 = 18$.
So 18 more stickers will fit on the paper.

4 The piece of cheese doesn't come to a point, so it is not like a pyramid. It has a triangular face at the top and at the bottom. It is most like a triangular prism.

5 The bottom layer will have 5×8 or 40 blocks.

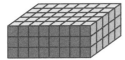

There will be 3 layers of blocks.
Now $3 \times 40 = 120$.
So altogether there will be 120 blocks in the box.

6 A right angle is a quarter of a turn.
So this is closest to a right angle.

7 The water tank is in the shape of a cylinder. A cylinder has circles at the top and bottom. When looking down at the top you will see a circle.

8 Count the squares for each letter:

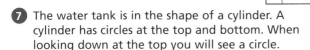

So, the letter E has the greatest area, followed by I, F, X and L.

9 The top view doesn't show the number of cubes, but the other view lets us see how high the cubes are in each position.

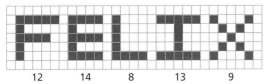

top view

The back row has $4 + 2 + 1 = 7$ cubes.
The second back row has $3 + 2 + 1 = 6$ cubes.
The middle row has 3 cubes and the front 2 rows both have just 1 cube.
Now $7 + 6 + 3 + 1 + 1 = 18$.
So there are 18 cubes altogether.

10 8 faces can be seen at the top so there will also be 8 faces on the bottom.
We can see 8 faces on the front, so there will be 8 faces on the back.
We can see 4 faces on the right side so there will be another 4 on the left side. These sides have a total of 8 faces together.
So there are 5 lots of 8 faces.
$5 \times 8 = 40$
So there are 40 faces altogether.

11 A square pyramid has one square face and the other faces are all triangles.

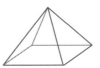

So there is 1 square and 4 triangles.

12 In the two pictures we can see the 4 faces next to the face with ●, but not the face opposite that one. That opposite face must have this symbol ✄.
In the first picture ✿ must be on the bottom.
So the face opposite ⊙ is ❖ .

SPELLING (Real Test)
Making adverbs, adding the suffix 'ful', and 'ie' and 'ei' words   Page 73

1 clearly   2 friendless   3 hopeful   4 cried
5 pitiful   6 dimly   7 fizzes   8 aircraft
9 kidneys   10 grief   11 merciful   12 cellar
13 complex   14 quickly   15 colourful
16 review   17 rescues   18 fiercely

EXPLANATIONS

1 The letter combinations *eer* and *ear* have the same sound. Get to know and use groups of words with *ear* spellings (e.g. spear, hear). Remember: You *hear* c*lear*ly with your *ear*.

2 *Friendless* is *friend* + *less*. *Friend* is a word that follows the '*i* before *e*' convention. Remember: You have a *friend* to the *end*.

3 When adding the suffix *ful* to a word it has only one *l*.

4 To add a suffix beginning with a vowel to a word ending with a consonant + *y* you change the *y* to *i* then add the suffix (e.g. try ➔ tried).

5 Two points to watch. When adding the suffix *ful* to a word it has only one *l*. If the word ends with a consonant + *y*, you change the *y* to *i* and add the suffix (e.g. beauty ➔ beautiful).

6 *Dimly* is *dim* + the suffix **ly**. Because *dim* ends in a consonant, and the suffix begins with a consonant, there is no need to double the **m** (**mm**).

7 The **zz** word ending is more common than the single **z** ending. Very few common words end with a single **z**. Examples of double z (**zz**) endings are *fizz, fuzz* and *buzz*.

8 This is a tricky word as *aircraft* is both singular and plural: *one aircraft* or *many aircraft*.

9 To make the plural form of a noun ending with a vowel + **y**, simply add **s** (e.g. valleys, trolleys).

10 *Grief* is a word that follows the '*i* before *e*' convention.

11 *Merciful* is *mercy* + **ful**. When a word ends with consonant + **y** change the **y** to **i** to add the suffix **ful** (e.g. pity ➔ pitiful). The suffix **ful** only has one **l**.

12 *Cellar* and *seller* are homonyms—words that sound the same but which have different meanings. A *seller* is a person who sells things. A *cellar* is a room under the house where things are stored. Make sure you use the words in the correct context.

13 *Ex* and *ecks* make a similar sound. Both sounds are in many words (e.g. apex/reflex; wrecks/necks). You will have to learn and remember such words.

14 *Quickly* is *quick* + **ly**. Make sure you have a **c** before the **k**. The **ck** ending is common.

15 *Colourful* is *colour* + **ful**. You may often see *colour* spelt as *color*. This is an American spelling which is not acceptable in Australia.

16 *Revue* and *review* are homonyms—words that sound the same but which are spelt differently. A *revue* is a fun musical stage show. A *review* is a report on something, often a movie or a book.

17 This is confusing **cue** with **que**. Both make the same sound. There are not many words ending with **cue** (e.g. rescue, barbecue). Try to remember which ones they are.

18 *Fiercely* is *fierce* + **ly**. You do not drop the **e** to add **ly**. *Fierce* is a word that follows the '*i* before *e*' convention.

GRAMMAR AND PUNCTUATION
(Real Test)   Pages 75–76
Verbs, tense and use of commas

1 B   **2** C   **3** D   **4** A   **5** store   **6** B   **7** D   **8** D
9 C   **10** A   **11** B   **12** C   **13** C   **14** A   **15** was
16 *The, Vampire*   **17** A   **18** B

EXPLANATIONS

1 Commas are used after introductory words in a sentence, often where someone is attracting attention.

2 Most adjectives of comparison simply add **er** and **est** for comparative adjectives (e.g. fast, faster, fastest). This doesn't happen with *good*. *Good* is used when describing one person. *Better* is used when comparing two people. *Best* is used when comparing more than two people. The comparison is between Charlie and other novelists as a single group.

3 *Write* is an irregular verb. Most verbs in English form their past tense by adding **ed** (e.g. he walked). Irregular verbs do not form their past tense this way. The past tense of *write* is the irregular verb *wrote* (not 'writed'). 'Writed' is not a word.

4 If the name of a roadway is shortened and still retains its last letter, no full stop is required (e.g. St —Street).

5 *Store* is a verb. It is what the drivers do. Don't be confused because *store* can also be a noun.

6 Writers use brackets to add information to a sentence without changing the meaning of the sentence. The words in brackets provide additional information for the reader.

7 The basic rule is that singular subjects (nouns) need singular verbs; plural subjects (nouns) need plural verbs. In this case *play* must be used because there are two people: *Sandy and Rocky. Sandy and Rocky* are the subject of the sentence—two people. Think of the sentence as: The two people *play*.

8 *Back* is unnecessary. It is a redundant word. *Refer* means 'check something that is already recorded'. No meaning is lost by omitting *back*.

9 *Which* is a pronoun used to refer to things. *But* is a conjunction indicating a point that may appear contrary to what has been stated.

10 This apostrophe indicates possession or ownership: they are his father's shoes. *His* is a possessive pronoun; *shoes, holes* and *soles* are plural nouns.

11 This is a tricky question. *That* is correct because it refers to a specific thing. It is emphasising a particular type of gem: ones *that sparkle. Which* is used for more general statements.

12 *Who's* is a contraction of *who is*. The sentence could be read as: Who is responsible? *Whose* is a pronoun.

13 A sentence has a verb (*laughs*) and a subject (*Sara*). None of the other options have a verb.

14 The response *"You've been in hospital!"* carries the implication of surprise because of the exclamation mark. It is important to know how various stops affect meaning.

15 Past tense is needed because the action has already happened. Remember: Singular subjects (nouns) need singular verbs; plural subjects (nouns) need plural verbs. In this case *was* must be used because there is only one kit (of tools). Think of the sentence as: *A kit … was removed.*

16 This is a punctuation question. Two words require capital letters. The correct words are *The* and *Vampire. The* is the first word in a sentence. *Vampire* is a proper noun—the name of a book.

17 Only the actual words spoken are in speech marks. The words spoken are broken to form two sentences: *This is my brother* and *He wants to join the team.* You will notice that the second sentence starts with a capital letter. It follows a full stop. The comma comes after *brother* and indicates a pause. It is inside the speech mark.

18 Use a comma to separate the items in a series of three or more things (or for a pause). This is a series of adjectives. Adjectives in series, unlike nouns, often do not require *and* between the last two adjectives.

READING (Test Your Skills)
Understanding descriptions
Page 77

Go to page 208 for a guide to question types.

School days
EXPLANATIONS

1 This is an **inferring type of question.** To find the answer you have to 'read between the lines'. You read that Mr Stark's announcements *usually meant new rules and how to obey them (see line 9)* and he *would often be seen sitting in his office 'dragging on a ciggie', and looking towards the ceiling. Dad reckons he was probably dreaming up new rules and devious ways to make the kids' school lives more miserable (see lines 18–20).* The narrator's father thought Mr Stark was spiteful and devious. *Spiteful* means 'unpleasant and nasty'. *Devious* means dreaming up 'skilful ways to use underhand tactics'.

2 This is a **fact-finding type of question.** The answer is a fact in the text. You read that *Of course, he smoked … It certainly helped to explain his BO (see lines 16–18). BO* are the initials for 'body odour'. Mr Stark's bad odour (smell) was most likely made worse by his smoking habit.

3 This is a **language type of question.** To find the answer you have to read the text carefully, especially the section that is quoted *"You think you've got it tough," Dad would say, with a far-off look (see line 21).* A far-off look is most often associated with someone thinking fondly of their past. They have pleasant memories.

4 This is an **inferring type of question.** To find the answer you have to 'read between the lines'. You read that Mr Stark would *look down on the class—and the class teacher (see line 8).* Some students called him Stinky *being very, very careful they weren't heard (see line 15).* The students would be cautious of Mr Stark. The repetition of the word *very* emphasises just how cautious they were.

5 This is a **fact-finding type of question.** The answer is a fact in the text. You read that *He wore a cardigan under his coat regardless of the weather … that had an effect on his smell (see lines 10–13).* Mr Stark's smoking contributed to his bad odour. He would often be seen *dragging on a ciggie* [cigarette] *(see line 18).* The narrator talks a lot about Mr Stark's smell.

READING (Real Test)
Understanding descriptions
Page 78

Careers
1 D **2** D **3** B **4** A **5** C **6** C **7** A
EXPLANATIONS

1 This is an **inferring type of question.** To find the answers you have to 'read between the lines'. You read the question *So you want to be a dog-trainer? (see line 2).* This text is a description of the duties of a dog trainer, a career, or an occupation that a person may take. It is not the description of a person or a dog.

2 This is a **fact-finding type of question.** The answer is a fact in the text. You read that *a dog trainer will teach a dog special ways to behave over several weeks (see lines 9–11).*

3 This is a **language type of question.** To find the answer you have to read the text carefully, especially the section that is quoted: *Dogs can be trained … as guides for people with impaired vision (see lines 2–6).* Combine this information with your own knowledge of problems people have with their eyes. *Impaired vision* is weak or damaged vision. *Impaired* means the eyes are not as good as they could be or once were.

4 This is a **fact-finding type of question.** The answer is a fact in the text. You read that *Training may have to cure a dog's bad habits, such as chasing cars, or barking too much (see line 17).*

5 This is a **judgement type of question.** You read that dogs can be trained to *help soldiers find bombs (see lines 2–4).* Combine this with your own knowledge of bombs. It is probably the most dangerous job for a dog. They could get killed.

6 This is a **fact-finding type of question.** The answer is a fact in the text. You read that *dogs are taught certain tasks by giving them rewards, such as small pieces of food (see line 19).*

7 This is a **language type of question.** To find the answer you have to read the text carefully, especially the section that is quoted: *They must be able to <u>master</u> these skills before advanced training can begin (see lines 15–16).* Then you combine this information with your own knowledge of how skills are acquired. If you *master* something, such as a skill, you know how to *do* it.

READING (Real Test)
Understanding recounts   Page 79

River meeting
1 C   2 He thought the island was uninhabited.
3 D   4 B   5 A   6 C

EXPLANATIONS

1 This is a **fact-finding type of question.** The answer is a fact in the text. The family landed on an unsettled place of the shore of an island *(line 3)*. Roko left this place one morning *(line 7)* to find a good place to settle.

2 This is a **fact-finding type of question.** The answer is a fact in the text. You read that *They thought the island was uninhabited (see line 4).*

3 This is a **language type of question.** To find the answer you have to read the text carefully, especially the section that is quoted: *They landed on the coast at a place called Vuda. They thought the island was uninhabited (see lines 3–4). Uninhabited* has a meaning similar to 'unpopulated'. *Uninhabited* means '**not** habitated—without habitants'.

4 This is a **fact-finding type of question.** The answer is a fact in the text. You read that *After some days he came to a wide river. The young man was hot and tired … He sat down (see lines 10–11).*

5 This is a **language type of question.** To find the answer you have to read the text carefully, especially the section that is quoted: *Standing up, he called out to the women but they could not hear him. Frustrated, he decided to resume his journey (see lines 20–22).* Combine this with your own knowledge of a feeling of frustration. A feeling of frustration is caused by being unable to do something. Even after trying very hard to call out to the women they didn't hear Roko's calls.

6 This is a **fact-finding type of question.** The answer is a fact in the text. You read that *While he was resting he was surprised to see some women fishing (see lines 15–16).*

READING (Real Test)
Understanding poetry   Page 80

The dog next door
1 B   2 A   3 A   4 C   5 D   6 B

EXPLANATIONS

1 This is a **fact-finding type of question.** The answer is a fact in the poem. You read that *There are many good reasons for owning a pet … / But the most common reason for those that I've met, / Seems just to annoy the neighbours (see lines 2–5).*

2 This is a **fact-finding type of question.** The answer is a fact in the poem. You read that *The owners go off to work each day / … Who quickly get tired of their solitary play, / So they bark and annoy the neighbours! (see lines 6–9).*

3 This is a **language type of question.** To find the answer you have to read the poem carefully, especially the section is quoted: *The owners go off to work each day / … Who quickly get tired of their solitary play (see lines 6–8).* Combine this with your own knowledge of how the pet must feel when there is no one in the house. *Solitary play* means 'playing by yourself—without company'.

4 This is a **fact-finding type of question.** The answer is a fact in the poem. You read the last line of each verse (except the last) which mentions how the dogs annoy the neighbours: *So they bark and annoy the neighbours! (see line 9)* and *'though it certainly upsets the neighbours! (see line 13)*

5 This is a **fact-finding type of question.** The answer is a fact in the poem. You read *They're supposed to guard and protect the house / Scaring intruders away. / But their yapping would hardly scare a mouse (see lines 10–12).*

6 This is a **fact-finding type of question.** The answer is a fact in the poem. You read *So if you have a dog, keep it under control / Take it walking, and teach it good manners (see lines 18–19).*

READING (Real Test)
Understanding timetables   Page 81

Indian Pacific train timetable
1 B   2 3   3 1, 4, 3, 2   4 A   5 D   6 B   7 4

EXPLANATIONS

1 This is a **fact-finding type of question.** The answer is a fact in the timetable in the text. In column three you can read that the trip from Sydney to Perth is over three days: Wednesday, Thursday and Friday. In the text you read *The Indian Pacific, which travels between the west coast and east coast on a three-day, 4352-km trek across Australia (see lines 2–3).*

2 This is a **fact-finding type of question.** The answer is a fact on the map. The trip passes through three states. This is shown on the map and indicated on the timetable in column 1. The states are: New South Wales, South Australia, Western Australia.

3 This a **fact-finding** and **sequencing type of question.** The correct order is Broken Hill (1), Adelaide (2), Cook (3), Kalgoorlie (4).

4 This is a **language type of question.** To find the answer you have to read the text carefully, especially the section that is quoted: *The three-day trip takes passengers through a wide variety of Australian landscapes (see lines 4–5).* Combine this with your own knowledge of what you might see on a long train trip. The word *landscapes* refers to the countryside. The train passes through much countryside. It includes a lot that can be seen at one time.

5 This is an **inferring type of question.** To find the answer you have to 'read between the lines'. You can see where the line starts and finishes. The purpose of the map is to show the route taken by the *Indian Pacific.* A small map gives no indication of size or distance. Other than Adelaide, none of the stops are shown.

6 This is an **inferring type of question.** To find the answer you have to 'read between the lines'. You read that the trip is a *4352-km trek across Australia (see line 3).* Combine this information with your own knowledge of how long it would take to travel thousands of kilometres. The journey takes so long because it's a long way from Sydney to Perth, in fact, 4352 km.

7 This is a **fact-finding type of question.** The answer is a fact in the text. You read that *the train departs Sydney every Wednesday and Saturday. The return journeys from Perth depart Saturdays and Wednesdays (see lines 7–8).* There are four trips between the two cities: two going to Perth and two returning to Sydney.

WRITING (Real Test)
Recount 1
Page 84

Tick each correct point.
Read the writer's work through once to get an overall view of their response.

Focus on general points
☐ Did it make sense?
☐ Did it flow?
☐ Did the events arouse any feeling?
☐ Did you want to read on? (Were the events interesting?)
☐ Was the handwriting readable?

Now focus on the detail. Read the following points and find out whether the writer's work has these features.

Focus on content
☐ Did the opening sentence(s) introduce the subject of the recount?
☐ Was the setting established, i.e. when and where the action took place?
☐ Was the reader told when the action takes place?
☐ Was it apparent who the main characters(s) is/are?
☐ Have personal pronouns been used (e.g. I, we, our)?
☐ Were the events recorded in chronological (time) order?
☐ Was the recount in past tense?
☐ Did the writing include some personal comments on the events (e.g. surprised, thrilled)?
☐ Did descriptions make reference to any of the senses (e.g. wet rocks, salty air)?
☐ Were interesting details included?
☐ Did the conclusion have a satisfactory summing-up comment?

Focus on structure, vocabulary, grammar, spelling, punctuation
☐ Was there a variation in sentence length and beginnings?
☐ Was there a new paragraph started for changes in time, place or action?
☐ Were subheadings used? (optional)
☐ Were adjectives used to improve descriptions (e.g. *smelly* bait)?
☐ Were adverbs used to make 'actions' more interesting (e.g. yelled *loudly*)?
☐ Were adverbs used for time changes (e.g. later, soon, then)?
☐ Were capital letters where they should have been?
☐ Was punctuation correct?
☐ Was the spelling of words correct?

Marker's suggestions (optional)

WRITING (Real Test)
Recount 2
Page 85

Tick each correct point.
Read the writer's work through once to get an overall view of their response.

Focus on general points
☐ Did it make sense?
☐ Did it flow?
☐ Did the events arouse any feeling?

☐ Did you want to read on? (Were the events interesting?)

☐ Was the handwriting readable?

Now focus on the detail. Read the following points and find out whether the writer's work has these features.

Focus on content

☐ Did the opening sentence(s) introduce the subject of the recount?

☐ Was the setting established, i.e. when and where the action took place?

☐ Was the reader told when the action takes place?

☐ Was it apparent who the main characters(s) is/are?

☐ Have personal pronouns been used (e.g. I, we, our)?

☐ Were the events recorded in chronological (time) order?

☐ Was the recount in past tense?

☐ Did the writing include some personal comments on the events (e.g. feeling cold, disappointed)?

☐ Did descriptions make reference to any of the senses (e.g. loud commentary, blue water)?

☐ Were interesting details included?

☐ Did the conclusion have a satisfactory summing-up comment?

Focus on structure, vocabulary, grammar, spelling, punctuation

☐ Was there a variation in sentence length and beginnings?

☐ Was there a new paragraph started for changes in time, place or action?

☐ Were subheadings used? (optional)

☐ Were adjectives used to improve descriptions (e.g. *frozen* ground)?

☐ Were adverbs used to make 'actions' more interesting (e.g. swam *strongly*)?

☐ Were adverbs used for time changes (e.g. later, soon, then)?

☐ Were capital letters where they should have been?

☐ Was punctuation correct?

☐ Was the spelling of words correct?

Marker's suggestions (optional)

WRITING (Real Test)
Description 1   Page 87

Tick each correct point.
Read the writer's work through once to get an overall view of their response.

Focus on general points

☐ Did it make sense?

☐ Did it flow?

☐ Did the description arouse the reader's interest?

☐ Did you want to read on to understand more about the place or scene?

☐ Was the handwriting readable?

Now focus on the detail. Read the following points and find out whether the writer's work has these features.

Focus on content

☐ Is the general scene and basic location clearly stated?

☐ Has the writer provided some physical description of the scene or landscape?

☐ Is the description broken up into parts (e.g. sea, sand, cliffs)?

☐ Has the writer tried to put the scene in a time frame (e.g. a late autumn day)?

(optional)

☐ Is relevant detail included (e.g. soft, golden sand)?

☐ Does the language create clear pictures?

☐ Does the writer make reference to reactions to the scene through several senses (e.g. cool water)?

☐ Does the writer convey any feelings created by the scene?

☐ Is there a concluding comment, opinion or reaction to the scene?

Focus on structure, vocabulary, grammar, spelling, punctuation

☐ Is the description written in present tense?

☐ Is there variation in sentence lengths and beginnings?

☐ Are there paragraphs separating different aspects of the scene?

☐ Has the writer used any similes (e.g. as clear as glass)?

☐ Is there a generous use of adjectives to enhance the writing (e.g. *cool, shady* grass)?

☐ Are adverbs used effectively (e.g. lying *lazily* on the sand)?

☐ Are capital letters used correctly?

☐ Is the punctuation correct?

☐ Is the spelling of words correct?

Practical suggestion: ask yourself if you can visualise the scene.

Marker's suggestions (optional)

WRITING (Real Test)
Description 2   Page 88

Tick each correct point.
Read the writer's work through once to get an overall view of their response.

Focus on general points
- ☐ Did it make sense?
- ☐ Did it flow?
- ☐ Did the description arouse the reader's interest?
- ☐ Did you want to read on to understand more about the person or animal?
- ☐ Was the handwriting readable?

Now focus on the detail. Read the following points and find out whether the writer's work has these features.

Focus on content
- ☐ Has the character to be described been established?
- ☐ Has the writer provided some physical description of the person?
- ☐ Is the description broken up into parts (e.g. appearance, mannerisms, age, interests)?
- ☐ Is relevant detail included (e.g. hair colour)?
- ☐ Does the language create clear pictures?
- ☐ Does the writer make reference to reactions to the person through several senses (e.g. wiry hair, soft skin)?
- ☐ Does the writer convey any feelings about the character?
- ☐ Is there a concluding comment, opinion or reaction to the character (can be reflective)?

Focus on structure, vocabulary, grammar, spelling, punctuation
- ☐ Is the description written in present tense?
- ☐ Is there variation in sentence lengths and beginnings?
- ☐ Are there paragraphs separating different aspects of the character?
- ☐ Has the writer used any similes (e.g. as thin as a rake)?
- ☐ Is there a generous use of adjectives to enhance the writing (e.g. *long, bony* fingers)?
- ☐ Are adverbs used effectively (e.g. smiled *happily*)?
- ☐ Are capital letters used correctly?
- ☐ Is the punctuation correct?
- ☐ Is the spelling of words correct?

Practical suggestion: ask yourself if you can visualise the scene.

Marker's suggestions (optional)

WEEK 4

MEASUREMENT AND GEOMETRY (Real Test)
Location, transformations and geometric reasoning   Pages 95–96

1 B, E   2 B   3 A   4 B   5 B   6 A   7 A   8 C
9 C   10 D

EXPLANATIONS

1 The shapes in B and E cannot be folded in two so that the two halves match exactly. So they have no lines of symmetry.

2 The counter moves left one square to B3 and then up two squares to B5.

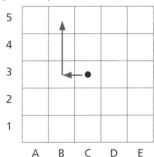

3 The shape turns a quarter of a turn clockwise.

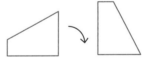

4 In the top row, bolts are on the right. Second from the right in the top row are nuts.

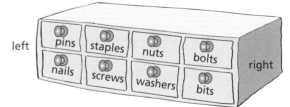

5 When flipped over the dotted line, the shape will be upside down.

6 Bill's room is 303.

301	Stairs	302	303 ↑	304	305
310	309	308	307	Lift	306

7 The arrow shows the direction of north. So the seating area is north of the house.
The pool is west of the house.

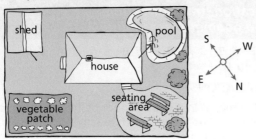

8 River Rd and Bunyip Rd meet in square E3.

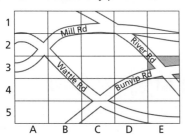

9 Imagine the completed pattern.

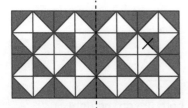

Sara should colour the square like this .

10 From the shop the customer will need to go left into Main Rd and then turn right into Bay Rd.

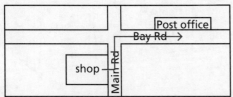

STATISTICS AND PROBABILITY
(Real Test)
Chance and data
Pages 101–102

1 D **2** B **3** 472 **4** 6 **5** A **6** B **7** A **8** C
9 C, E **10** D

EXPLANATIONS

1 The tally marks for brown eyes are 𝍷𝍷𝍷𝍷𝍷 ||||
This means 1 lot of 5 plus 4.
Now 5 + 4 = 9. So, 9 students had brown eyes.

2 There are red, white and blue balloons in the packet, but no green. It is impossible to take a green balloon from the packet.

3 Ben has 512 sheep and 40 goats.
Now 512 − 40 = 472.
So Ben has 472 more sheep than goats.

4 There are 3 symbols for *Mattie*. The key tells us that each symbol means 2 students.
Now 3 × 2 = 6.
So 6 students chose *Mattie*.

5 The spinner that has the largest sector of red on it is more likely to stop on red. This spinner is most likely to stop on red.

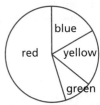

6 If Frances takes a red jellybean and eats it there are now 3 jellybeans left in the dish. One jellybean is red, one is white and one is black. So Alex is more likely to get a jellybean that is not red than one that is red. The chance of getting a red jellybean could be described as unlikely.

7 From the graph we can see that John took 7 wickets. Now 3 more than 7 is 10.
The boy who took 10 wickets is James.
So James is the boy who took 3 more wickets than John.

8 It doesn't matter what happened in the rolls before. In any roll of the dice there are many more chances of getting a number that is not 6 than of getting a 6. So the dice is unlikely to show 6 on the next roll.

9 From the graph we can see that Emily won 13 badges, Rose won 16, Max won 7 and Dan 10.

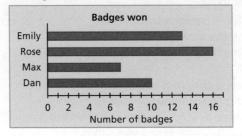

So Emily won fewer badges than Rose.
Max won fewer badges than Emily.
Dan won fewer badges than Emily.
Rose won more badges than Dan.
Dan won more badges than Max.
The true statements are 'Dan won fewer badges than Emily.' and 'Dan won more badges than Max.'

10 There must be one tile from each box. Consider the options:

■○△⬡ has no tiles from the last box.

●■▭▱ has no tiles from the third box.

◤⬡■△ has no tiles from the last box.

▱◤⬡■ has tiles from every box, so this is the correct option.

SPELLING (Real Test)
Adding suffixes to words ending in y; homonyms and demons
Page 104

1 uniform **2** sleeveless **3** careful **4** sign
5 tough **6** fourteen **7** here **8** tomorrow
9 highway **10** pear **11** right **12** sunny
13 nouns **14** film **15** tunic **16** gluing
17 throat **18** Which

EXPLANATIONS

1 Make sure you pronounce the word correctly. *Uniform* is *uni–form*. **Uni** is a prefix meaning 'one' (e.g. unicycle).

2 *Sleeveless* is *sleeve* + the suffix *less* (meaning 'without').

3 When adding the suffix **ful** to a word it only has one *l*.

4 *Sign* has a silent **g**. A silent **g** often comes before an **n** (e. g. reign, gnat, gnome).

5 *Tough* is an **ough** word. These words have to be learned and remembered. Other **ough** words include *rough* and *enough*. 'Tuff' is a fun spelling of the word.

6 *Fourteen* is a compound word: *four* + *teen*. *Fore* and *four* are homonyms—words that sound the same but which are spelt differently. *Four* is the number four (4). *Fourteen* is 14. *Fore* means 'at the front'.

7 *Here* and *hear* are homonyms—words that sound the same but which are spelt differently. **Hear** is what you do with your **ear**. *Here* means 'this place'. Learn to use the words in their correct context.

8 *Tomorrow* is *to* + *morrow*. *Morrow* has a double **r** (**rr**). Double **r** is common in many similar two-syllable words (e.g. horror, barrow).

9 *Highway* is a compound word: *high* + *way*. *Hi* is a fun or short way to spell *high* but is incorrect spelling in that context.

10 *Pear* and *pair* are homonyms—words that sound the same but which are spelt differently. *Pear* is the fruit. *Pair* means 'two of the same thing'. Learn to use the words in their correct context.

11 *Right* and *write* are homonyms—words that sound the same but which are spelt differently. *Right* means 'correct'. *Write* is what you do with a pen or pencil. Learn to use the words in their correct context.

12 *Sunny* and *Sonny* are homonyms—words that sound the same but which are spelt differently. *Sunny* refers to the weather. *Sonny* is a friendly name for a young boy. Learn to use the words in their correct context.

13 *Ou* and *ow* can make the same sound. Both sounds are in many words (e.g. count/cloud and brown/town). You will have to learn and remember such words.

14 Many people incorrectly say 'fil-um'. Make sure you pronounce the word correctly.

15 *Chu* and *tu* are sounds that can be easily confused. *Tunic* is a common school word you should remember. Other **tu** words include *tulip*, *tuba* and *tunes*.

16 Many words that end with **ue** drop the **e** before adding the suffix **ing** (e.g. arguing, issuing).

17 *Ote* and *oat* can make the same sound. Both sounds are in many words (e.g. wrote/note; coat/float). You will have to learn and remember such words.

18 *Which* and *witch* are homonyms—words that sound the same but which are spelt differently. A *witch* is an imaginary evil woman. *Which* is often used to begin a question. It has a silent **h** after the **w**. Learn to use the words in their correct context.

GRAMMAR AND PUNCTUATION (Real Test)
Pronouns, prepositions and adverbs; apostrophes and commas
Pages 106–107

1 B **2** D **3** A **4** A **5** joke **6** C **7** C **8** wet
9 D **10** purposely, cheerfully, never **11** A **12** C
13 B **14** B **15** D **16** A **17** C **18** D

EXPLANATIONS

1 The comma indicates a pause. It is inside the speech marks (quotation marks).

2 Pronouns stand for nouns. They save speakers from continually repeating the noun.

3 *We'd* is a shortened word (contraction) for *we would*. The letters **woul** have been replaced with an apostrophe.

4 *Slowly* is an adverb adding meaning to the verb. It tells how Gerry ran. Adverbs often end in *ly*. *Slow* and *slowest* are adjectives.

5 *Joke* is a common noun. A clue is in the indefinite article (a) that precedes the word: *a joke*. It is something that can be heard. *Gaylene* is a proper noun.

6 Pronouns stand for nouns. They save speakers from continually repeating the noun. *His* is a possessive pronoun. *He's* is a contraction of *he is* and is incorrect in this context.

7 The basic rule is singular subjects (nouns) need singular verbs and plural subjects (nouns) need plural verbs. In this case, *mixes* must be used because Omar is one person.

8 *Wet* is unnecessary. It is a redundant word. *Rain* is water which is obviously *wet*. No meaning is lost by omitting *wet*.

9 *It's* is a shortened word (contraction) of *it is*. The letter *i* has been replaced with an apostrophe.

10 This is a grammar question. Adverbs modify other words, expressing manner, place, time or degree. Most end with the prefix *ly* but not all (*never*).

11 *It* is a pronoun and stands in place of a noun. *Our new car* is the subject of the first sentence in this short paragraph. The car is still the subject in the next sentence. *It* saves repeating the words *Our new car*.

12 *Who's* is a shortened word (contraction) of *who is*. The letter *i* has been left out. It has been replaced with an apostrophe.

13 Questions usually expect an answer. This question can be answered. Not all sentences that start with *How* are asking questions.

14 The comma after *stated* indicates a pause before the actual words spoken are quoted.

15 An exclamation sentence is one that is often said suddenly through surprise, anger or excitement.

16 Singular subjects (nouns) need singular verbs; plural subjects (nouns) need plural verbs. In this case, *provide* must be used because *twins* refer to more than one person.

17 There are two distinct parts joined by a conjunction (because). The first part has the subject (the machine) and a verb (stopped) that relates to it. In the second part the subject again is *the machine* represented by *it*. The verb is *ran*. The other options become confusing.

18 *She* is a personal pronoun referring to *princess*. *She* is correct because it is the subject of the sentence. (*Her* is used as the object of a sentence.) There is only one princess. *They* is incorrect.

READING (Test Your Skills)
Understanding legends   Page 108

Go to **page 208** for a guide to question types.

The story of Muyim
EXPLANATIONS

1 This is a **language type of question.** To find the answer you have to read the whole text carefully, especially the introduction *A long time ago there was a young man and a young woman* (see lines 2–4). Then you combine it with your own knowledge of text types. A legend is a narrative and a traditional way of explaining something that can be observed, especially in nature. It is presented as history but is unlikely to be true.

2 This is a **fact-finding type of question.** The answer is a fact in the text. You read that *an evil spirit lived there who became very jealous of the young man the woman loved. The evil spirit decided to take the woman for himself* (see lines 12–18).

3 This is a **fact-finding type of question.** The answer is a fact in the text. You read that a bulrush will *bend in the gentle wind* (see line 40). A bulrush has tall thin stems that bend in the breeze. Yimbin was turned into a bulrush.

4 This is a **language type of question.** To find the answer you have to read the text carefully, especially the section that is quoted: *The young man felt great heartache at the loss of his companion* (see lines 23–24). Then you combine it with your own knowledge of how you might feel if you lost something you really liked. A person who has heartache is a grieving person. They feel grief.

5 This is a **fact-finding type of question.** The answer is a fact in the text. You read that the evil spirit *turned her into a blue flowering waterlily called Muyim. Keeping her this way he would always be reminded of her beauty* (see lines 20–22).

6 This is a **language type of question.** To find the answer you have to read the text carefully, especially the section that is quoted: *the evil spirit, seeing the forlorn young man searching day after day for his companion, finally felt sorry for him* (see lines 29–31). Then you combine it with your own knowledge of synonyms. A synonym is another word with a very similar meaning. A suitable synonym for *forlorn* is *sad*.

READING (Real Test)
Understanding legends — Page 109

The legend of Devota
1 D 2 B 3 A 4 A 5 C 6 B

EXPLANATIONS

1 This is a **fact-finding type of question.** The answer is a fact in the text. You read that Devota was tortured in jail *because of their faith (see line 6):* her Christian belief. Christians were persecuted by the Roman administration. *Faith* refers to a religious belief. Devota was a *young Christian woman (see line 7).*

2 This is a **fact-finding type of question.** The answer is a fact in the text. You read that *Each year, on 27 January … The royal family burns a fishing boat (see lines 20–21).*

3 This is a **fact-finding type of question.** The answer is a fact in the text. You read that *Unfortunately, a storm overtook the boat. Then, a dove … guided the boat to Monaco on the French coast where it ran aground (see lines 14–15).* Devota's body ended up in Monaco because her boat was blown off course. It did not go to Africa.

4 This is a **language type of question.** To find the answer you have to read the text carefully, especially the section that is quoted: *Diocletian … persecuted the Christians because of their faith (see lines 5–6).* Devota was *imprisoned and tortured (see line 8).* Combine this information with your own knowledge of prison conditions and torture to understand that a persecuted believer could be treated unfairly and very badly because of their religion.

5 This is a **fact-finding type of question.** The answer is a fact in the text. You read that 27 January is important because it is the day (or close to) when Devota's body originally arrived in Monaco: her boat *ran aground on a day which is close to the present 27 January (see lines 15–16).*

6 This is a **language type of question.** To find the answer you have to read the text carefully, especially the section that is quoted: *the dove … guided the boat to Monaco on the French coast where it ran aground (see lines 14–16).* Combine this information with your own knowledge to understand that the boat sailed into shallow water and got stuck. It became stranded and couldn't go any further.

READING (Real Test)
Understanding procedures — Page 110

How to make a spaghetti pie
1 C 2 D 3 A 4 B 5 A 6 D

EXPLANATIONS

1 This is a **language type of question.** To find the answer you have to read the text carefully, especially the headings *How to make a spaghetti pie (see line 1)* and *Things you'll need (see line 3).* Combine this information with your own knowledge of recipes *(see line 6).* A recipe is the instructions for preparing/cooking a meal. It is a procedure. Procedures explain how to do something. Recipes are a very common form of procedure. The *How to* in the title is an obvious clue.

2 This is a **language type of question.** To find the answer you have to read the text carefully, especially the section that is quoted *This is a very easy and delicious dish to make (see line 2).* The adjective *delicious* is a clue. *Dish* can have many meanings. In the sentence it is used to mean food prepared for eating. It is a *delicious* dish.

3 This is an **inferring type of question.** To find the answer you have to 'read between the lines'. You read that the items included in a box on the right of the list are *bowl, spoon, pan* and *plate (see lines 3–6).* Combine this with your own knowledge of the difference between food and non-food items. The items in the second list are non-food items.

4 This is a **fact-finding type of question.** The answer is a fact in the text. You read *Heat the olive oil in the frying pan (see line 17).* The spaghetti mixture is cooked in the heated oil. The oil is not intended as an ingredient.

5 This is an **inferring type of question.** To find the answer you have to 'read between the lines'. You read *Do not drop the plate! (see line 22).* The words are meant as a warning. This is part of the preparation where the cook has to be very careful. A dropped plate could mean a smashed plate and spoiled food. A clue that this is a warning is the writer's use of the exclamation mark!

6 This is an **inferring type of question.** To find the answer you have to 'read between the lines'. You read the writer's statement: *This is a very easy and delicious dish to make (see line 2).* Combine this with your own knowledge of how people describe food. The writer is quite enthusiastic about the dish. The writer calls it a *delicious* dish and states that it is a *fun way to use leftover spaghetti (see line 12).* The writer finishes up with the words: *This is great as a snack or a meal (see lines 24–25).*

How does a match work?

1 A **2** glass powder **3** D **4** D **5** C **6** C

EXPLANATIONS

1 This is a **language type of question.** To find the answer you have to read the text carefully, especially the section that is quoted: *A safety match can only ignite when it is struck against the striking surface on the side of a matchbox (see lines 8–9).* Combine this with your own knowledge of how a match is used. The word *ignite* means 'to catch on fire'. There are clues in the text that mention flame and fire.

2 This is a **fact-finding type of question.** The answer is a fact in the text. If you read the text carefully you will see that the match head *contains … glass powder (see line 11)*, as does the side of the matchbox: *striking surface is made of … glass powder (see lines 9–10).*

3 This is an **inferring type of question.** To find the answer you have to 'read between the lines'. You read that *Rub your hands together … You feel the warmth that the rubbing makes (see lines 2–3).* You have to read the text carefully and relate facts in the first paragraph to other points in the text: *When a match is struck on the striking surface of its box, the friction caused by the glass powder on both surfaces produces enough heat (see lines 13–15)* to start a flame. The powdered glass and sand make the surfaces rougher creating more friction heat when rubbed together.

4 This is a **fact-finding type of question.** The answer is a fact in the text. You read that a *safety match can only ignite when it is struck against the striking surface on the side of the matchbox (see lines 8–9).*

5 This is a **fact-finding type of question.** The answer is a fact in the text. By reading the text carefully you will identify the correct order of events. The last thing to catch on fire is *the matchwood (see line 18).* It only ignites after the sulphur has burst into flame.

6 This is a **language type of question.** To find the answer you have to read the text carefully, especially the section that is quoted: *the two different types of matches work—safety matches and 'strike anywhere' matches (see lines 5-7).* Combine this with your own knowledge of literary techniques. A literary technique is used to add impact to a point being made by the writer. This dash (—) is used to quickly add additional information for the reader, the two match types.

Tricia's report

1 A **2** B **3** 3, 1, 2, 4 **4** C **5** D **6** A

EXPLANATIONS

1 This is a **fact-finding type of question.** The answer is a fact in the text. You read that to get to the top of the hill, the family *took the lift (see line 9).*

2 This is a **fact-finding type of question.** The answer is a fact in the text. You read that the family did not see the waterfall lit up at night. Tricia writes *I'd love to … see the waterfall flooded in light, but we didn't do that (see line 18).*

3 This is a **fact-finding and sequencing type of question.** The correct order is: played in a playground (1), looked at ruins (2), visited a cemetery (3) and found a waterfall (4).

4 This is a **fact-finding type of question.** The answer is a fact in the text. You read that the waterfall was found by accident. Tricia writes *Imagine my surprise when we discovered a huge waterfall (see lines 15–16).*

5 This is an **inferring type of question.** To find the answer you have to 'read between the lines'. You read that Castle Hill *is the best place to get a view of Nice (see lines 6–7)* and *we were soon in an area of grassy, shady parks and a playground where we had a play (see lines 10–11)* and *Imagine my surprise when we discovered a huge waterfall (see lines 15–16).* Combine this with your own knowledge of exploring new places and you will decide that the best word to describe the visit to the park at Colline du Chateau is *enjoyable. Exciting* is too strong for a visit to a park and a cemetery.

6 This is an **inferring type of question.** To find the answer you have to 'read between the lines'. You read that when at the cemetery *Mum laughed and said the people there had the best views of anybody! (see lines 13–14).* Mum laughed because the people that were there permanently were all dead and in the ground. They couldn't enjoy the view. Mum was making a joke.

Tick each correct point.
Read the writer's work through once to get an overall view of their response.

Focus on general points
☐ Did it make sense?
☐ Did it flow?

☐ Did the procedure seem clear?
☐ Was the handwriting readable?

Now focus on the detail. Read the following points and find out whether the writer's work has these features.

Focus on content
☐ Does the title clearly advise the reader of the topic?
☐ Is the goal/aim of the writing clearly presented in the first sentences?
☐ Is the equipment to be used listed and/or briefly described?
☐ Is there some advice on what NOT to do? (optional)
☐ Is there some advice on the topic chosen?
☐ Are the steps listed in sequence (can be numbered) and each one on a new line?
☐ Is the instruction in each step clear?
☐ Are the main sections readily defined or spaced and do any headings stand out?
☐ Have helpful tips or suggestions been included?
☐ Has a last comment or suggestion been included?
☐ Were interesting details included?
☐ Did the conclusion have a satisfactory summing-up comment?

Focus on structure, vocabulary, grammar, spelling, punctuation
☐ Are sentences short and clear?
☐ Were subheadings used? (optional)
☐ Are action verbs used to start most steps (e.g. make, lift, speak)?
☐ Were adverbs used to describe how to carry out actions (e.g. talk *clearly*)?
☐ Were capital letters where they should have been?
☐ Was punctuation correct?
☐ Was the spelling of words correct?

Practical suggestion: follow the steps as written and see if the explanation really works.

Marker's suggestions (optional)

WRITING (Real Test)
Procedure 2
Page 116

Tick each correct point.
Read the writer's work through once to get an overall view of their response.

Focus on general points
☐ Did it make sense?
☐ Did it flow?
☐ Did the procedure seem clear?
☐ Was the handwriting readable?

Now focus on the detail. Read the following points and find out whether the writer's work has these features.

Focus on content
☐ Does the title clearly advise the reader of the topic?
☐ Is the goal/aim of the writing clearly presented in the first sentences?
☐ Is the equipment to be used listed and/or briefly described?
☐ Is there some advice on what NOT to do? (optional)
☐ Is there some advice on the topic chosen?
☐ Are the steps listed in sequence (can be numbered) and each one on a new line?
☐ Is the instruction in each step clear?
☐ Are the main sections readily defined or spaced and do any headings stand out?
☐ Have helpful tips or suggestions been included?
☐ Has a last comment or suggestion been included?
☐ Were interesting details included?
☐ Did the conclusion have a satisfactory summing-up comment?

Focus on structure, vocabulary, grammar, spelling, punctuation
☐ Are sentences short and clear?
☐ Were subheadings used? (optional)
☐ Are action verbs used to start most steps (e.g. make, lift, speak)?
☐ Were adverbs used to describe how to carry out actions (e.g. talk *clearly*)?
☐ Were capital letters where they should have been?
☐ Was punctuation correct?
☐ Was the spelling of words correct?

Practical suggestion: follow the steps as written and see if the explanation really works.

Marker's suggestions (optional)

WRITING (Real Test)
Explanation 1
Page 118

Tick each correct point.
Read the writer's work through once to get an overall view of their response.

Focus on general points
☐ Did it make sense?
☐ Did it flow?
☐ Did the writing and subject arouse the reader's interest?
☐ Did you want to read on?
☐ Was the handwriting readable?

Now focus on the detail. Read the following points and find out whether the writer's work has these features.

Focus on content

☐ Do the introductory sentences clearly identify (and define) the subject?

☐ Are the features of the subject precisely described (colour, size, shape, etc.)?

☐ Does the information sound factual?

☐ Are the uses of the subject explained?

☐ Is there any information explaining specific or unusual instances of use? (optional)

☐ Does the writer suggest who would use the item selected?

☐ Does the writer give a concluding comment, opinion or personal judgement of the subject?

Focus on structure, vocabulary, grammar, spelling, punctuation

☐ Is there variation in sentence lengths and beginnings?

☐ Have 'longer' sentences been used (including multiple clauses beginning with words such as *so, because, when* and *if*)?

☐ Are the sections broken up into clear paragraphs?

☐ Are the paragraphs based on single topics (e.g. shape, colour, how to use, etc.)?

☐ Have subheadings been used? (optional)

☐ Have technical or scientific (correct) words been used?

☐ Is the explanation written in the present tense?

☐ Are adjectives used to enhance the writing (e.g. *colourful* pattern)?

☐ Are capital letters used correctly?

☐ Is the punctuation correct?

☐ Is the spelling of words correct?

Practical suggestion: ask yourself if this explanation provides enough information for you to use the object or draw a picture of it.

Marker's suggestions (optional)

WRITING (Real Test)
Explanation 2   Page 119

Tick each correct point.
Read the writer's work through once to get an overall view of their response.

Focus on general points

☐ Did it make sense?

☐ Did it flow?

☐ Did the writing and subject arouse the reader's interest?

☐ Did you want to read on?

☐ Was the handwriting readable?

Now focus on the detail. Read the following points and find out whether the writer's work has these features.

Focus on content

☐ Do the introductory sentences clearly identify (and define) the subject?

☐ Are the features of the subject precisely described (colour, size, shape, etc.)?

☐ Does the information sound factual?

☐ Are the uses of the subject explained?

☐ Is there any information explaining specific or unusual instances of use? (optional)

☐ Does the writer suggest who would use the item selected?

☐ Does the writer give a concluding comment, opinion or personal judgement of the subject?

Focus on structure, vocabulary, grammar, spelling, punctuation

☐ Is there variation in sentence lengths and beginnings?

☐ Have 'longer' sentences been used (including multiple clauses beginning with words such as *so, because, when* and *if*)?

☐ Are the sections broken up into clear paragraphs?

☐ Are the paragraphs based on single topics (e.g. shape, colour, how to use, etc.)?

☐ Have subheadings been used? (optional)

☐ Have technical or scientific (correct) words been used?

☐ Is the explanation written in the present tense?

☐ Are adjectives used to enhance the writing (e.g. *colourful* pattern)?

☐ Are capital letters used correctly?

☐ Is the punctuation correct?

☐ Is the spelling of words correct?

Practical suggestion: ask yourself if this explanation provides enough information for you to use the object or draw a picture of it.

Marker's suggestions (optional)

SAMPLE TEST PAPERS
SAMPLE TEST 1

LITERACY—WRITING — Page 122

Tick each correct point.
Read the writer's work through once to get an overall view of their response.

Focus on general points

☐ Did it make sense?
☐ Did it flow?
☐ Did the story arouse any feeling?
☐ Did you want to read on? Did the story create any suspense?
☐ Was the handwriting readable?

Now focus on the detail. Read the following points and find out whether the writer's work has these features.

Focus on content

☐ Did the opening sentence(s) 'grab' your interest?
☐ Was the setting established (i.e. when and where the action took place)?
☐ Was the reader told when the action takes place?
☐ Was it apparent who the main character(s) is? (It can be the narrator, using *I*.)
☐ Was there a 'problem' to be 'solved' early in the writing?
☐ Was a complication or unusual event introduced?
☐ Did descriptions make reference to any of the senses (e.g. cold nose, warm coat)?
☐ Was there a climax (a more exciting part near the end)?
☐ Was there a conclusion (resolution of the problem) and was it 'believable'?

Focus on structure, vocabulary, grammar, spelling, punctuation

☐ Was there variation in sentence length and beginnings?
☐ Was a new paragraph started for changes in time, place or action?
☐ In conversations or speaking were there separate paragraphs for each change of speaker?
☐ Were adjectives used to improve descriptions (e.g. *careful* movements)?
☐ Were adverbs used to make 'actions' more interesting (e.g. tail wagged *joyfully*)?
☐ Were capital letters where they should have been?
☐ Was punctuation correct?

☐ Was the spelling of words correct?
Marker's suggestions (optional)

LITERACY—READING — Pages 123–128

Alice in Wonderland
1 C **2** D **3** (4, 1, 3, 2) **4** D **5** C, E **6** B **7** A
EXPLANATIONS

1 This is a **fact-finding type of question.** The answer is a fact in the text. You read that Alice *began by taking the little golden key from the table, and unlocking the door to a passage (see lines 13–14).*

2 This is a **fact-finding type of question.** The answer is a fact in the text. You read that *roses … were white, but there were three gardeners at it, busily painting them red (see lines 17–18).* The gardeners were painting white roses red.

3 This is a **fact-finding type of question.** The answer is a fact in the text. By reading the text carefully you will identify the correct order of events. The correct order of events is: Alice leaves the tea party (1), finds a door in a tree (2), enters a hall (3), takes a key from a table (4).

4 This is a **language type of question.** To find the answer you have to read the text carefully, especially the section that states when Alice sees a tree with a door in it she thinks it's *very curious! … But everything's curious today (see lines 8–9)* and when she discovers the gardeners painting roses she thinks that's *a very curious thing (see line 18).* Some words, like *curious,* have several meanings. For Alice *curious* meant that the strange things that were happening around her were hard to explain.

5 This is an **inferring type of question.** To find the answer you have to 'read between the lines'. You read that when Alice finds a strange door she says *"I think I may as well go in at once." And in she went (see lines 9–10).* Alice does things without much thought—such as going into strange places—she doesn't hesitate. Alice could be described as *rash* and she was an inquisitive character.

6 This is a **fact-finding type of question.** The answer is a fact in the text. You read that Alice noticed that *one of the trees had a door leading right into it (see lines 7–8).*

7 This is an **inferring type of question**. To find the answer you have to 'read between the lines'. You read that when Alice finds the tree with a door in it she has the thought *"I think I may as well go in at once" (see lines 9–10)*. Alice's discoveries make her inquisitive.

What are mountain devils?

8 the shape of its woody 'fruit'/seed capsule   **9** C
10 C **11** B **12** D **13** D

EXPLANATIONS

8 This is a **fact-finding type of question**. The answer is a fact in the text. You read that the *mountain devil … is named after the shape of the woody 'fruit' it bears—the seed capsule—which has a beak and two horns, resembling a horned devil (see lines 8–11)*.

9 This is a **language type of question**. To find the answer you have to read the text carefully, especially the section that is quoted: *The name makes a person think of mysterious, evil spirits that lurk in dark mountains (see line 2)*. The woody seedpods are called mountain devils. The word *lurk* has a slightly sinister meaning. It means 'to wait in hiding in a shadowy place with the intention of doing some harm'.

10 This is a **fact-finding type of question**. The answer is a fact in the text. You read that mountain devils are *vivid red native Australian flowers (see line 3)*. Mountain devils cannot be wicked as they are plants. The true statement is: 'The mountain devils are not wicked at all'. This is confirmed in the last line of the text: *There is nothing evil about this native Australian (see line 16)*.

11 This is a **language type of question**. To find the answer you have to read the text carefully, especially the section that is quoted: *the mountain devil (Lambertia formosa) is named after the shape of the woody 'fruit' it bears (see lines 8–10)*. The words *Lambertia Formosa* are in brackets as they are the scientific name for mountain devils (or honey flowers). Brackets are used to add a bit of additional information without interfering with the flow of the text. The use of brackets is a literary technique.

12 This is a **fact-finding type of question**. The answer is a fact in the text. You read that *the tubes fill with a nectar which attracts ants and birds, especially honeyeaters (see line 7)*. Some birds, especially honeyeaters, are attracted to the flowers because they like the nectar that forms in the tubes.

13 This is a **fact-finding type of question**. The answer is a fact in the text. By reading the text carefully you will identify the correct order of events. The seed capsules start off green then *become grey and harden like the wood as they get older (see lines 14–15)*.

Bedroom scene

14 B **15** A **16** A **17** C **18** D, X **19** *Mountain devils* A, B; *Bedroom scene* A, C **20** D

EXPLANATIONS

14 This is a **language type of question**. To find the answer you have to read the text carefully, especially the section that describes parts of Pippa's bedroom: *Pippa's room was covered in pictures of animals (see line 2)* and *on her bookshelf were books of glossy photographs (see line 9)*. Combine this with your own knowledge of how text is constructed. The text is a description. The reader gets a 'look' at Pippa's bedroom.

15 This is a **fact-finding type of question**. The answer is a fact in the text. You read that Pippa's Australian collection was *a collection of cuddly Australian animals (see lines 18–19)*. They are toy animals. The rest of her collection was posters and photographs.

16 This is a **fact-finding type of question**. The answer is a fact in the text. You read that *Above her head hung a poster of two pandas feeding in a bamboo clump (see lines 2–4)*.

17 This is a **language type of question**. To find the answer you have to read the text carefully, especially the section that states that some pictures *had been replaced by new pictures when Pippa discovered something that took her eye (see lines 15–16)*. *Took her eye* is a common saying meaning 'attracted her attention or interest'.

18 This is a **judgement type of question**. You read that Pippa had *On a coffee table in the corner was her favourite display—a collection of cuddly Australian animals (see lines 18–19)* and *Pippa's room was covered in pictures of animals (see line 2)*. She has posters, movies and books about animals. Combine this with your own knowledge of what a collector is and you can work out that Pippa could be described as a collector. She collected animal pictures and furry animal toys. Pippa was also a researcher. She read books, and watched films and documentaries to better understand animals.

19 This is a **synthesis type of question**. To find the answer you have to read both texts. The *Mountain devils* text **describes** the mountain devils as well providing some **information** for the reader. The *Bedroom scene* text **describes** Pippa's room for the reader, as well as **amuses** readers regarding the extremes Pippa has gone to with her animal interests.

20 This is an **inferring type of question**. To find the answer you have to 'read between the lines'. You read that Pippa has a room full of posters and pictures. You read that *shoved in behind the bookcase were more posters and photographs. Their*

corners poked out at various angles (see lines 14–15). Combine this with your own knowledge of how things can look untidy. Pippa could be untidy.

Beautiful glass

21 D **22** cullet **23** C **24** A **25** D **26** C **27** B

EXPLANATIONS

21 This is a **fact-finding type of question.** The answer is a fact in the text. You read that the writer is impressed by the fact that glass *can be recycled forever (see line 9).* It can be recycled many times.

22 This is a **fact-finding type of question.** The answer is a fact in the text. You read that *Crushed recycled glass is called 'cullet' (see line 12).*

23 This is a **fact-finding type of question.** The answer is a fact in the text. You read that *To make full use of recycled glass, recyclers separate the clear glass from coloured glass. Only clear glass can be recycled to make new, clear glass containers (see lines 16–18).*

24 This is a **fact-finding type of question.** The answer is a fact in the text. You read that *Glass from other sources is collected separately (see line 13).* This tells you that the text is only concerned with one form of glass: glass food and drink containers.

25 This is an **inferring type of question.** To find the answer you have to 'read between the lines'. You read that the *common glass container in the home is made of simple materials (see line 2).* You read that the materials are readily available. They include mined salt, sand from sand dunes and crushed limestone rock. The materials to make glass are very common.

26 This is a **language type of question.** To find the answer you have to read the text carefully, especially the heading *Beautiful glass (see line 1).* The word *beautiful* in this text is not used literally. The writer is referring to a special quality of glass that he finds appealing.

27 This is a **fact-finding type of question.** The answer is a fact in the text. You read that the writer says that *We should be recycling all glass food and drink containers (see line 14).*

Pool rules!

28 B **29** C **30** A **31** B **32** A **33** D
34 *Beautiful glass* B, D; *Pool rules!* A, C

EXPLANATIONS

28 This is a **fact-finding type of question.** The answer is a fact in the text. You read *The first thing I saw was a brand-new sign at the entrance gate: Rules for the Pool (see line 3–4).*

29 This is a **fact-finding type of question.** The answer is a fact in the text. You read that the writer

agrees with the rule about spitting. She states *spitting in pools is Yuk! (see line 13)*

30 This is a **language type of question.** To find the answer you have to read the text carefully, especially the section that states *It's more fun running through a sprinkler (see line 21)* than obeying all the pool rules. You also read the *rules take all the fun out of a pool visit (see line 13).* When the writer says, *Pool rules! Phooey! (see lines 21–22)* she is expressing disgust. The exclamation mark helps to make her feelings clear.

31 This is an **inferring type of question.** To find the answer you have to 'read between the lines'. You read that *There were over fifteen rules to obey if you wanted to* enjoy *the pool (see line 6–7).* The writer is astounded by the number of rules, and what the rules are about. She says *I was flabbergasted! (see line 6). Astounded* means 'flabbergasted' or 'amazed' or 'astonished'.

32 This is a **fact-finding type of question.** The answer is a fact in the text. You read *Obviously spitting in pools is Yuk! but the other rules take all the fun out of a pool visit (see line 13).*

33 This is a **fact-finding type of question.** The answer is a fact in the text. You read *Little kids love to run around. This is banned! Try telling that to an excited four-year-old (see line 19).*

34 This is a **synthesis type of question.** To find the answer you have to read both texts. The *Beautiful glass* text **explains** the value of glass. However, it also attempts to **persuade** the reader to be more socially responsible. The *Pool rules!* text **entertains** the reader. It is quite amusing. It also **exposes** what the writer feels is a foolish situation.

John Flynn

35 D **36** A **37** C **38** (2, 1, 3, 4) **39** D

EXPLANATIONS

35 This is a **judgement type of question.** You can find the answer to the question by reading the whole text carefully and then working out the answer. You will have to combine the facts that you read with your own knowledge. You have to make a judgement about the information provided, in order to work out the final answer. John Flynn was caring and understanding. He spent his life trying to improve the lives of others, especially those living under harsh, lonely conditions.

36 This is a **fact-finding type of question.** The answer is a fact in the text. You read that Flynn's early mission work was in Victoria. You are told he paid for his studies to become a minister by *working in missionary centres around Victoria (see lines 4–5).*

37 This is a **language type of question.** To find the answer you have to read the text carefully, especially the section that is quoted: *From Beltana, Flynn patrolled far and wide and his ideas for better services for the outback were developed (see lines 12–13).* Words can often have more than one meaning. In the text *patrolled* means 'visiting remote places and gathering information to help people'.

38 This is a **fact-finding type of question.** The answer is a fact in the text. By reading the text carefully you will identify the correct order of events. The order of events in John Flynn's early life is: becomes a teacher (1), trains as a Presbyterian minister (2), goes to Beltana Mission (3) and sets up nursing homes in remote towns (4).

39 This is an **inferring type of question.** To find the answer you have to 'read between the lines'. You read that *From Beltana, Flynn patrolled far and wide ... [in] the outback (see line 12)* and *Nursing homes were opened at remote inland towns (see line 13).* Combine this with your own knowledge of the remoteness of outback Australia and you can appreciate that the writer finds it strange that Flynn got the idea for a modern Flying Doctor Service in such a small and remote location.

LITERACY—CONVENTIONS OF LANGUAGE
Pages 129–132

GRAMMAR AND PUNCTUATION
1 an 2 B 3 C 4 C 5 B 6 A 7 A 8 D 9 C
10 D 11 B 12 A 13 down 14 A 15 B 16 D
17 A 18 C 19 A 20 many, artistic, striking 21 D
22 C 23 model truck 24 B 25 B

SPELLING
26 galaxies 27 bridge 28 handball 29 slinks
30 lunches 31 limb 32 fresh 33 dried 34 wood
35 action 36 plum 37 golfer 38 hole 39 fairway
40 peace 41 fought 42 enemy 43 rabbit
44 welder 45 money 46 vacuum 47 muffin
48 quite 49 splendid 50 something

EXPLANATIONS

1 The indefinite article *an* is used because it does not refer to a particular hole. *An* is used before nouns or adjectives that begin with a vowel sound: *an escape hole.*

2 Remember *bad, worse* and *worst* when describing items. *Bad* or *poor* can be used when describing one person. *Worse* is used when comparing two people. *Worst* is used when judging more than two people. The comparison is between Misty and the younger girls as one group. 'More poorer' is incorrect.

3 *Place* is a common noun which in this sentence refers to a space where the car can be left.

4 *Swim* is an irregular verb. Most verbs in English form their past tense by adding *ed* (e.g. he walked). Irregular verbs do not form their past tense this way. The past tense of *swim* is the irregular verb *swam* (not 'swimmed'). *Swum* needs another verb to help it such as *have* e.g. *have swum.*

5 If a title is shortened and still retains its last letter then no full stop is required. *St* is a proper noun and must have a capital letter.

6 Commands ask someone to do something. They end with a full stop.

7 *Its* is a possessive pronoun. It stands for *Australia's.* No apostrophe is required. *It's* is a contraction of *it is.*

8 *There* is the beginning of a new sentence. *There* is used as a pronoun in this sentence. *Their* shows ownership and *they're* is a contraction of *they are.*

9 *Many* is used when there is a countable number. *Much* is used for things that are not counted (e.g. water). *More* is incorrect because the towns are not being compared.

10 *From* is used to indicate a distance. Certain prepositions tend to go with particular situations (e.g. *in* winter but *on* weekends).

11 *Do* is the last word in a question. The next sentence starts with a capital letter.

12 *And* joins things that are similar or which go together.

13 *Down* is unnecessary. It is a redundant word. The only way something can drop is down! No meaning is lost by omitting *down.*

14 Questions usually expect an answer. Remember: Not all sentences that start with *when* are question sentences.

15 The year dates are additional information that the writer may feel the reader would appreciate.

16 Singular subjects (nouns) need singular verbs; plural subjects (nouns) need plural verbs. In this case *were* must be used because there are *few days.* This is more than one day.

17 Only the actual words spoken are within speech marks (quotation marks). Dad makes a statement. All other words are not part of the spoken words. The comma goes inside the speech marks after the last spoken word.

18 *Through* is a preposition indicating movement from the end or past something to the other side.

19 Use a comma to separate the items in a series of three or more things, or for a pause. There is no comma where *or* is used in the series: *tomato, cheese or sliced ham*. Remember: Two or more words can make a single item (e.g. sliced ham).

20 Adjectives are describing words. *Many* describes the number of skills, and *artistic* and *striking* describe the paintings.

21 *Which* is a pronoun used to refer to things. *So* is a conjunction indicating a reason for a decision.

22 This apostrophe indicates possession or ownership: it was *Fay's explanations*. *Yours* is a possessive pronoun, *mistakes* and *explanations* are plural nouns.

23 Pronouns, such as *it*, do the work of nouns. They are used to refer to something previously mentioned, i.e. the model truck.

24 Make sure you read the question carefully. In this case, *because, regardless* and *even though* cannot be followed by *the fact that. Despite* has a similar meaning to *regardless of*. Something is done even though there are difficulties.

25 The comma indicates a pause before asking the question.

26 *One galaxy, many galaxies*. When a word ends in a consonant + *y*, you change the *y* to *i* and add *es* to make the plural form.

27 Take care not to reverse letter order in words.

28 *Handball* is a compound word: *hand + ball*. It ends with a double *l* (*ll*). This is common with the names of most ball games (e.g. football, softball).

29 One person *slinks*. Many people *slink*. When a verb ends with two consonants you simply add the *s* to get the correct (singular) form.

30 *One lunch, many lunches*. Make sure you pronounce the word carefully. Most nouns ending with *ch* take *es* to make the plural form (e.g. leech ➔ leeches).

31 *Limb* has a silent *b*. A silent *b* will often follow an *m* (e.g. plumber).

32 The letters *esh* are not a common word ending, however a few common words have the *esh* ending (e.g. flesh, mesh). *Fresh* is spelt as it sounds.

33 When a word ends with a consonant + *y* to add a suffix beginning with a vowel you change the *y* to *i* then add the suffix (e.g. try ➔ tried).

34 *Wood* and *would* are homonyms—words that sound the same but which are spelt differently. *Wood* comes from trees. *Would* is often used to ask a question. Learn to use the words in their correct context.

35 The letters *tion* sound like *shun* in most words (e.g. nation, motion).

36 *Plum* does not have a silent *b*. Do not confuse *plum* with *plumber* which does have a silent *b*. Other words without a silent *b* include *drum, strum* and *grim*.

37 Both *er* and *or* can change a noun or verb into the name of a person's pastime or occupation. The ending *er* tends to be the more common (e.g. baker, player) whereas *or* often follows *ct* (e.g. actor, doctor).

38 'Whoal' is not a word. *Ole* and *oal* make the same sound. Both letter combinations are in many words (e.g. hole/pole; coal/foal). *Hole* and *whole* are homonyms—words that sound the same but which are spelt differently. A *hole* is a hollow space. *Whole* refers to the total of something. It has a silent *w* before the *h*. Learn to use the words in their correct context.

39 *Fairway* is a compound word: *fair + way*. *Fair* and *fare* are homonyms—words that sound the same but which are spelt differently. *Fair* is an adjective for something attractive. *Fare* refers to a payment to travel.

40 *Piece* and *peace* are homonyms—words that sound the same but which are spelt differently. *Peace* is the time without war. *Piece* is a small part of something (e.g. *piece* of *pie*). Learn to use the words in their correct context.

41 The pattern *ough* spells many sounds. In *fought* it sounds like *or*. Other words in this group include *sought* and *bought*.

42 Spelling *enemy* can be tricky with the *m* and *n*. There is no double *m* (*mm*).

43 Make sure you pronounce the word carefully. It is *rabbit*, not 'rabbert'.

44 *Welder* does <u>not</u> have a silent *h* like a number of similar words (when, whether).

45 *Money* is a very common word and one you should know. *Money* has a similar spelling to *honey*.

46 *Ume* and *uum* can make the same sound. Double *u* (*uu*) is in very few words.

47 Don't be tempted to add *e* to words. There are only a few common words with the *ffin* letter combination (e.g. coffin).

48 *Quite* and *quiet* are words that sound very similar but which are spelt differently. *Quite* suggests a considerable degree of something (e.g. quite a lot). *Quiet* refers to a lack of sound. A trick is to imagine someone being told very forcefully to be *qui-et*!

49 Make sure you pronounce the word carefully. It is *splendid*, not 'splen<u>derd</u>'.

50 *Something* is a compound word: *some* + *thing*. Make sure you pronounce the word carefully. It is *some<u>thing</u>*, not 'some<u>think</u>'.

NUMERACY   Pages 133–140

1 C **2** A **3** B **4** A **5** B **6** C **7** B **8** C **9** B **10** B **11** D **12** 6 **13** A **14** C **15** D **16** 3 **17** D **18** $4.35 **19** A, E **20** B **21** B, C **22** 34 **23** A, B **24** D **25** A **26** A **27** 63 **28** B **29** A **30** 79 **31** 400 mL **32** D **33** Mary, Ned, Olivia, Tom, Ramy **34** 35 **35** 36 **36** 0.4, 0.15, 0.06 **37** C **38** 7 **39** 8 **40** 8 **41** 8, 3, 7 **42** D

EXPLANATIONS

1 This object is a rectangular prism.

2 Three thousand and twenty-seven has 3 thousands, 0 hundreds, 2 tens and 7 ones.
It is 3027.

3 Imagine the paper folded along the dotted line. The two parts must match exactly. This shows the picture flipped over the dotted line.

4 The stopwatch is used to measure time.
[It is used to measure the time to run a race, for example.]

5
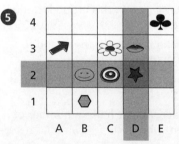

The stamp at D2 is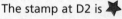

6 The shape was a trapezium.
When cut into two pieces, both new pieces are the same sort of shape as the original.
The two pieces are trapeziums.

7 The time on the clock is half-past six.
[The long hand is halfway around the clockface and the short hand is halfway between 6 and 7.]
Now half an hour is 30 minutes so it is 30 minutes after 6 o'clock. This can also be written as 6:30.

8 A triangular prism has 2 triangular faces and 3 rectangular faces.
So it has 5 faces altogether.

9 If a shape is cut into quarters it is cut into 4 **equal** parts.
Only this shape has been cut into equal parts.
So this is the shape that has been cut into quarters.

10

Left   Right

11 This angle is the largest.
[The arrow shows how far one arm has turned from the other arm.
So this angle is a bit less than a full turn.]

12 From the key we can see that each flower symbol means 2 students.

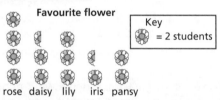
Favourite flower
Key = 2 students
rose daisy lily iris pansy

From the graph we can see that there are 3 symbols for lily.
Now $3 \times 2 = 6$.
So 6 students chose lily.

13 Starting at the price of $2.75, Heath will need 25 cents to make $3 and then another $7 to make $10.
The change will be $7.25.
[$10.00 – $2.75 = $7.25]

14 By counting, we can see that Kel has 12 cars at the start.
Now $12 - 3 = 9$
So Kel had 9 cars left after he gave 3 to Sam.
Now $9 - 4 = 5$
So Kel had 5 cars left after he gave 4 cars to David.

15 The rectangle has exactly two lines of symmetry.
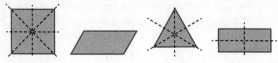

16 $6 \times 4 = 24$
So 6 rows of 4 cards is 24 cards altogether.
Those 24 cards are now going to be divided into 8 rows.

$24 \div 8 = 3$

So there will be 3 cards in each row.

17 This spinner is most likely to stop on 2.

The sector showing 2 covers more than half of this spinner so the chance of landing on 2 is greater than fifty-fifty.

18 Ned could use these coins to buy the apple.

He would have these coins left.

This means Ned would have $4.35 left.

19 Kelly has more than 18 hectares but less than 23 hectares of land.

Two of the choices are between 18 and 23.

So Kelly could have 19.5 hectares of land or 22 hectares.

20 There are 9 blocks altogether. There are 3 blocks in the second layer, but from the top view the layers can't be seen. From the top Sally will see 4 blocks in the back row and two in the front row.

This is the view from the top.

21 [Try each pattern.]

3, 13, 23, 33, …

This pattern is going up by 10 each time so this is not Isabel's pattern.

3, 6, 9, 12, …

$3 + 3 = 6; 6 + 3 = 9; 9 + 3 = 12$

This pattern is going up by 3 each time so it could be Isabel's pattern.

5, 8, 11, 14, …

$5 + 3 = 8; 8 + 3 = 11; 11 + 3 = 14$

This pattern is going up by 3 each time so it could be Isabel's pattern.

6, 9, 13, 18, …

$6 + 3 = 9; 9 + 4 = 13; 13 + 5 = 18$

This pattern is going up by a different number each time so this is not Isabel's pattern.

Isabel's pattern could be 3, 6, 9, 12, … or 5, 8, 11, 14, …

22 There are 5 rows of 6 blocks.

Now $5 \times 6 = 30$.

So there are 30 blocks altogether in those rows.

Suzy has 4 more blocks.

$30 + 4 = 34$

So Suzy has 34 blocks altogether.

23 Count the squares, matching halves.

18　　　18　　　16　　　19

The first two shapes both have 18 squares.

So options A and B cover the same area.

24 The box has 5 blue, 6 green, 4 red and 2 yellow marbles. There are no black marbles in the box. So it is impossible to take a yellow and a black marble from the box.

25 The ruler shows centimetres. The small marks are millimetres.

The nail starts at 10 mm on the ruler and finishes at 67 mm.

Now $67 - 10 = 57$.

So the length of the nail is 57 mm.

26 The third Saturday in July is 18 July.

JULY						
SUN	MON	TUE	WED	THU	FRI	SAT
			1	2	3	4
5	6	7	8	9	10	11
12	13	14	15	16	17	18
19	20	21	22	23	24	25
26	27	28	29	30	31	

Two weeks after that will be the first day of the next month.

So Stephanie's birthday is 1 August.

27 $38 + 25 = 38 + 2 + 23$
$= 40 + 23 = 63$

28

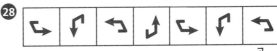

29 Ruby could be going to the cinema.

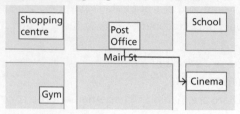

30 100, 99, 97, 94, 90, 85, …
100 − 1 = 99; 99 − 2 = 97; 97 − 3 = 94
94 − 4 = 90; 90 − 5 = 85; 85 − 6 = 79
The next number will be 79.

31 The jug holds 600 mL.
The bottle held 1 litre or 1000 mL.
Now 1000 − 600 = 400.
So, 400 mL of juice is still in the bottle.

32 Odd numbers end in 1, 3, 5, 7 or 9.
So there are 5 odd numbers between 10 and 20, (11, 13, 15, 17 and 19).
There will also be 5 odd numbers between 20 and 30, 5 between 30 and 40, and 5 between 40 and 50.
Counting by fives, there are 20 odd numbers between 10 and 50.

33 Ned collected the most stickers, so Ned has 31.
Tom collected the least stickers, so Tom has 19.
This leaves, in order, 23, 26 and 28 stickers.
Now Ramy collected more than Olivia but less than Mary. So Ramy has the middle of those amounts.
Ramy collected 26 stickers.
Olivia collected 23 and Mary collected 28.

Student	Mary	Ned	Olivia	Tom	Ramy
Number of stickers	28	31	23	19	26

34 82 − 47 = 85 − 50 = 35

35 Each new shape uses 7 extra sticks.

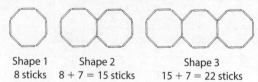

Shape 1   Shape 2   Shape 3
8 sticks   8 + 7 = 15 sticks 15 + 7 = 22 sticks

Shape 4 will use 22 + 7 = 29 sticks.
Shape 5 will use 29 + 7 = 36 sticks.

36 0.06 has no tenths (and 6 hundredths).
0.4 has 4 tenths (and 0 hundredths).
0.15 has 1 tenth (and 5 hundredths).
So 0.4 is the largest and 0.06 is the smallest.
In order, from highest to lowest, the numbers are 0.4, 0.15 and 0.06.

37 Difference = 74 − 39
= 75 − 40
= 35

38 Each tray holds 6 cakes.
Now 42 ÷ 6 = 7.
So 7 trays will be needed for 42 cakes.

39 By counting we can see that there are 24 marbles.
The marbles are divided into 3 shares.
Now 24 ÷ 3 = 8.
So each boy will get 8 marbles.

40

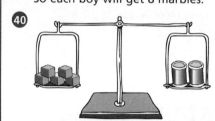

2 cans balance 5 blocks.
Doubling, 4 cans will balance 10 blocks.
Doubling again, 8 cans will balance 20 blocks.

41 Begin with the units:
1 + 6 = 7
So the last number in the answer of the number sentence must be 7.
Now look at the tens:
missing number + 4 = 2 ?
No, that doesn't work so it must be
missing number + 4 = 12.
So the missing number is 8.
The first number in the sum is 581.
This means that 1 must be carried to the hundreds.
So 5 + 1 + new missing number = 9.
This missing number must be 3.
The number sentence is 581 + 346 = 927.

42 From the graph we can see that there are 9 boys and 7 girls in Year 3.
9 + 7 = 16

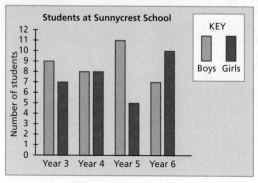

So there are 16 students in Year 3.

Also from the graph we can see that there are 8 boys and 8 girls in Year 4.

8 + 8 = 16

So there are 16 students in Year 4.

We can see that there are 11 boys and 5 girls in Year 5.

11 + 5 = 16

So there are 16 students in Year 5.

We can see that there are 7 boys and 10 girls in Year 6.

7 + 10 = 17

So there are 17 students in Year 6.

So Year 6 has the most students.

SAMPLE TEST 2

LITERACY—WRITING   Page 141

Tick each correct point.
Read the writer's work through once to get an overall view of their response.

Focus on general points

☐ Did it make sense?
☐ Did it flow? Were the arguments logical and relevant?
☐ Did the opinions expressed arouse any feelings/reactions?
☐ Was the body of the writing mainly in the third person?
☐ Did you want to read on to understand/appreciate the writer's point of view?
☐ Were the arguments convincing?
☐ Was the writer assertive (e.g. the use of *is* rather than a less definite term)?
☐ Was the handwriting readable?
☐ Was the writing style suitable for a persuasive text (objective; not casual or dismissive)?

Now focus on the detail. Read the following points and find out whether the writer's work has these features.

Focus on content

☐ Did the opening sentence(s) focus on the topic?
☐ Was the writer's point of view established early in the writing?
☐ Did the writer include any evidence to support his or her opinion?
☐ Did the writer include information relevant to his or her experiences?
☐ Were the points/arguments raised by the writer easy to follow?

☐ Did the writing follow the format with an introduction, the body of the text and a conclusion?
☐ Were personal opinions included?
☐ Was the concluding paragraph relevant to the topic?

Focus on structure, vocabulary, grammar, spelling, punctuation

☐ Was there a variety of sentence lengths, types and beginnings?
☐ Was a new paragraph started for each additional argument or point?
☐ Has the writer used any similes (e.g. as clear as crystal) to stress a point raised?
☐ Did the writer avoid approximations such as *probably, perhaps* and *maybe*?
☐ Did the writer use such phrases as *I know …* and *It is important to …*?
☐ Did the writer refer to the question in the points raised? (A good way to do this is to use the key words from the question or the introduction.)
☐ Has the writer used any less common words correctly?
☐ Was indirect speech used correctly?
☐ Were adjectives used to improve descriptions (e.g. *expensive* buildings)?
☐ Were adverbs used effectively (e.g. firstly)?
☐ Were capital letters used correctly?
☐ Was punctuation used correctly?
☐ Was the spelling of words correct?

Marker's suggestions (optional)

LITERACY—READING   Pages 142–147

Happy Christmas for pets

1 D **2** C **3** B **4** A **5** B **6** A **7** D

EXPLANATIONS

1 This is a **fact-finding type of question.** The answer is a fact in the text. You read that *Many people forget that pets are for life, not just for Christmas* (see lines 2–3). You also read *Unfortunately many families get tired of the new pet by the end of the summer holidays and a sad puppy or kitten is given to the pound* (see lines 5–8).

2 This is a **fact-finding type of question.** The answer is a fact in the text. You read that *The new pet needs exercise and to be toilet trained. This can be a frustrating task that requires patience* (see lines 17–18). The writer suggests that many families get tired of an untrained pet. *Families must think about protecting items that can be chewed or scratched (see lines 14–15)*. The joy of a owning a pet soon wears off and the pet *is given to the pound (see line 8)*.

3 This is a **judgement type of question.** You read that *many families get tired of the new pet by the end of the summer holidays and a sad puppy or kitten is given to the pound (see lines 6–8)*. Think how the pet must feel after all the fuss and attention over Christmas then suddenly it's off to the pound. Most puppies or kittens would feel unwanted if left in a pound.

4 This is a **language type of question.** To find the answer you have to read the text carefully, especially the section that is quoted: *The new pet needs … to be toilet trained. This can be a frustrating task that requires patience and a calm response to those little 'accidents' (see lines 17–18)*. The writer uses the word *accidents* to be polite. He has put the word in inverted commas to indicate that it has a special meaning. He uses it rather than say wee or poo—the kind of accidents young animals might have until they are trained.

5 This is a **fact-finding type of question.** The answer is a fact in the text. You read that *Firstly, there is the cost … the new pet has to be registered (see lines 10–11)*. An important cost in owning a pet is getting it registered. It is one of the costs the writer lists.

6 This is a **judgement type of question.** You read that *pets are for life, not just for Christmas (see lines 2–3)* and *Make it a happy Christmas for a pet too! (see line 20)*. The language used suggests that this information is friendly advice. It is informing people that being a pet owner has its responsibilities. Pets are not toys.

7 This is an **inferring type of question.** To find the answer you have to 'read between the lines'. You read that gates should be secured (shut) because *Roads are dangerous (see lines 15–16)*. Combine this with your own knowledge of how traffic can be dangerous to small and young pets, especially if they accidentally wander onto roads.

The swim
8 B   **9** A   **10** C   **11** D   **12** B   **13** D

EXPLANATIONS

8 This is a **fact-finding type of question.** The answer is a fact in the text. You read that *[a]fter leaving the farmhouse we* [the family] *arrived at a little rise overlooking a paddock of corn (see line 4)*.

9 This is a **language type of question.** To find the answer you have to read the text carefully, especially the section that is quoted: *A flock of birds screeched up from the scraggly stalks (see lines 4–5)*. Combine this with your own knowledge of what corn stalks look like when they start to die, especially if parrots are in amongst them ripping corn cobs apart. *Scraggly* means 'messy and uneven in shape'.

10 This is an **inferring type of question.** To find the answer you have to 'read between the lines'. You read that the group *arrived at a little rise overlooking a paddock of corn. A flock of birds screeched up from the scraggly stalks (see lines 4–5)* when Jenny asks her question. Nigel can see the corn stalks and it is very obvious to him that the birds are eating the corn.

11 This is a **fact-finding type of question.** The answer is a fact in the text. You read that Nigel said, *"Why don't we eat it? I love corn" (see line 13)*. His father thought this was a good idea. He said, *"Good idea Nigel! We can pick some on the way back. I like fresh corn on the cob—with plenty of butter" (see lines 14–16)*. Freshly picked corn was going to be a 'treat'.

12 This is a **synthesis type of question.** To find the answer you have to read the whole text. The text is about the father and his two children exploring a farm. They find the paddock of corn, they see birds, they plan to pick some corn and they swim in the stream. You read: *The swim was fun (see line 20)*. You then combine these ideas to come up with the conclusion that the day was generally peaceful.

13 This is a **synthesis type of question.** To find the answer you have to read the whole text. The title for a passage should give some idea of what the *whole* passage is about. The text is about 'exploring the farm' from the corn paddock to the stream.

Cartoon
14 in the morning   **15** D   **16** C   **17** B   **18** D   **19** A

EXPLANATIONS

14 This is an **inferring type of question.** To find the answer you have to 'read between the lines'. You read that the grandfather says, *"Look what Fido's dragged in! He's been doing this ever since I started reading my daily newspaper online" (see lines 1–6)*, meaning he is acting strangely by pulling a computer into the room. Combine this with your own knowledge of when newspapers are mainly delivered (morning) and how some dogs are trained to fetch them. The cartoon most likely has a morning setting.

15 This is an **inferring type of question.** To find the answer you have to 'read between the lines'. You can see the look on the grandmother's face. A suitable comment would be, "Do you think it's time to retrain Fido?" Fido should be discouraged from wanting to please the grandfather by getting the computer.

16 This is an **inferring type of question.** To find the answer you have to 'read between the lines'. You can see the look on the boy's face. A suitable comment would be "Here we go again!" The boy has his eyes raised indicating a feeling of disbelief.

17 This is an **inferring type of question.** To find the answer you have to 'read between the lines'. You can see the reaction of the dog. It is trying to please the grandfather. It wants approval for what it has done. It most likely got approval for fetching the morning paper.

18 This is a **synthesis type of question.** To find the answer you have to look at the complete cartoon. The caption for a cartoon should give some idea of what the *whole* cartoon is about. The best caption is 'Man's best friend!' The exclamation mark suggests that this should not be taken literally. The actions of Fido hardly qualify him as a 'best friend'.

19 This is an **inferring type of question.** To find the answer you have to 'read between the lines'. You read that the grandfather says *"I started reading my daily newspaper online" (see lines 4–6)*. This implies he once read it as a delivered newspaper. Obviously, Fido used to enjoy fetching the paper. Fido feels fetching the computer might be as satisfying.

Who is Robbie Paul?

20 B **21** D **22** A **23** C **24** B **25** A **26** C

EXPLANATIONS

20 This is a **fact-finding type of question.** The answer is a fact in the text. You look at the cards to see that they include an Indigenous Santa who is dressed for the north Queensland climate. You also read they contain *an Indigenous Santa in thongs (see line 14)*.

21 This is an **inferring type of question.** To find the answer you have to 'read between the lines'. You read that *Robbie says he put the croc on the card for a bit of north Queensland humour (see lines 15–16)* and his kangaroo *has a really mischievous look on his face (see line 10)*. Robbie appears to enjoy his culture and where he lives.

22 This is a **fact-finding type of question.** The answer is a fact in the text. You read that *Robbie says completing university studies not only improved his illustrations but also introduced him to computer graphics (see line 12–13)*.

23 This is an **inferring type of question.** To find the answer you have to 'read between the lines'. You read that *Robbie says he put the croc on the card for a bit of north Queensland humour (see line 16)* and his *kangaroo has a really mischievous look on his face (see line 10)*. The cards are intended to amuse because they are not typical Christmas cards.

24 This is a **language type of question.** To find the answer you have to read the text carefully, especially the section that is quoted: *Robert 'Robbie' Paul (see line 2)*. Inverted commas around a name is a literary technique. It is a way of telling the reader that this is not as it seems. In this case it is intended to give the name that Robert Paul is commonly known by.

25 This is a **language type of question.** To find the answer you have to read the text carefully, especially the section that is quoted: *The kangaroo has a really mischievous look on his face in the way he winks at us! (see lines 10–11)*. Combine this with your own knowledge of what winking can mean. The kangaroo is being cheeky. *Cheeky* is a synonym for *mischievous*.

26 This is an **inferring type of question.** To find the answer you have to 'read between the lines'. You read that *Robbie says he put the croc on the card for a bit of north Queensland humour (see lines 15–16)* and his *kangaroo has a really mischievous look on his face (see line 10)*. Robbie's Santa has short sleeves and wears thongs. A quirky picture would include something amusing and unusual— something out of the ordinary.

Snapshots

27 D **28** *Who is Robbie Paul?* B, D; *Snapshots* A, C
29 A **30** B **31** It's Spring—Stanza 4 **32** A **33** C

EXPLANATIONS

27 This is an **inferring type of question.** To find the answer you have to 'read between the lines'. You read that each stanza starts with the name of a season *It's Summer (see line 2), It's Autumn (see line 8), It's Winter (see line 14)* and *It's Spring (see line 20)*. These are the seasons as they change over a full year.

28 This is a **synthesis type of question.** To find the answer you have to read both texts. The *Who is Robbie Paul?* text is a factual **recount** of Robbie Paul's life (biography) and highlights some **differences** in the way Christmas is celebrated. The *Snapshots* poem **describes** some aspects of the seasons while **entertaining** readers with a stimulating word picture.

29 This is a **language type of question.** To find the answer you have to read the poem carefully. Combine this with your own knowledge of how a snapshot (photo) might be a brief record of a family event such as a holiday. So the poem's title *Snapshots* has the meaning of a brief summary of an event. The event in the poem is the changing of the seasons. Each stanza is a brief description of a season.

30 This is a **language type of question.** To find the answer you have to read the text carefully, especially the section that is quoted: *The leaves are falling off the trees / They drift to earth upon a breeze (see lines 11–12).* Then you combine it with your own knowledge of how leaves gently fall from trees in a light wind (breeze). A synonym for *drift* is 'float'.

31 This is a **synthesis-type question.** You have to read all four stanzas to get the answer. In *It's Spring* you read *The gardens start to come alive (line 21)* with bees and blossom and *The days are getting longer (line 23).* Stanza 4 is full of the poet's positive reactions.

32 This is a **language type of question.** To find the answer you have to read the text carefully, especially the section that is quoted: *clouds are building in the sky (see line 4).* Combine this with your own knowledge of how clouds form. Clouds usually build up, or get bigger, before a storm. The clue is in the line in the same stanza, *Perhaps we'll get a storm again (see line 6).*

33 This is a **judgement type of question.** You can find the answer to the question by reading the whole poem carefully and then working out the answer. You will have to combine the facts that you read with your own knowledge. You know that the seasons are in a cycle. They always follow the same order. The poet has left the last stanza (of two words) unfinished because the poem is back to summer, which was the first stanza. It starts with the same words.

The lollipop man

34 B **35** C **36** D **37** a lollipop **38** *The swim* **YES** A, D; *Lollipop man* **YES** B, C **39** A

EXPLANATIONS

34 This is a **fact-finding type of question.** The answer is a fact in the text. You read that *Mr Rhodes was placing orange witchhat markers down the centre of Elm Road (see lines 2–4).*

35 This is a **fact-finding type of question.** The answer is a fact in the text. You read that *the new project [was] to widen Elm Road (see line 21).*

36 This is an **inferring type of question.** To find the answer you have to 'read between the lines'. You read that Mr Rhodes *had a very responsible job to do (see lines 9–10).* Combine this with your own understanding of responsibilities and it can be said that Mr Rhodes had an important job to do. Part of his job was to see that there were *no accidents*

(see lines 19–20). You read that *Mr Rhodes would … proudly turn the sign one way, then the other (see line 18).* His pride in his job indicated that he thought it an important job.

37 This is a **fact-finding type of question.** The answer is a fact in the text. You read that Mr Rhodes had *a long pole with a round sign on the top (see lines 12–13).* The *sign looked like a giant lollipop (see lines 14–15).*

38 This is a **synthesis type of question.** To find the answer you have to read both texts. In *The swim* text you read that the family had just moved to a remote farm *(line 2).* They had also enjoyed a swim in a local waterhole *(line 20).* In *The lollipop man* text you read that Mr Rhodes worked with a road crew *(line 6)* and he was in a team that repaired roads *(lines 7, 8).*

39 This is a **fact-finding type of question.** The answer is a fact in the text. You read that *Mr Rhodes had to put out markers before the start of work and collect them at the end of each day (see lines 22–23).* The last job of the day was to collect the orange traffic markers.

LITERACY—CONVENTIONS OF LANGUAGE Pages 148–151

GRAMMAR AND PUNCTUATION

1 C **2** and, but **3** A **4** D **5** A **6** B **7** B
8 behind **9** D **10** C **11** D **12** D **13** A **14** Sara
15 A **16** A **17** B **18** C **19** B **20** D **21** A
22 C **23** D **24** C **25** B

SPELLING

26 wiping **27** daily **28** wonderful **29** flash
30 scared **31** spoon **32** swamp **33** travelled
34 sister **35** coming **36** usually **37** yank
38 simple **39** tricks **40** wrist **41** chew **42** drain
43 soccer **44** shadow **45** against **46** mountain
47 cheesy **48** herd **49** narrow **50** fleeing

EXPLANATIONS

1 The comma indicates a pause. It goes immediately before the words in the speech marks (quotation marks).

2 Conjunctions are joining words. They join single words or parts of a sentence.

3 *You're* is a shortened word (contraction) of *you are.* The letter *a* has been replaced with an apostrophe.

4 *Quickly* is an adverb adding meaning to the verb. It tells how the class *did* their work. Adverbs often end in **ly**. *Quicker* is an adjective.

5 A sentence starts with a capital letter. Proper nouns (names of people) have capital letters and so does the first word spoken in direct speech.

6 Pronouns stand for nouns. They save speakers from continually repeating the nouns. *Hers* is a possessive pronoun, therefore an apostrophe *s* is not required.

7 *Sleep* is an irregular verb. Most verbs in English form their past tense by adding 'ed' (e.g. he walked). Irregular verbs do not form their past tense this way. The past tense of *sleep* is the irregular verb *slept* (not 'sleeped'). 'Sleped' is not a real word.

8 *Behind* is unnecessary. It is a redundant word. If you are *following* a team you are *behind* that team. No meaning is lost by omitting *behind*.

9 The actual words spoken are: "*Good morning, I've come to see the coach.*" The words spoken are broken by the information about the person who spoke. Because the actual words spoken are 'broken', each part of the spoken words must be in speech marks.

10 The only person owning something is a *girl*. The apostrophe goes before the *s* (*girl's bracelet*). *Boys, swings* and *weeds* are plural nouns. No apostrophes are required.

11 *Done* is a verb that needs a helper: another verb to help it. We say <u>has</u> done. *Have, has* and *had* can be helping verbs. *Has* is present tense. The helping verb is always close to the verb it is helping.

12 Brackets are used to include additional information that may be useful. The year dates are additional information that the writer may feel the reader would appreciate.

13 *Hers* is a possessive pronoun.

14 *Her* is a pronoun and stands in place of a female person. *Sara* is the subject of the first sentence in this short paragraph. *Sara* is still the subject in the second half of the next sentence. *Her* saves repeating the name *Sara* in the final sentence.

15 *Whose* is a possessive pronoun and does not require an apostrophe to show ownership. *Who's* is a shortened word (contraction) of *who is*.

16 Singular subjects (nouns) need singular verbs; plural subjects (nouns) need plural verbs. In this case, there is more than one bat. The plural verb *have* is required. The verb does not refer to the singular *cricket kit bag*.

17 Statements provide information. They have a subject (I) and a verb (*went*) and may have an object (*to sleep*).

18 *But* is a conjunction. It joins two opposing ideas. Trevor had two options but chose the second: to save his money.

19 The comma after *there* indicates a pause. It separates the person spoken to from the rest of the sentence.

20 *Which* is a pronoun used to refer to things. *So* is a conjunction indicating a reason for a decision.

21 Singular subjects (nouns) need singular verbs; plural subjects (nouns) need plural verbs. Mistakes with subject–verb agreement can easily be made with pronouns. *Everybody* is a pronoun. In this case, *wears* must be used because *everybody* is one of a group of pronouns that takes a singular verb. Other such pronouns include *each, someone* and *anyone*.

22 There are two distinct parts joined by a conjunction (*although*, which just happens to be at the beginning of the sentence). The first part has the subject (*the rains*) and a verb (*were*) that relates to it. In the second part the subject is *the creeks*. The verb is *were*. The other options become confusing.

23 *Which* is a pronoun that refers to non-human subjects. *That* is incorrect because it is used to refer to a specific thing. *Which* is used for more general statements. *What* is generally used to ask questions.

24 *From* is used to indicate where something originates. The $2 originated with Ingrid's sister. That's where it came <u>from</u>. *Off* is used to indicate movement down: the boy fell <u>off</u> the fence.

25 *Sweep* is an irregular verb. Most verbs in English form their past tense by adding *ed* (e.g. he walked). Irregular verbs do not form their past tense this way. The past tense of *sweep* is the irregular verb s*wept* (not 'sweeped').

26 When a word ends in a consonant + *e* you drop the *e* before adding *ing* (e.g. hope ➜ hoping).

27 In some short words if there is a vowel before the *y* you may have to change the *y* to an *i* before adding the suffix beginning with a consonant (e.g. gay ➜ gaily). *Daily* is a common word you should learn and remember.

28 *Wonderful* is *wonder* + *ful*. When adding the suffix *ful* to a word it only has one *l*.

29 *Flash* is one of the many *ash* family of words (e.g. crash, ash, dash). *Sch* is an uncommon word ending.

30 *Scared* and *scarred* have two different meanings. *Scared* means 'frightened'. *Scarred* means 'to have a mark on one's skin'. *Scared* is scare + *ed*. Simply add the *d*. *Scarred* is scar with the suffix *ed*. The *r* is doubled (*rr*) before *ed* is added.

31 *Une* and *oon* can make the same sound. Both letter combinations are in a number of words (e.g. June/prune; soon/moon). You will have to learn and remember such words.

32 *Swamp* isn't spelt as it sounds. Most other *amp* words do <u>not</u> rhyme with it (e.g. camp, clamp, tramp).

33 In most two-syllable words that end with *l* you double the *l* (*ll*) before adding the suffix *ed* (e.g. labelled, equalled).

34 *Sister* is a common word. It does not have a double *s*.

35 *Coming* is *come* + *ing*. Many words that end with a consonant + *e* drop the *e* before adding the suffix *ing* (e.g. hope ➔ hoping, care ➔ caring).

36 *Usually* is *usual* with the suffix *ly*. *Usually* has a double *l* (*ll*).

37 *Nck* is an uncommon word ending in English. Most *ank* words rhyme with *yank* (e.g. crank, thank, rank).

38 The syllable *ple* is a very common word ending in English (e.g. ample, apple, people).

39 *Trix* is a fun spelling of *tricks*. *Tricks* belongs to a big family of *icks* words (e.g. licks, bricks, sticks).

40 *Wrist* begins with a silent *w*. There are quite a few words where a silent *w* is followed by an *r* (e.g. write, wrong).

41 *Ue* and *ew* can make the same sound: either the long *u* sound as in *cue* and *few* or the long *oo* sound as in *grew* and *glue*. In this case *ew* in *chew* has the long *oo* sound. You will have to learn and remember to spell these words.

42 *Ain* and *ane* can make the same sound. Both letter combinations are in a number of words (e.g. train/brain; sane/crane). Remember: <u>Rain</u> goes down a <u>drain</u>. You will have to learn and remember the words in each group.

43 Double *c* (*cc*), double *k* (*kk*) and *ck* can all make the same sound. *Soccer* has a double *c* (*cc*). You should learn it as it is a common sporting word.

44 Make sure you pronounce the word correctly. It is *shad<u>ow</u>*, not 'shad<u>er</u>'.

45 The suffix *est* is used with comparative adjectives (e.g. best, fastest). *Against* does not have this suffix. *Against* is a preposition meaning 'opposed to'.

46 Think of *mountain* as *mount* + *ain*. *Mount* rhymes with a few common words (e.g. count, fount). *Mountain* has a very similar spelling to *fountain*.

47 *Cheesy* is *cheese* + *y*. When adding *y* to words that end with a consonant + *e* you drop the *e* before adding the *y* (e.g. breeze ➔ breezy, ease ➔ easy).

48 *Heard* and *herd* are homonyms—words that sound the same but which are spelt differently. *Heard* is the past tense of *hear*. *Herd* is the name given to a group of some animals. Learn to use the words in their correct context.

49 Make sure you pronounce the word correctly. It is *nar<u>row</u>*, not 'nar<u>rer</u>'.

50 *Flee* and *flea* are homonyms—words that sound the same but which are spelt differently. *Flee* means 'escape quickly'. A *flea* is a small biting insect. When adding *ing* to words that end in double *e* (*ee*) you simply add the *ing* (e.g. seeing, freeing).

NUMERACY
Pages 152–159

1 A **2** A **3** C **4** B **5** 24 **6** B **7** D **8** A **9** C
10 raspberry, lemonade, lime, orange **11** B **12** B
13 23 **14** A **15** 24 **16** 15 **17** C **18** D **19** 32
20 24 **21** A **22** A, B, C **23** B **24** C **25** 28 **26** C
27 73 **28** 35 km **29** D **30** D **31** $2, 15
32 1.05 kg, 1 kg 80 g, 1200 g, 1.4 kg **33** 53 **34** 70c
35 1 **36** B, D **37** C **38** Abi, Shae, Pia, Jane
39 D **40** 6 **41** A **42** 170 cm

EXPLANATIONS

1 Triangles have 3 sides.
Peter drew 3 triangles.

2 A cylinder has circles at the top and bottom and a curved surface between them. A can of drink is shaped liked a cylinder.

3 Three thousand and forty is 3 thousands, 0 hundreds, 4 tens and 0 ones.
It is 3040.

4 The picture shows kitchen scales. Scales are used to measure mass.

5 By counting, we can see that there are 12 buttons left.
So Justin must have used 12 of the buttons.
Now 12 + 12 = 24.
So there were 24 buttons in the packet.

6 Blackbutt Road crosses Rosewood River in B2.

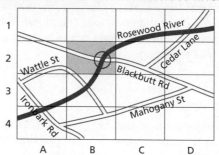

7 $3 \times 6 = 18$

So 3 groups of 6 students is 18 students altogether.
Now $18 \div 2 = 9$.
So 2 groups of 9 students will be the same as 3 groups of 6 students.

8 A quarter to seven is 15 minutes before 7 o'clock or 45 minutes after six o'clock.
It is 6:45.

9 $2 + 40 + 500 = 500 + 40 + 2$
$\quad\quad\quad\quad\quad\quad = 542$

10 There are more raspberry iceblocks than any other flavour, so a raspberry iceblock is most likely to be taken.

There are more lemonade iceblocks than either lime or orange, so a lemonade iceblock is the second most likely.

There are less orange iceblocks than any other flavour, so an orange iceblock is least likely to be taken.

In order, the flavours are raspberry, lemonade, lime and orange.

11 There are 60 minutes in an hour.
A quarter of an hour is 15 minutes.

12 This is the paper folded then unfolded.

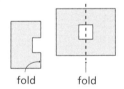

fold   fold

13 7, 11, 15, 19, …
$7 + 4 = 11$
$11 + 4 = 15$
$15 + 4 = 19$
The numbers are going up by 4 each time.
Now $19 + 4 = 23$.
So the next number in the pattern is 23.

14 The students start basketball at 10:30. After basketball they have morning tea at 11:15. So at 11:00 they will still be playing basketball.

Start time	Activity
9:00	Bus to swimming pool
9:15	Swimming
10:15	Bus back to school
10:30	Basketball
11:15	Morning tea
11:30	Cricket
12:45	Lunch
1:30	Walk
2:45	Awards presented

15 One quarter is one of four equal parts.
So each orange will be cut into four pieces.
There are 6 oranges. Now $6 \times 4 = 24$.
So Kylie will have 24 quarters.

16 $37 + 18 = 37 + 3 + 15$
$\quad\quad\quad\quad\quad = 40 + 15$

17 Gemma's picture has 6 lines of symmetry.

18 From 5 am until 5 pm is 12 hours. From 5 pm until 8 pm is 3 hours.
Now $12 + 3 = 15$.
So Toby was away from home for 15 hours.

19

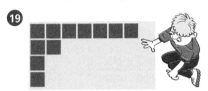

We can see that 8 tiles fit across the floor one way and 4 fit the other way.
So there are 4 lots of 8 tiles.
Now $4 \times 8 = 32$.
So 32 tiles will fit on the floor altogether.

20 $43 - 19 = 24$
So $43 - 24 = 19$.
The number is 24.

21

There are 6 beads that are repeating.

The last bead in the necklace is the fourth bead in the repeating pattern.
So the fifth bead will be next in the necklace.
The next bead will be .

22 [Try each option.]
$9 + 17 = 17 + 9$ because the same two numbers are being added together.
$20 + 6 = 17 + 3 + 6 = 17 + 9$
$16 + 10 = 16 + 1 + 9 = 17 + 9$
$14 + 14 = 14 + 3 + 11 = 17 + 11$
So $14 + 14$ is not the same as $17 + 9$.
So $9 + 17$, $20 + 6$ and $16 + 10$ all have the same value as $17 + 9$.
[Or $17 + 9 = 26$. Try each option to see which add to 26.]

23 Khaled could pay for the sandwich with the $2 coin and one of the 50c coins. He would get 10c change. Khaled would then have these coins; $1, 50c, 20c, two 10c and 5c.

This means he would have $1.95.

Or, by counting, we can see that Khaled has $4.35. The sandwich cost $2.40.

Now $4.35 − $2.40 = $1.95.

24 If tomorrow is Wednesday then today is Tuesday. So yesterday was Monday. The only statement that is certain is 'Yesterday was Monday'.

25

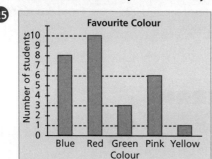

From the graph we can see that 8 students voted for blue, 10 voted for red, 3 for green, 6 for pink and 1 for yellow.

Now $8 + 10 + 3 + 6 + 1 = 8 + 10 + 10$
$= 28$

So altogether 28 students voted.

26 We can see that that the section of the number line between 1 and 2 is divided into 4 parts. So, the marks on the number line are counting by quarters.

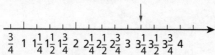

The arrow is pointing to $3\frac{1}{4}$.

27 $56 + 17 = 53 + 3 + 17$
$= 53 + 20$
$= 73$

28

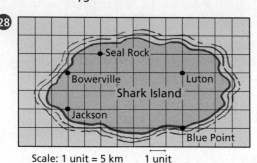

Scale: 1 unit = 5 km   1 unit

By counting, we can see that it is 7 units from Bowerville to Luton.

The scale tells us that each unit is 5 km.

Now $7 \times 5 = 35$.

So it is 35 km from Bowerville to Luton.

29 Edward's answer was 7. Before dividing by 2 his answer must have been 14 because $14 \div 2 = 7$. Before adding 5 he must have had 9 because $9 + 5 = 14$.

Edward must have started with 9.

30 The box holds 5 blue, 2 yellow, 4 red, 1 white and 3 green marbles.

So Billy could take 3 blue marbles.

He could take 1 yellow and 2 green marbles.

He could take 1 red, 1 blue and 1 green marble.

Billy cannot take 2 white marbles because there is only one white marble.

It is impossible for Billy to take 1 red and 2 white marbles.

31 6 drinks cost $12.

Now $12 \div 6 = 2$.

So 1 drink costs $2.

Now $30 \div 2 = 15$.

So 15 drinks can be bought for $30.

32 1 kg = 1000 g

So 1.4 kg = 1400 g

1 kg and 80 g = 1080 g

1.05 kg = 1050 g

So, in order from least to greatest mass, the weights are 1050 g, 1080 g, 1200 g and 1400 g.

So, in order, the masses are 1.05 kg, 1 kg 80 g, 1200 g and 1.4 kg.

33 $90 − 37 = 53$.

Bree needs 53 more points to go to the next level.

34 The pencils cost 50 cents each.

Now $7 \times \$0.50 = \$3.50$.

So altogether the 7 pencils cost $3.50.

5 pens cost the same as 7 pencils.

So 5 pens cost $3.50.

Now $\$3.50 \div 5 = \$0.70$.

So each pen cost 70 cents.

35 Each book symbol means 4 books. Half a symbol means 2 books and a quarter of a symbol means 1 book.

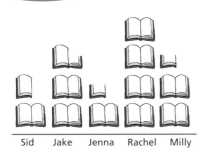

| | Key
= 4 books |

Sid Jake Jenna Rachel Milly

Rachel has 4 symbols.

4 × 4 = 16

So Rachel read 16 books.

Sid has one symbol (4 books) plus half a symbol (2 books).

So Sid read 6 books.

Milly has 2 symbols (2 × 4 = 8 books) plus a quarter of a symbol (1 book).

So Milly read 9 books.

Now 6 + 9 = 15.

So altogether Sid and Milly read 15 books.

So Rachel read one more book than Sid and Milly together.

36 0.17 means 1 tenth and 7 hundredths.

So $0.17 = \frac{1}{10} + \frac{7}{100}$

$= \frac{10}{100} + \frac{7}{100}$

$= \frac{17}{100}$

So $\frac{1}{10} + \frac{7}{100}$ and $\frac{17}{100}$ are both the same as 0.17.

37 ♥○♥☆♥□♥☆♥○♥☆♥□♥☆♥○♥☆♥□♥☆...

This part of the pattern, ♥○♥☆♥□♥☆, is being repeated. There is 1 of ○ but 4 of ♥.

So 4 ♥ are needed for each ○.

38 Find the number of blocks in each prism.

Shae:

Number of blocks = 5 × 2 × 3
= 30

Abi:

Number of blocks = 2 × 4 × 4
= 32

Jane:

Number of blocks = 3 × 3 × 3
= 27

Pia:

Number of blocks = 7 × 2 × 2
= 28

So Abi used the most blocks, followed by Shae, Pia and Jane.

39 Mel puts 6 eggs in each of 5 cartons.

Now 5 × 6 = 30.

So Mel put 30 eggs in cartons.

Now 40 − 30 = 10.

So Mel will have 10 eggs left.

40 The green cube has 6 faces altogether.

Each face will have one block in the centre with just one face painted green.

So there will be 6 blocks with green paint on only one face.

41 Molly sees the reflection of the clock in the mirror. The real clock will be like this.

reflection

The hour hand is pointing to 5 so the time is 5 o'clock.

42 1 metre = 100 centimetres.

On the measuring stick, 1 metre is divided into 10 parts.

Now 100 ÷ 10 = 10.

So each part is 10 cm.

Counting by 10s, we can see that John is 170 cm tall.

SPELLING WORDS FOR REAL TESTS

To the teacher or parent

First read and say the word slowly and clearly. Then read the sentence with the word in it. Then repeat the word again.

Give the student time to write their answer. If the student is not sure, then ask them to guess. It is okay to skip a word if it is not known.

Spelling words for Real Test Week 1

Word	Example
1. pianos	The music teacher has two pianos in her house.
2. stresses	Driving in the city stresses out my big sister.
3. displays	The butcher displays the meat he has for sale in a glass case.
4. thinks	Emma thinks she will get one hundred per cent for spelling.
5. branches	The bank has two branches in Parramatta.
6. believes	Jay believes that people who litter should be put in jail!

Spelling words for Real Test Week 2

Word	Example
1. afternoon	It was late in the afternoon when Uncle James arrived.
2. captain	The school has a boy captain this year.
3. meat	The butcher has meat for sale on white trays.
4. almonds	Dad buys packets of mixed nuts that include almonds.
5. boiled	We used boiled water to make our coffee.
6. bulbs	Tulips are bulbs that flower well in cool regions.

Spelling words for Real Test Week 3

Word	Example
1. clearly	The children spoke clearly on the night of the awards.
2. friendless	The new boy in our class felt friendless.
3. hopeful	We are hopeful that the floods don't come into our street
4. cried	Angela cried all night when she had a sore throat.
5. pitiful	It was a pitiful result. We lost without scoring!
6. dimly	My torch shone dimly in the dark shed.

Spelling words for Real Test Week 4

Word	Example
1. uniform	Did you wear your school uniform to school this week?
2. sleeveless	Lindy's blouse was sleeveless.
3. careful	We are all careful to keep the carpet clean in wet weather.
4. sign	Angela put a sign on her bedroom door.
5. tough	It was a tough match. We lost by one point.
6. fourteen	There are fourteen days in two weeks.

SPELLING WORDS FOR SAMPLE TESTS

To the teacher or parent

First read and say the word slowly and clearly. Then read the sentence with the word in it. Then repeat the word again.

Give the student time to write their answer. If the student is not sure, then ask them to guess. It is okay to skip a word if it is not known.

Spelling words for Sample Test 1

Word	Example
26. galaxies	There are millions of galaxies in the sky.
27. bridge	The bus drives across the bridge into the city.
28. handball	Our class plays handball after school on Tuesday.
29. slinks	Amy's cat slinks around the yard looking for food!
30. lunches	The children next door take packed lunches to school.
31. limb	A limb fell off the tree in a windstorm.
32. fresh	"Do you want fresh fruit or an energy bar?" asked Mum.
33. dried	During the drought the dams on the farm dried up.
34. wood	We put some wood on the campfire to keep the insects away.
35. action	"I prefer to watch an action movie rather than a cartoon," stated Bonny.
36. plum	The skin of the plum was yellow but the flesh was bitter.
37. golfer	Mum is a golfer but Dad is a bowler.
38. hole	Mum got a hole in one for her first shot!
39. fairway	The club mowed the fairway after the storm had passed.
40. peace	The army wanted peace in the land but the rebels had other ideas.

Spelling words for Sample Test 2

Word	Example
26. wiping	"It's your turn to do the wiping up," said Dad.
27. daily	"It is now time for your daily piano lesson," said Ms Taylor.
28. wonderful	We had a wonderful time at the fete.
29. flash	We saw a flash of lightning before we heard the thunder.
30. scared	You're not really scared of little spiders!
31. spoon	Put the spoon next to the knife please.
32. swamp	The ibis stood in the water at the edge of the swamp.
33. travelled	The crew had travelled many kilometres to reach safety.
34. sister	Your sister is in the same class as my brother.
35. coming	Spring is coming and the grass is growing.
36. usually	Renee usually gets all her spelling right but today she made a mistake.
37. yank	We tried to yank the weeds out of the garden but it was too hard.
38. simple	The sum was so simple I could do it in my head!
39. tricks	The magician showed us how to do some tricks.
40. wrist	When I fell I jarred my wrist and grazed my elbow.

Notes

Notes